ANTICHRIST AND HIS TEMPLE

BY ROMAN BERESNEV

Copyright © 2020 by Roman Beresnev
Published by Roman Scripts Press

All rights reserved

No part of this publication may be reproduced, stored in a retrieval system, or transmitted in any form or by any means electronic, mechanical, photocopying, recording, or otherwise, without the written permission of the author or publisher.

Art and illustrations provided by the author
Translated by Natalia Chumpalova
Edited by Tammie Knauff

ISBN: 978-1-7352560-0-9 (Paperback Edition)
ISBN: 978-1-7352560-1-6 (Hardcover Edition)
ISBN: 978-1-7352560-2-3 (eBook Edition)

Library of Congress Catalog Card Number: 2020913231

Unless otherwise indicated, all Scripture quotations are taken from the Holy Bible, New King James Version. Copyright © 1982 by Thomas Nelson, Inc. Used by permission. All rights reserved.

Printed in U.S.A.

10 9 8 7 6 5 4 3 2 1

Contents

Introduction 1

Chapter 1. When Will the Antichrist Come? 9

   1. What does the Bible tell us about the antichrist? 12
   2. Is the antichrist/beast a person or a kingdom? 20
   3. So when will the antichrist come? 25
   What to do with doubts and is it easy to notice the extraordinary? 29

Chapter 2. Unmasking the Antichrist 35

   1. Different views of antichrist's identity 35
   2. What the reformers of the church thought of the antichrist ... 42
   3. Does the Papacy fit the role of the antichrist? 43
   Conclusion 64

Chapter 3. Will the Temple Be Rebuilt? 69

   1. What do the Jews believe? 69
   2. What do Evangelicals believe? 73
   3. The prophecy of Daniel 9:27 76
   5. Jesus' words about "the 'abomination of desolation' " in Matthew 24:15 84
   Conclusion 87

Chapter 4. Where Will the Antichrist Sit? 93

1. Other prophecies on this subject 95
2. Are the "representatives" truly representatives? 108
3. *In persona Christi* or the art of impersonation 116
4. Old Testament examples 119
5. How has the antichrist pretended that the basilica is the sanctuary? 125
6. Original or fake? 137
7. Architectural theology 138
8. The development of architectural theology 142
Conclusion 148

Chapter 5. What Is the "Abomination of Desolation"? 155

1. All that glitters is not gold 156
2. What have we missed? 159
3. Daniel's prophecies about the "abomination of desolation" ... 160
4. How will the antichrist set up the "abomination of desolation?" 161
Conclusion 204

Chapter 6. Who Is the False Prophet? 211

1. What do we know about the false prophet? 212
2. What do we know about the true prophet? 214
3. What will be the content of the message of the true prophet? . 219
4. What will be the message of the false prophet? 227
5. There is nothing new under the sun 228
6. Who are "the rest of her offspring?" 232

Epilogue 235

Introduction

The mystery of the antichrist is one of the puzzles in the prophetic books of the Bible, Daniel and Revelation. Understanding this mystery, as well as the study of these prophetic books themselves and how their interpretations have developed and changed during history will not only be a revelation but a shocking revelation. For many centuries, this issue of the antichrist majorly concerned Bible scholars, but, for various reasons, they failed to find answers to some key questions. There is an explanation for this failure—it was anticipated by the antichrist prophecy itself. According to the angel's words, the book of Daniel was to be sealed. Finishing his instruction to Daniel, the angel told him:

> "But you, Daniel, shut up the words, and seal the book until the time of the end; many shall run to and fro, and knowledge shall increase." . . .
> And he said, "Go your way, Daniel, for the words are closed up and sealed till the time of the end. Many shall be purified, made white, and refined, but the wicked shall do wickedly; and none of the wicked shall understand, but the wise shall understand" (Daniel 12:4, 9, 10).

This means that according to God's plan it was not possible to understand this book until the time determined by Him. That is, in order to make clear the message of the book, at least two conditions have to be met: (1) the time determined by God must be finished and (2) the Holy Spirit must give wisdom and understanding in order to unveil it since "no prophecy of Scripture is of any private interpretation, for prophecy never came by the will of man, but holy men of God spoke as they were moved by the Holy Spirit" (2 Peter 1:20, 21).

At this point, we should probably ask a natural question: Why is this book supposed to be open for understanding only after a certain time?

The answer is manifold. First, because the prophecies themselves deal with end-time events, according to God's plan, the necessity of learning the truth at that time will be more critical than it has ever been. The power of deception will be so great that God will give His light to destroy the darkness of delusion. Does this mean that God wanted people to be unaware of the truths in the book of Daniel until a certain time? Of course not. We shall see that those who have made the Bible the foundation of their faith understood the truths Daniel had spoken about, but they never connected them with his book nor were they able to understand the prophetic periods or the time of the fulfillment of the prophecies. That is why, according to the plan of God, when a certain time comes the truth is to be proclaimed in new power and with new biblical discoveries.

Second, the prophecy could confuse many people if they understood the timing prematurely. Christians of all centuries have been waiting for Christ's second coming. This has been their hope and encouragement. But, nevertheless, the prophetic periods indicated a delay of hundreds to thousands of years. This perspective could have ruined the faith of many, especially those living during times of persecution. But why did God allow this delay to be such a long one? Because He is not a human being, His love and patience are surprising—even to the angels. God sought and is seeking the salvation not only of those who were persecuted and had to run for their lives because of their faithfulness to the gospel but also the salvation of those who carried out this persecution—those who rebel against Him.

The apostle Peter assures us that just as God saved Saul, who persecuted the early Christians, and transformed him into the apostle Paul, "the Lord is not slack concerning His promise, as some count slackness, but is longsuffering toward us, not willing that any should perish but that all should come to repentance" (2 Peter 3:9).

Third, one can interpret these prophecies with a great degree of certainty only after their fulfillment. They were given mainly, not to let us know what *would* happen, but to cause us to believe *after* the events had happened. Jesus said, "And now I have told you before it comes, that when it does come to pass, you may believe" (John 14:29).

Why is that so? God must communicate something that hasn't yet happened, and this task is not an easy one. How would you foretell the inventions of the radio, television, the Internet, Skype, and things such as these? What words would you use to explain them to a person perhaps from the nineteenth century? The task would not be easy, would it? But God told Daniel about events that would happen hundreds to thousands of years after the end of his life. That is why He used symbols and images—just as we would use symbols and images trying to convey the idea of what a computer is and how it functions to those living a century before us. Therefore, most prophetic messages are given in symbols. The advantage of symbols is that they make it possible to explain and describe things that do not yet exist. But on the other hand, this is also their most vulnerable aspect. The risk of failing to interpret a symbol in the one and only right way is high. For example, if we were to describe FaceTime calls to a person living in the eighteenth or nineteenth century, we may want to say that it looks and sounds very much like a fortune-teller is talking with someone on the other side of a mirror. Such an image might be helpful to some extent, but certainly not perfect. The eighteenth-century person would think that in the future mirrors will be able to talk! But the only thing in common between a mirror and a smart phone is that both have glass. This common trait is external, and if we are to interpret a prophecy based only on this characteristic, it will easily and often lead us to wrong conclusions. Therefore, in the prophecies, God provides several specific details, and only by putting them together are we able to identify a phenomenon or a character in a prophecy with minimal risk of an error.

Sure, God could have told us much about our future. He could have told us things that for centuries would cause us to wonder and admire His knowledge about the universe's laws, human beings, and earth's history. But the God of the Bible is not a prestidigitator; He is not an actor who entertains His audience with His ability to foretell the future. On the contrary, many people find the study of His prophecies to be a rather boring and useless. The God of the Bible pays no attention to many subjects that thrill the minds of modern people. But why not? There could possibly be only one reason—the significance of what He revealed through His prophets couldn't be compared to anything that might occupy our minds. The knowledge God reveals is the most crucial knowledge we can possess. Why is this so? Because the redeemed will have an eternity to learn history and politics, to examine conspiracy theories and science, but right now we need to set priorities and go deep into another science—the plan of redemption. "The fear of the Lord is the beginning of knowledge, but fools despise wisdom and instruction" (Proverbs 1:7), and this means that knowing God is the primary step to all the other knowledge, which only puffs up if it is gained without Him.

For this reason, it is the worship of the living God, the truth and deception about His Son's sacrifice for our sins that we recall each

INTRODUCTION

time we participate in the Lord's Supper—not the things that will happen to kings, presidents, and men of authority, which always remain the focus of prophecy. God passes by and neglects politics and the most arrogant underhanded plots. In the Bible, they receive His attention only if they affect the fate of His people and challenge His plan of salvation.

Misunderstanding this basic principle of prophetic interpretation has led thousands to misinterpret the Bible. Sometimes these misunderstandings look convincing and plausible. However, after a careful study, one notices that racial, cultural, political, and gender issues, along with other prejudices, have been artificially imposed on the Bible text. Such interpretations use the Bible text for their own purpose.

But still, if Daniel wrote about us and for us—about our worship of God and the events of our time—why didn't he do so more clearly? Why doesn't God call things by their proper names in the prophecies? Those names or words didn't exist yet and would have meant nothing to Daniel. But then we can ask another question: Why did God speak to a prophet who lived and spoke in the past instead of one who lived in our time so that we would be able to understand him? In other words, wouldn't it have been easier for God to convey His message to the world through a contemporary person who would call things by their actual names, avoiding symbols? The answer to this question is also not very difficult.

First, God conveys His message not to everyone, but to His prophets. Sin brought separation between God and human beings. As a result, man lost his ability to speak with God face to face. But God didn't leave us ignorant. He started to choose prophets to communicate His will to people. These individuals were different from others mainly because they desired to do His will more than anything else. They were looking for the light of His truth as persistently as others look for silver and gold. And God gave them a promise: "Those who seek me diligently will find me" (Proverbs

8:17). In our days, so few seek God, so few study the Scriptures and examine the prophecies with the same dedication as Daniel did. Because of this, God chose Daniel to convey His message.

Second, whether God's message is conveyed in symbols or in plain, common language is not the crucial question. In fact, it is a peripheral question. The major question is this: Are we going to believe that this message and the messenger have been sent by God, bearing in mind that the message is one of rebuke? There are a lot of examples in the Bible when people labeled true prophets as false prophets. Their messages and their standing were denied because they rebuked human delusions.

Third, history shows us an important example. Jesus Christ, the greatest prophet of all, preached a message to His contemporaries. He was God incarnate. And how did He choose to present His message? Jesus used a language of parables, the language of images and symbols. But why? He wanted to avoid alienating most of the people. Speaking too plainly would have aroused their desire to kill Him for the truth He spoke, shedding light on their human actions. Using parables, Jesus was able to communicate the truth without being specific. This way, a listener could see himself from another perspective and be brought to repentance before his heart became hardened. But it takes time and effort to understand parables, just as it takes time and effort to understand prophecy. Jesus' listeners had to understand whom or what He was speaking about. That means that the contemporaries of a prophet do not always have the benefit of listening to a message that doesn't need interpretation. The same is true of those who study prophecy. That is why the Bible says, "He who has an ear, let him hear what the Spirit says to the churches" (Revelation 3:22). Prophecy, such as Jesus' parables, sheds light on our actions, and it is our responsibility to accept this light and to ask Jesus to keep our hearts from hardening.

Understanding these principles becomes a key to proper treatment of all apocalyptic prophecy and to the prophecy about the antichrist in particular. It is necessary to study history, but it is even more crucial to study and know the Bible. But the main factor that enables an explorer to dig deeper into the mysteries of God will always be a humble heart and submission to the Holy Spirit—not one's secular or religious education.

The books of Daniel and Revelation do not only contain unique apocalyptic prophecy but also embrace, to a certain extent, all the other books of the Bible. This fact requires their readers to not only have a good understanding of the basic concepts of the Scriptures but also the ability to study the history and culture of those nations that existed in the ancient Near East and experience studying books of different genres, skill in treating texts carefully,* and a knowledge of other hermeneutical principles. But most importantly the explorer of Bible prophecy needs to be obedient to the Holy Spirit. As it is impossible to learn algebra without knowing addition, subtraction, and multiplication, thus the study of apocalyptic prophecy won't lead to the correct answers without previously studying all the Bible books, having a converted heart, and a personal relationship with God.

Like apocalyptic prophecy, this book is intended to reach a wide range of readers, but it would be unrealistic to think that all of them will be able to equally understand the prophecies. It is assumed that the reader is not only familiar with all the other books of the Bible but that he also has a sufficient knowledge of prophecy and the different principles of their interpretation.† The reader should understand not only such basic prophetic symbols as a woman representing a church—either God's true church or an apostate church (Babylon)—but also understand even more complicated concepts, such as the parallels between the second and the seventh chapters of the book of Daniel; why Antioch Epiphanes cannot be the one who fulfills the prophecy of Daniel 8 concerning the casting down of the

---

* Preferably in the original languages.
† According to this approach, the principles of interpretation are usually divided into four groups: preterism, futurism, idealism, and historicism.

sanctuary; or how, where, and when the day-year principle can be applied. We also assume that the reader already knows that the birth of Jesus took place before the beginning of the Christian Era (A.D.) and is also familiar with other basic dates of biblical events. As a matter of practicality, this book does not deal with these and other similar questions. The reason for this is a reluctance to overload with extra details a book that is already replete with them and the desire to help the reader focus on the major issue—that is, to trace the development of the topic under discussion from the beginning of the book to its end without getting stuck in the details.

Another reason why there is no thorough argumentation for each statement is not the lack thereof, but the genre of this volume. It is not a scientific paper nor a thesis, but an ordinary book. When choosing between the former and the latter, we decided to prefer the latter, as this volume is intended for study not only by the community of scholars but also anyone who studies the Bible and who would probably prefer that the book be easier to follow.

If the reader has never studied the apocalyptic prophecies yet wants to do so, we would recommend reading the following books: Mark Finley's *The Next Superpower: Ancient Prophecies, Global Events, and Your Future* and a wonderful overview of church history in Ellen White's book, *The Great Controversy*. For a more profound study see Daniel and Revelation Committee Series, research encompassing seven volumes made by the above-mentioned committee.

fanaticism; it can be traced to Scripture itself. Second, if we take an unbiased look at these texts, we'll find that according to them any person who "denies that Jesus is the Christ" or who "does not confess that Jesus Christ has come in the flesh" is an antichrist. It is very simple. Everyone who does either of these things can be called an antichrist on a biblical basis. However, no matter how earnestly we try to find something in these texts that will shed light on the time or place of the antichrist's coming, we won't be able to do it.

One can ask, "Then why do Christians believe that, when the antichrist comes, he will sit in the temple of God and have power for three and a half years, persecuting and blaspheming? Where do such ideas come from?" If such questions come to your mind, I'm glad that they have been asked. This is a good example of how we too often follow stereotypes, trusting the "experts" and not looking at the details or studying the Bible for ourselves. And the "experts" often do not bother to provide extra explanations. Sometimes this can be justified—the simpler the answer the easier it can be understood. But at the same time, such an answer can lead to error just as eating ready-made food just because we trust those who have made it can sometimes be a mistake.

However, we need to give weight to these interpretations because the antichrist really will do all the things mentioned above. We can read about this not in cryptic manuscripts but in the Bible itself. But since the word, *antichrist,* is not specifically identified in these texts, we'll have to prove who is being written about. In the process of laying out these arguments, we'll learn some other important lessons.

Other texts about the antichrist in the Bible

The antichrist in the book of Revelation. "Then I stood on the sand of the sea. And I saw a beast rising up out of the sea, having seven heads and ten horns, and on his horns ten crowns, and on his heads a blasphemous name. Now the beast which I saw was like a leopard, his feet were like the feet of a bear, and his mouth like the mouth of a lion. The dragon gave him his power, his throne, and great authority" (Revelation 13:1, 2).

In Revelation 12, we can learn who the dragon is "so the great dragon was cast out, that serpent of old, called the Devil and Satan, who deceives the whole world; he was cast to the earth, and his angels were cast out with him" (Revelation 12:9).

Let's continue reading Revelation 13, beginning with verse 3:

> And I saw one of his heads as if it had been mortally wounded, and his deadly wound was healed. And all the world marveled and followed the beast. So they worshiped the dragon who gave authority to the beast; and they worshiped the beast, saying, "Who is like the beast? Who is able to make war with him?"
>
> And he was given a mouth speaking great things and blasphemies, and he was given authority to continue for forty-two months. Then he opened his mouth in blasphemy against God, to blaspheme His name, His tabernacle, and those who dwell in heaven. It was granted to him to make war with the saints and to overcome them. And authority was given him over every tribe, tongue, and nation. All who dwell on the earth will worship him, whose names have not been written in the Book of Life of the Lamb slain from the foundation of the world (Revelation 13:3–8).

If you are reading these verses for the first time, you may be wondering what all this medieval fantasy means. What a bizarre beast this is! He is even talking! Don't worry. To tell the truth, even those who have read these lines many times sometimes ask the same questions. But this is what the language of prophecy requires. A cursory reading is not enough to understand it, and even the most thoughtful reading won't help. We need something more. We need two conditions to be met. Mathematicians talk about "necessary conditions" and "sufficient conditions." First, we need a knowledge of the entire Bible, and this is not an overstatement. The book of Revelation is the last book of the Bible, and we can't understand it without a knowledge of the contents of all the other books. This overall knowledge of the Bible is a necessary condition to understanding prophecy, but by itself it is not enough to do so. We also need another condition to be met—the guidance of the Holy Spirit, the One who authored and inspired the prophetic word. We need to be in a living connection with Him. That is, we need to know Him personally. Only then will we be able not only to understand *what* God has told us but also to understand *why* it was told. We will be able to read between the lines, understand the text, and even feel as if we were reading a letter from a beloved person whom we have known for a long time. When this happens, the words become vivid, and we see a 3D picture of the things that are described in the prophecy. The Holy Spirit brings us to the very center of the events where we can emphasize and grasp the inner sense of each word.

Why is the beast of Revelation 13 the antichrist? We need to answer the question, "What do this beast and the antichrist have in common?" Let's take a thorough look at what we know about the life of Jesus and at what we know about this beast and compare one with the other. Table 1 below shows the results of such a study.

Christ and the Antichrist, table 1

Christ	Antichrist
He receives His power from the Father. (Matthew 28:18)	He receives his power from the dragon. (Revelation 13:2)
The Father gave Him His throne. (Revelation 3:21)	The dragon gave him his throne. (Revelation 13:2)
Three and a half years are given to Him. (Daniel 9:27)*	Forty-two months are given to him. (Revelation 13:5)
He was dead, but is alive. (Revelation 1:18)	He receives a deadly wound but comes back to life. (Revelation 13:3)
He accepts worship as God. (John 20:28)	He accepts worship as God. (Revelation 13:4, 8)
He is the Lamb of God. (John 1:29)	He confronts the Lamb of God. (Revelation 13:8)
He leads to the Father. (John 14:6)	He leads others to the dragon. (Revelation 13:4)
He is part of a heavenly trio. (Matthew 28:19; 2 Corinthians 13:14)	He is part of an ungodly trio. (Revelation 16:13)

---

* The "week" in Daniel 9:27 is a prophetic week and represents seven years. Half of a week then represents three and a half years of Christ's public ministry, at the conclusion of which He brought His sacrifice and abolished the sacrifices and offerings of the temple.

As we have noticed, the word, *antichrist,* does not appear anywhere in the description of the beast in Revelation 13. Nevertheless, we can clearly see in table 1 that the opposing parallels are frequent and intentional, a vivid example of how the Bible points to the antichrist without ever naming him. A thorough comparison shows us that it is the antichrist who is spoken about here—*the* antichrist with the definite article "the"—the one specific antichrist that was predicted by the apostle John. Though anyone can become an antichrist according to the first and the second epistles of John, the only antichrist who fulfils the prophecy of Revelation 13 is the beast/antichrist. Perhaps this is the reason John doesn't mention him by name—then we will not confuse the former with the latter. But this antichrist, the second and most important one, is more dangerous than all his forerunners put together. He doesn't deny that Jesus is the Christ or that Jesus has come in the flesh. On the contrary, he has a form of godliness and even more, he imitates Christ. Here lies his deceptive power that makes people worship him.

It is important for the purposes of our study to understand and agree that this beast of Revelation 13 is the antichrist even though John doesn't mention his name. To illustrate why, I'm going to tell you a story.

A minister of the gospel once asked his wife during the congregational hymn in the church if she liked his singing. This was not a casual curiosity. His wife had a good musical education; she was the conductor of a choir. She could easily listen to the polyphony of voices in a choir and distinguish if someone was slightly off key or not harmonizing. Of course, it was even easier for her to listen to her husband singing right by her. Her answer was not only truthful, but wise. She replied, "I like your preaching!"

Praise the Lord for wise ladies who can find the right words! Are not her words a good example of how to explain something while saying practically nothing? Did she say anything about the preacher's singing? No. One might say that her answer had nothing to do with singing since she didn't say the words, *singing, to sing,* or *sing.*

Nevertheless, one does not need to be a philologist or a theologian, and one needn't produce an independent, expert assessment of her words to understand what she meant. Similarly, the fact that John did not use the word, *antichrist,* in Revelation 13 doesn't mean that he is not speaking of him. John lays down this principle from the beginning of the book, saying, "He who has an ear, let him hear" (Revelation 2:7). That is why it is so important to know the biblical text, but it is even more important to know the Author of the text.

The antichrist in the book of Daniel. When we read the description of the beast in Revelation, we can't help being reminded of the fourth beast in Daniel 7. Let's compare them.

The Beast of Daniel 7 and the Beast of Revelation 13, table 2

Beast in Daniel 7	Beast in Revelation 13
10 horns (Daniel 7:7)	10 horns (Revelation 13:1)
Blasphemies (Daniel 7:8, 11, 25)	Blasphemies (Revelation 13:1, 6)
Worldwide dominion (Daniel 7:23)	Worldwide dominion (Revelation 13:8)
Persecutions of the saints (Daniel 7:21, 25)	Persecutions of the saints (Revelation 13:7)
3 ½ years* (Daniel 7:25)	42 months (Revelation (13:5)

* This prophetic period is mentioned in the Bible seven times. Three times it is referred to as "time and times and a half time" (Daniel 7:25; 12:7; Revelation 12:14), two times as forty-two months (Revelation 11:2; 13:5), and two times as 1,260 days (Revelation 11:3; 12:6). All these descriptions are describing one and the same prophetic period of time. Revelation 12:6 and 12:14 prove the identity of the "time, times and a half" with the "1,260 days," while Revelation 11:2 and Revelation 11:3 prove the identity of the 1,260 days with the "42 months."

As we can see from table 2, John is not too original when writing about this beast. Speaking in modern language, we could easily blame him of plagiarism—at least in some passages taken from the book of Daniel. But to be serious, the issue here is not that John was well-acquainted with the book of Daniel, but the fact that both books were inspired by the Holy Spirit. He is the One who is in charge, the One who showed John in vision the same beast that He showed to Daniel as well. When we compare the description and the behavior of these beasts, it becomes obvious that they are not two different beasts—but one and the same beast. So we inevitably conclude that this beast is another description of the antichrist without specifically mentioning this name. In this case, if the beast in Revelation 13 equals the antichrist, and if the beast in Revelation 13 also equals the beast in Daniel 7, then the beast in Daniel 7 equals the beast in Revelation 13, and they both equal the antichrist. We can express our findings in the form of a simple mathematical formula:

$$\text{If } a = b \text{ and } a = c,$$
$$\text{then } a = b = c.$$

Thus, we can find in Scripture two very extensive descriptions of the antichrist. These will form the basis of our research and will help us answer the main question of this chapter: When can we expect the coming of the antichrist?

Possibly you are now asking, "Who is this beast? If it is a person, then who is he? If it is not a person, then what is it?" Ironically, in searching for the answer to this question we'll be able to find answers to many other questions, including the main question of this chapter—the time of his coming.

2. Is the antichrist/beast a person or a kingdom?

Surprisingly, when speaking about the antichrist, people today rarely turn to Daniel 7 and Revelation 13. More often they turn to other texts of Scripture. In addition, the influence John's words in his epistles—where he speaks of the antichrist as a certain person—has formed the solid belief that the antichrist must be a specific individual. Thus, we only need to find out who he is and when to expect him. But it is not that easy. See, for example, here is what Daniel himself says about the beast/antichrist: "Thus he said: 'The fourth beast shall be a fourth kingdom on earth, which shall be different from all other kingdoms, and shall devour the whole earth, trample it and break it in pieces' " (Daniel 7:23).

We have already proven that this beast is the antichrist, and we learn from this text that this beast is a particular "kingdom," that is, a certain political or politico-religious entity, structure, or a social institution that has great power and authority comparable to the power and authority of the state.

Who is right? Is it possible that most Christians who truly believe that the antichrist is a certain person are mistaken and are leading others astray? We would suggest for you to consult church history. People were searching for the answers to these questions long before us, and they have left not only a rich heritage of their research but, even more so, firmly established traditions of faith, including traditions that concern the antichrist. The generations that followed passed on these traditions as a baton, without any serious analysis, because they believed that the older a tradition or interpretation is, the closer it is to the truth. Today we have a lot of pseudobiblical beliefs that are tremendously strong but have nothing to do with the Bible's teaching. That is why by no means can the authority of a tradition be compared to the authority of the Bible. As the light of the moon cannot be equated to the light of the sun, so the light of a tradition cannot be equated to the light of the

Bible. Besides, in the case of the book of Daniel, the Bible says that our predecessors would be in a less advantageous situation than we are. Daniel was told that his book would be sealed until the end time (Daniel 12:9, 10). This means that the last generations would understand this book better than previous ones.

Then why to consult any external, extrabiblical testimony? We hold the position that the extant tradition that is often represented in the writings of the church fathers is valuable for two reasons: (1) it is helpful to study the history of the interpretation of Scripture, and (2) it is helpful to study the history of the church itself. The study of various traditions enables us to see how theological thought has evolved or degraded in the course of centuries while the Bible itself has remained unaltered. To our surprise, we often find that a modern interpretation of the Bible can be traced to tradition and not to the Bible. Sometimes this is the only way to find an answer to the question of why modern Christians have come to believe in this or that idea. With this in mind, let's read two testimonies of the church fathers.

> So now, since the true Christ is to come a second time, the adversary, taking occasion by the expectation of the simple, and especially of them of the circumcision, brings in a certain man who is a magician, and most expert in sorceries and enchantments of beguiling craftiness; who shall seize for himself the power of the Roman empire, and shall falsely style himself Christ; by this name of Christ deceiving the Jews, who are looking for the Anointed, and seducing those of the Gentiles by his magical illusions.
>
> But this aforesaid Antichrist is to come when the times of the Roman empire shall have been fulfilled, and the end of the world is now drawing near. There shall rise up together ten kings of the Romans,

reigning in different parts perhaps, but all about the same time; and after these an eleventh, the Antichrist, who by his magical craft shall seize upon the Roman power and of the kings who reigned before him, *three he shall humble*, and the remaining seven he shall keep in subjection to himself. At first indeed he will put on a show of mildness (as though he were a learned and discreet person), and of soberness and benevolence: and by the lying signs and wonders of his magical deceit having beguiled the Jews as though he were the expected Christ, he shall afterwards be characterized by all kinds of crimes of inhumanity and lawlessness, so as to outdo all unrighteous and ungodly men who have gone before him; displaying against all men, but especially against us Christians, a spirit murderous and most cruel, merciless and crafty. And after perpetrating such things for three years and six months only, he shall be destroyed by the glorious second advent from heaven of the only-begotten Son of God, our Lord and Saviour Jesus, the true Christ, who shall slay Antichrist *with the breath of His mouth*, and shall deliver him over to the fire of hell.[1]

This quite interesting passage was penned by Cyril of Jerusalem (A.D. 313–386) and is nothing else than an early comment on Daniel 7:9–14. That is its value. As you can see, he not only answers the question whether the antichrist is a real person but also points to the time of his coming.

And now let us give the floor to Irenaeus of Lyons (A.D. 130–202), who lived two centuries before Cyril.

> For when he (Antichrist) has come, and of his own accord concentrates in his own person the apostasy, and accomplishes whatever he shall do according to his own will and choice, sitting also in the temple of God, so that his dupes may adore him as the Christ; . . . whose coming John has thus described in the Apocalypse: "And the beast which I had seen was like a leopard, and his feet as of a bear, and his mouth as the mouth of a lion; and the dragon conferred his own power upon him, and his throne, and great might" [Revelation 13:2][2]

In fact, when you read Irenaeus of Lyons, you are convinced that Cyril of Jerusalem borrowed his conclusions from his predecessor. In this sense, he faithfully carried the baton further. There were certainly other participants in this race, but let us pause here and summarize what we have learned.

First, we find that from the earliest church fathers, the fourth beast of Daniel 7, and the first beast of Revelation 13 were regarded as the antichrist. Undoubtedly, we should give the church fathers credit for this insight. They understood well the principle, "He who has an ear, let him hear" (Revelation 2:7, 11, 17, etc.) and were able to point to these passages of Scripture as ones speaking of the antichrist.

Second, commenting on the prophecy, they accurately identified the four beasts as four kingdoms: Babylon, Media-Persia, Greece, and Rome. They specified that the antichrist would come after the Roman kingdom and would emerge out of it. In other words, they pointed to the time of the fall of the Roman Empire, specifically to the time of the ten kings responsible for Rome's fall, as the time when the antichrist would come to the stage.

Third, they maintained that the antichrist would be a man or a person. Besides that, he would probably be a kingly person, as he would appear at the time of these ten kings and would subdue three of them.

Fourth, the antichrist would sit in the temple of God, showing himself that he is God.

The first three points are more or less clear, but how did these church fathers come to the idea that the antichrist would sit in the temple of God? Indeed from what we have learned from the Bible, there is no mention that this would happen. Is this a Bible teaching or some baseless tradition of interpretation?

Here is the text that Irenaeus gives to prove his statement. "Let no one deceive you by any means; for that Day will not come unless the falling away comes first, and the man of sin is revealed, the son of perdition, who opposes and exalts himself above all that is called God or that is worshiped, so that he sits as God in the temple of God, showing himself that he is God" (2 Thessalonians 2:3, 4). So far, we haven't examined this passage. However, we must do so in order to decide whether or not we agree that it speaks of the antichrist.

On one hand, the apostle Paul doesn't state explicitly that he is speaking about the antichrist or that this person has anything to do with the beast-antichrist of Daniel and Revelation. On the other hand, the blasphemy of this personage is so outstanding and challenging that one is driven to the conclusion that anyone doing something like this, must be that same antichrist. We will not make a definite conclusion at this point in our study; but will leave the question to be answered in the process of our further research.

The only thing that is left, then, is to resolve the following question: Is the antichrist a person or a kingdom? As you will recall, Daniel referred to the fourth beast as a kingdom, but all the church fathers (and most modern Christians as well) believe that the antichrist is a person. Which view is correct?

Let's read Daniel again.

Those great beasts, which are four, are four kings which arise out of the earth (Daniel 7:17).

"Thus he said:
'The fourth beast shall be
A fourth kingdom on earth,
Which shall be different from all other kingdoms,
And shall devour the whole earth,
Trample it and break it in pieces' " (verse 23).

As you can see, the contradiction is easy to resolve when we turn to Scripture. The angel explained to Daniel that this fourth beast is both a king (a person) and his kingdom. This appears to be logical and a more comprehensive view of the fulfillment of the prophecy. We cannot limit the interpretation to one or the other option. Any kingdom has a king who personifies it and acts on its behalf. At the same time, the antichrist will have to rely on state institutions in order to carry out his ideas and give them life. That's why the only correct conclusion is to say that the antichrist is both a person and a state of which he is the head.

3. So when will the antichrist come?

As we have seen, the prophet Daniel, followed by the early church fathers, predicted that the antichrist would come after the fall of the Roman Empire during the time of the ten kings. Moreover, the antichrist would come while there are still ten, but later three of them would disappear (Daniel 7:8, 24).

According to the common opinion, the Roman Empire ended in A.D. 476. Ten barbarian tribes took its place. By the end of the middle of the sixth century, three out of the ten tribes ceased to exist—the Heruli, Vandals, and Ostrogoths. Daniel's prophecy was fulfilled accurately, and this gives us reason to pay the most serious attention to this given time period in order to be able to recognize the antichrist.

However, we should observe that many modern interpreters disagree with the idea that the antichrist would come at the time of the fall of the Roman Empire and the ten kings. For many Christians, the antichrist's coming is a future event. Let's give the floor to a brilliant representative of this view, Dr. Jimmy DeYoung, a biblical prophecy teacher and a journalist. Here are his thoughts on the issue of when the antichrist comes:

> The revived Roman Empire has to be in place. The 10 horns of Daniel 7:7, 24 would be the revived Roman Empire. When they come to power the antichrist is then going to appear. Not necessarily the leadership that is in place today. For example, as the president of the European Union we have mister Van Rompuy and then as the Chief Foreign Policy person we have Catherine Ashton. These two are major players today but ultimately there is going to be a political figure that comes out of the ten horns. Let me just use an illustration. There is a perfect prototype of the antichrist. I would say that this individual is the former Prime Minister of Great Britain Tony Blair. Tony Blair today is speaking on how to bring the resolution of world conflict through religion. And that is going to be what the antichrist is going to do. What Tony Blair is doing today is what the antichrist is going to do.[3]

Immediately we want to draw your attention to the fact that Dr. DeYoung confirms that the antichrist will come during the time of the ten kings. But this is the only point in which he doesn't depart from the text of the prophecy. Then he begins doing some imperceptible conceptual substitutions and eisegesis (the insertion of ideas into the Bible text that do not exist in it, a process that violates all the laws of hermeneutics, or Bible interpretation). These errors are not obvious to an unsophisticated audience, but they lead to incorrect conclusions. For instance, DeYoung speaks of the Roman Empire, but then he subtly introduces the term, *revived*—"the revived Roman Empire."

First, by introducing this term, he unwittingly admits that the Roman Empire has fallen or has been destroyed, as the prophecy claimed it would be. Second, what is the meaning of the "revived" Roman Empire? DeYoung is fully aware that, according to the prophecy, the antichrist would come after Rome's decline, but how can something that does not exist decline? So he is facing an unsolvable dilemma. Rome collapsed in A.D. 476, but DeYoung is still unable to determine who the antichrist is! For him, the only logical way out is to state that the Roman Empire will be revived in the future. Otherwise, he would have to search for the antichrist in the past, not in the future.

Here is a summary of the arguments against this position:

> *1. The Bible doesn't say that the Roman Empire will ever be "revived."* On the contrary, no matter how fervent the European nations that once constituted the Roman Empire have been in their efforts to unite, they have not—and will not—be able to do it (see Daniel 2:41–43). The collapse of the Roman Empire was marked by its division into ten parts. This means that for its revival, it is necessary to unite them again, but according to the prophecy this will not happen. All efforts to compare or to call the European Union the "revived" Roman Empire are a mere substitution of concepts.

2. The Bible says that the antichrist will come during the time of the ten kings and "pluck up" three of them. At present, the European Union consists of twenty-eight countries, and if we count all the countries in Europe, there would be even more. But the Bible tells us that the antichrist will come at the time of the *ten* kings. This contradiction is obvious, isn't it? Any application of the prophecy to our time would require a serious stretch of the imagination and would be a strained interpretation. Wouldn't it be more natural to look to the period of the end of the fifth century and the beginning of the sixth? Rome collapsed in A.D. 476. At that time, the empire was divided into ten kingdoms, three of which had disappeared by the middle of the sixth century.

3. In the prophecy of Daniel there is no indication that an interval of more than fifteen hundred years would elapse between the collapse of Rome and the ten kings among which the antichrist appears. On the contrary, all the previous empires in the same prophecy replaced each other almost immediately. There may be a gradual decay of one empire followed by the rise of a new power, but usually, the end of an empire is reckoned as the day its capital falls or the day its ruler is killed or deposed. The fall of Rome and the rise of the ten kings follow this pattern; the ten kings replace Rome immediately, not after fifteen hundred years. The defeat of an empire takes place because there is already a new leader on the political, economic, and military horizon able to confront the old world order. To put it in a different way, nature abhors a vacuum, especially for fifteen hundred years.

Based on all that has been stated above, we can conclude that according to the prophecy, the time of the coming of the antichrist is the time of the ten kings that replaced the Roman Empire. Daniel states that three of them should be "plucked out" (Daniel 7:8). This could happen only once in history, and it did take place soon after the Roman Empire's fall. This event happened in Europe during the sixth century. To interpret the prophecy as applying to the twenty-first century is to ignore both Scripture and history. It is nothing more than a witch hunting and tilting at windmills.

What to do with doubts and is it easy to notice the extraordinary?

By now you might have questions, and if you have read attentively enough, you probably have a lot of them. One of them might be, "If the antichrist came in the sixth century, why did the world not recognize him?" This question is fair and logical. Isn't it silly to assume that such an extraordinary person as the antichrist came to the world long ago, but remained unnoticed and unrecognized?

The broader question here is, "Is it easy for us to notice the extraordinary?" It seems that the answer is obvious, but let's not rush to a conclusion. The story that we are going to present shows that the answer to this question is not as clear as it seems.

> The following actually happened on an ordinary gloomy and cold January morning. A violinist came to a Washington, DC metro station at rush hour when it was full of people hurrying to work. He took out his violin and started to play for the people passing by. Three minutes went by before a passerby paid him any attention at all. A middle-aged man paused for a split second to listen to the musician and then kept walking. A few moments later, without slowing

down, a woman threw a small bill in his violin case and went on as quickly as she had come. Not long after, someone actually stood against the wall and listened but then looked at his watch and walked on again.

The person who paid the most attention was a three-year-old boy. He would probably have stayed there the whole time that the violinist was playing, but his mom, after repeatedly trying to distract him, decided at last not to waste any more time and took him by hand, dragging him to the escalator. The boy, however, kept his eyes on the musician and followed his mother, looking back until the walls hid him from sight. Something similar occurred with other children.

During the forty-five minutes that the musician played, only six people stopped for a few moments. About twenty people threw him some money as they passed by. When the music was over, nobody noticed. There were no appreciative listeners. Moreover, some people were even grateful that he was leaving. Not far from the spot where the violinist was playing, there was a lady who made her living polishing the shoes of passersby. When street musicians played, she couldn't hear her customers, so she often called the cops to complain, and the musicians seldom lasted long. When the violinist left she gave a sigh of relief.[4]

On that cold morning, January 12, 2007, busy commuters had no idea that the *Washington Post* was carrying out a social experiment. The violinist playing for passersby at the metro station was Joshua Bell, one of the most famous musicians in the world. He was playing a violin worth $3.5 million dollars. He played six Bach masterpieces that morning that were not only profound and emotionally moving but were among the most difficult pieces to play. On that morning, Joshua Bell made thirty-two dollars playing in the metro station. Two days before he had played to a full house in Boston where the average ticket price was one hundred dollars.

The questions that interested the sociologists and caused them to conduct this experiment are like our questions: Is it easy to notice the extraordinary? Do we notice something important when it happens at a wrong or inappropriate time or place? Can we recognize talent in an atypical situation? Considering the results of this experiment, we can confidently state that for most people, time and circumstances play a significant role in how they view a person or an event. The time and the circumstances of the antichrist's coming will play a key role in how easily many are able to identify him.

In many ways the antichrist parallels the real Christ. But let me ask a question: Did the world recognize Jesus when He came to earth? When Jesus came, not as a king but as a humble, poor man, did this not cause many to be confused? Who would expect that the greatest "musician" of all time would be playing, not in the royal palace of Herod but in the metro station where the poor polish passersby shoes and that no one would pay attention when He did? Did Jesus get applause from grateful listeners after He had finished His "performance"? Unlike Jesus, will perhaps the antichrist make his coming known, announcing it publicly so that he will be noticed and recognized? Certainly not. The antichrist wants to stay unrecognized; he wants to do everything possible in order to keep people from knowing the time of his coming. His coming to this world is to take place at a time and location to make certain that no one recognizes him. If the world were to recognize the coming of the antichrist, how could he ever lead into deception as many people as the Bible states he will? How could he make them worship him? These people worship him, not because they see him to be the antichrist. On the contrary, they worship him because they see him as worthy of worship. They don't believe that they are worshiping the antichrist; they believe they are worshiping God. Indeed, there is nothing amazing about the fact that the antichrist remains unrecognized. How else would he be able to deceive nearly the entire world?

But this question concerning why the world failed to recognize the antichrist if he has come, is not the only question that comes to mind. Someone might ask, "How could it ever be that the antichrist came, had power for three and a half years, then disappeared—and we still don't know who he is?" Or some might say, "I've heard that when the antichrist comes he will build a temple in Jerusalem. But we know that the temple is still in ruins following its destruction in A.D. 70. Why hasn't it been rebuilt yet?" "Has the antichrist ever sat in the temple, setting up 'the abomination of desolation,' as the prophecy foretold?"

We will present reasonable answers to each of these questions, but let's do so in turn. Therefore, we invite you to turn the page and read the next chapter.

Notes

1. S. Cyril, *S. Cyril of Jerusalem: Catethetical Lectures*, A Select Library of Nicene and Post-Nicene Fathers of the Christian Church, vol 7, eds. Henry Wace and Philip Schaff (New York: Christian Literature Company, 1894), 107, 108. This quote is included as commentary on Daniel 7:9–14.

2. Irenaeus, "Irenaeus Against Heresies" *Irenaeus*, The Ante-Nicene Fathers, Translations of the Writings of the Fathers down to AD 325, vol. 1, eds. Alexander Roberts and James Donaldson (New York: Charles Scribner's Sons, 1903), 557.

3. You can listen to the full version of the opinion expressed here at The John Ankerberg Show, accessed January 26, 2020, https://www.youtube.com/watch?v=eKQ971XVq2U.

4. See Gene Weingarten, "Pearls Before Breakfast Can One of the Nation's Great Musicians Cut Through the Fog of a DC Rush Hour? Lets Find Out, *Washington Post,* April 8, 2007, https://www.washingtonpost.com/lifestyle/magazine/pearls-before-breakfast-can-one-of-the-nations-great-musicians-cut-through-the-fog-of-a-dc-rush-hour-lets-find-out/2014/09/23/8a6d46da-4331-11e4-b47c-f5889e061e5f_story.html?utm_term=.b14bce083f60.

Chapter 2

Unmasking the Antichrist

1. Different views of antichrist's identity

The antichrist is a Jew

As we have already mentioned, attempts to understand who the antichrist would be and how to recognize him can be traced to the time of the early Christian church. Ever since John, in his epistles, exhorted readers to be alert for the coming of the antichrist, each new generation has been anxious to unravel the mystery.

Let us see, for instance, how Hippolytus of Rome (A.D. 170–236) dealt with these issues:

> Thus did the Scriptures preach before time of this lion and lion's whelp. And in like manner also we find it written regarding Antichrist. For Moses speaks thus: "Dan is a lion's whelp, and he shall leap from Bashan." But that no one may err by supposing that this is said of the Saviour, let him attend carefully to the matter. "Dan," he says, "is a lion's whelp;" and in naming the tribe of Dan, he declared clearly the tribe from which Antichrist is destined to spring. For as Christ springs from the tribe of Judah, so Antichrist

> is to spring from the tribe of Dan. And that the case stands thus, we see also from the words of Jacob: "Let Dan be a serpent, lying upon the ground, biting the horse's heel." What, then, is meant by the serpent but Antichrist, that deceiver who is mentioned in Genesis, who deceived Eve and supplanted Adam (πτερνίσας, bruised Adam's heel)?[1]

Although Hippolytus is not able to tell us the exact name of the antichrist, he obviously suggests narrowing down the search to the Jews. To prove his point, he uses the texts from Scripture that to his mind seem to affirm unmistakably that the antichrist was to come not only from the Jews, but specifically from the tribe of Dan.

The view of Hippolytus was almost certain to be accepted and approved by at least a part of the early church, not due to infallible biblical evidence but clearly because from the very beginning of the New Testament church there was conflict between Jewish Christians and Gentile Christians. Unfortunately, Hippolytus (a Gentile Christian) was held hostage by the attitudes of his time. We see that instead of following an unbiased study of the Scripture, he imposed on the Scriptures ideas that are not only alien to it but that were also keeping with the thinking of his day. These ideas were popular because they appeared to be plain and clear. They also appealed to the carnal human nature in this Jewish/Gentile conflict rather than to the higher nature that calls on Christians to be willing to give one's life for one's neighbor regardless of nationality.

Without a careful study of the Scriptures (if indeed there were any biblical studies at all in such interpretations), it was easy to let one's enmity towards the Jews influence one's interpretation of the prophecies. Also, the interpreter could be seen, not as an anti-Semite but as a follower of Christ—pious, prudent, and sophisticated in Scripture. However, even if the contemporaries of Hippolytus could not afford to pay attention to his loose interpretation of the Bible, we cannot because the difficulties in his views have now become not only evident but also insoluble. For instance, what are we to make of his identifying the antichrist with the tribe of Dan? Where can we locate the tribe of Dan today? From the time of the second temple most Jewish families have not been able to prove their connection to one tribe or another, and that is even more true today. Why would God point to the tribe of Dan as the tribe from which the antichrist would come, especially if it is not possible to identify this tribe?

Nevertheless, the idea of searching for the antichrist among the Jews has not been abandoned. Some people still believe that the Jews will be the first to worship the antichrist. Why? Is such a belief based on new discoveries in the biblical prophecies? Or is it simply a new form of the old animosity towards Jews?

The antichrist is a Muslim

In our day, there some Christians who are ready to assert that the antichrist will originate from the Islamic world. Some even refer to features of his appearance in order to make it easier to recognize him. According to Sunan Abi Dawud, "The Prophet said: The Mahdi will be of my stock and will have a broad forehead [and] a prominent nose. He will fill the earth with equity and justice as it was filled with oppression and tyranny, and he will rule for seven years."[2]

Comparing the prophecy about the Mahdi, the last prophet of Mohammed, who is to come before the end of the world, with the biblical prophecy about the antichrist, some people come to the following conclusion: "We see that several of the most unique and distinguishing aspects of the biblical Antichrist's person, mission, and actions are matched to quite an amazing degree by the description of the Mahdi as found in the Islamic traditions."[3] Certainly it would be helpful to know what the antichrist looks like, but we find it difficult to agree with this view for the following reasons.

First, it is based on the description of the Mahdi in the Islamic tradition. This means acknowledging that the Islamic prophets spoke the truth and that we can trust them as well as the Bible. The conclusion in this case is made based on the sacred books of both Christians and Muslims, and thus their authority is equated. But if that is so, then Christians should add the books of the Islamic tradition to their canon. However, Christians who believe this is an accurate description of the antichrist's appearance must hold the position—perhaps unwittingly—that the words of the Islamic prophets about the Mahdi are trustworthy, but as for everything else they wrote, we do not have to trust it. This is nothing but selective theology and double standards at work.

Second, an anti-Islamic attitude became the new standard in the Western world after September 11, 2001. The events in Syria, the spread of ISIS, immigration concerns, terrorist acts in Europe—all these have escalated the hostility between Christians and Muslims. Given this background, the idea of an Islamic antichrist can easily find a lot of supporters, but, as has happened many times in the course of history, the credibility of this view is based on newspaper headlines and not on the Bible. In fact, few in the Western world would probably pay attention to what is written in the sacred books of Islam if it were not for the attention given to Islam as a result of the connection between Islam and the concerns about terrorism and immigration.

Third, if we accept the Mahdi to be the antichrist, how do we justify the fact that Muslim texts predict him to come directly before the end of the world, not at the end of the fifth or the beginning of the sixth century, as the Bible prophecy says? The time factor still inexorably contradicts these pseudo-biblical teachings.

The antichrist is some well-known politician

Not everyone sticks with generalities; some go further and want to specifically name the antichrist, leaving no room for ambiguity. For instance, the following figures have been identified as the antichrist:

- Peter the Great
- Emperor Frederick II
- Napoleon
- Kaiser Wilhelm
- Adolf Hitler
- Joseph Stalin
- Benito Mussolini
- Nikita Khrushchev
- John F. Kennedy
- Margaret Thatcher
- Mikhail Gorbachev
- Ronald Reagan
- Boris Yeltsin
- Bill Clinton
- Prince William
- Barack Obama

This list is not exhaustive, but it is sufficient to demonstrate the principle by which the candidates have been chosen to assume their place of "honor." The major criterion is to be an outstanding political figure of one's time—preferably a negative one. The more atrocities you commit, the more chance you must be thought of as the antichrist and the more convincing the arguments are to the broader public.

Let's examine some figures in this list. For instance, how was Ronald Reagan chosen? In his case, he was included by someone whose hobby it was to count the number of letters in names. It turns out that there are exactly six letters in each of Reagan's three names: Ronald Wilson Reagan.[4] And since the Bible tells us something about the fearsome number, 666, that was enough to put Ronald Reagan on the list. But Bill Clinton wasn't "fortunate," like Reagan, to have the number 666 hidden in his name, nor were there any details of the prophecy about the antichrist that could be clearly pointing to him. The reasons for putting him on the list are much less dramatic. For some, it was enough to say of Clinton that he can present the truth in such a way that it seems to us like a lie. However, some biblical parallels were needed to make Bill Clinton a more credible candidate—and they were found! As it is known that the antichrist would commit atrocities together with a false prophet, it became necessary to find someone to accompany Bill and who could fill the role of a "false prophet." Guess who was chosen! Sure enough, it was Hillary! (It didn't hurt, either, that her reputation as an honest politician wasn't great.) Then some archive photos were found of an American Indian, apparently a shaman, praying over Hillary. Could anyone wish for better evidence? Bill Clinton was definitely on the list!

But the most "unshakable" argument of all is connected to Barak Obama. Some people identify Obama as the antichrist, quoting Luke 10:18, "And He said to them, I saw Satan fall like lightning from heaven." Then they solemnly remind us that although the text was written in Greek, Jesus spoke these words in Aramaic. According to their argument, the phrase, "*lightning from heaven,*" in Aramaic, sounds like "*baraq obamah.*" So we are to read the text as, "And he said to them I saw Satan fall like '*baraq obamah.*'" If you are not yet convinced by this interpretation of Luke 10:18, you are out of step with the 24 percent of Republicans and 14 percent of all Americans who, according to a Harris poll, believe Barack Obama to be the antichrist.[5]

But seriously, it should be counterargument enough to simply point out that those taking this view have deliberately replaced the word "heaven" (*shamaim*) in the phrase, "lightning from heaven," with the word "hill" (*bama*), because that is the only way they can arrive at something sounding similar (and we stress that it's just *similar*) to "baraq obamah." This flimsy argument not only imposes an alien interpretation on Scripture, but it also inserts an arbitrary text into it and then presents the desired result as genuine and credible!

Such attempts to identify the antichrist with some well-known, contemporary political figure make it difficult not to agree with the unknown authors of the following quotations:

> Sadly, "newspaper exegesis" is one of the most popular hermeneutics of our day. People practice newspaper exegesis when they mistakenly take biblical prophecy as describing what is happening right now in the news. They read Scripture through the lens of the news. Suddenly the president is *the* Antichrist. Computer chips are the mark of the beast. Helicopters are locusts. Myopia may be to blame.*

> Egocentrism. Ethnocentrism. Sociocentrism. Many other centrisms besides. We tend to view ourselves, and those around us, as being at the center of world history. Thus, if our life, culture, or country are coming to an end, we mistakenly believe the *world* is coming to an end. Hence, newspaper exegesis maintains credibility. At least in our eyes.[6]

In order to help us not to be tempted to impose an alien interpretation on the Bible or insert our own ideas into it, God gave us timelines. Remember that according to the prophecy, the time of the coming of the antichrist is the time of the ten kings who succeeded the Roman Empire, three of whom were to be "plucked up." This could happen in history only once and could occur only shortly after the fall of the Roman Empire.

---

* The inability to see the world as a big picture when our culture, religion, and even our own country do not hold a central or leading position.

That's exactly what happened in Europe in the sixth century. To interpret the prophecy as applying to the twenty-first century is to ignore both Scripture and history. It is to conduct a witch hunt and tilt at windmills. When we take into consideration the time factor, we will easily be able to detect the fraudulent from the truth as we read the interpretations of the Bible prophecies. The time factor is the foundation upon which we ought to build the whole structure. In its light, all the speculations about the antichrist as a politician of the present or the future have not a single chance to mislead us. If our dear reader is still not convinced, we suggest reading the first chapter of this book one more time.

2. What the reformers of the church thought of the antichrist

We should examine one more opinion—that the head of the Catholic Church is the antichrist. Though this view appeared much earlier, it took shape and became widely accepted during the time period of the Protestant Reformation. During this time, a shift in the theological paradigm occurred in which the idea that the antichrist was an individual person gave way to understanding the prophecy as referring to a system controlled by the antichrist. As Ron Rhodes, a professor of theology at Dallas University, states, "Indeed, most Reformers tended to see the successive popes and the Roman Church as antichrist."[7]

We can agree with the Reformation view of the papacy, but the Roman Catholic Church is more than the papacy; it is also millions of lay Catholics who were deceived as the Reformers thought. This is the very reason that although the Reformers opposed the pope, they considered it their mission to educate these countless Catholics and not to fight with them. That's why we, too, feel it is crucial to realize this difference. "Among the Catholics there are many who are most conscientious Christians and who walk in all the light that shines upon them, and God will work in their behalf."[8] Thus, like the Reformers, we agree that the key to success is not opposition, but education and freedom of choice. Our goal is to make the light shine brighter in the life of those who want to follow the light of the Bible rather than traditions, those who don't want to live in the moonlight but want to see the dawn.

The most prominent Reformers who encouraged the idea of the papacy as the antichrist were Martin Luther, Philip Melanchthon, John Calvin, Ulrich Zwingli, Nicolas Ridley, Hugh Latimer, William Tyndale, Thomas Cranmer, John Foxe, John Knox, and many others. All of them believed that the papacy or the papal system (not to be confused with Catholic Christians) is the antichrist. "Never in the history of the church were so many responsible scholars, preachers, linguists, theologians and Bible expositors convinced that the antichrist was alive and living in Rome."[9] It's worthwhile to pay attention and examine this view diligently.

3. Does the Papacy fit the role of the antichrist?

We have heard a lot about the coming of the antichrist. We have heard of what he is to do and when he will come. Why then do we have difficulty identifying him by name? It is like trying to recognize a person in a crowd whom we have never met though we have heard much about him. We have been told what he looks like, but we haven't been shown a picture. That reminds me of a story that happened to me at an airport in Hawaii.

My plane was to land at the large international airport in Honolulu. I had made an appointment in advance to be met there by a certain friend. I hadn't been to Honolulu before, and his help would be most valuable to me. But what I did not know was that shortly before my plane was to land, my friend had asked someone else to meet me because some unexpected circumstance had come up that made it impossible for him to do so. I'd never met this new person before. He didn't have my picture. It would be worthless for him to make a sign with my name on it, as I would be looking for my friend and would not be paying any attention to signs. I didn't have a cell phone with me to answer a call. I was depending completely on the prior arrangement I had made with my friend. The person who was to meet me realized all of that. If you were in his place, what question would you ask?

That's right: *How can I recognize someone I've never met among the crowds in the Honolulu International Airport? What does he look like?* My friend had no idea what clothes I would have on. It isn't easy to describe someone with enough detail so that a stranger can pick him out of the crowd.

My friend, however, was not at a loss. He said, "It's simple. He is not Hawaiian; he is not Filipino; he is not Spanish; he is not Japanese or Korean; he is not Mexican; he is not Chinese or Vietnamese, and he is not African-American. He is Russian, like me."

The other person immediately replied, "That's enough; I'll recognize him."

When I landed in Honolulu, I got my luggage and went out to the place where people gathered to meet those who had landed. For some reason, I noticed a person who was carefully scanning everyone's face. As soon as our eyes met, his face brightened, and he moved in my direction. I didn't know what to expect. Walking up to me, he called me by name and explained what had happened and why he was the one to meet me. It was surprising to me that he was able to recognize me based on such a limited description.

In the Bible there is a description of the antichrist that we need to be able to recognize. His description as a "terrible" beast is limited as well, but nevertheless it is good enough for us to be able to recognize him, because God Himself has given the description. This description is not limited to a single detail. It has a lot of peculiarities and characteristic traits that together are designed to eliminate any chance of error. But we still hold that the time of his appearing is the basic identifying characteristic with which we are to start. Just imagine what would have happened if the person meeting me at the airport in Honolulu would have been mistakenly waiting for me an hour or two hours later. Most likely I would have left the airport by that time. There would have been little chance of us meeting each other—that's exactly what happens when some people look for the coming of the antichrist in the future while that "plane" has already landed, and the passengers are all gone.

But besides time, God has given us some other descriptions by which to identify the antichrist. And here is another mistake that people often make. They focus on only one characteristic of the antichrist out of the list of many, and when they see an analogy to someone or something, they happily announce to the world that they have uncovered the identity of the antichrist. But is he truly uncovered?

Imagine that I ask you to meet me at the airport and give you a short description of my appearance—white shirt, blue tie, no mustache or beard, green eyes, light brown hair. Only when *all* the details of the description are found in one and the same person, can you be able to claim that you have found the right person. But in searching to identify the antichrist what happens too often in reality? Many stop their search as soon as they spot a white shirt and a blue tie. In the case of the antichrist, things are even worse. A white shirt alone is enough for many people! Their candidate might also have a beard to the waist and be blind with a black patch over both eyes, but nevertheless they are sure he is the antichrist. Otherwise, it would be necessary for them to throw their theological books into the trash basket because they would be exposed as falsehoods. The fact is that many so-called Bible scholars will soon not need the Bible anymore; a personal dislike will be enough for them to declare someone to be the antichrist. Scriptural passages that do not support their position are ignored as if they do not even exist. They have found one specific criterion—a "white shirt"—and everything else is excluded from consideration.

What description of the antichrist does the Scripture give us, and is it possible to line up that description with the papacy as the Reformers believed? Here is what we have been able to learn about the antichrist from the Bible. Let's summarize everything in one list:

1. He will come after the fall of the Roman Empire (Daniel 7:23, 24).
2. He is both a real man and a kingdom (Daniel 7:17, 23).
3. He will arise among the ten kings who follow Rome's fall, and as three of these kings are subdued (Daniel 7:24).
4. He will persecute God's saints (Daniel 7:25).
5. He will attempt to change God's law (Daniel 7:25).
6. He will have dominion for three and a half years (Daniel 7:25; Revelation 13:5).
7. He will receive a "deadly wound" (Revelation 13:3).
8. His deadly wound will be healed (Revelation 13:3).
9. He will blaspheme (Daniel 7:8, 11, 20; Revelation 13:5, 6).
10. He will sit in the temple of God, claiming to be God (2 Thessalonians 2:4).

As you can see, God took time to see to it that we would have a rather detailed description of the antichrist. No doubt, it involves peculiar symbols and images,* but it is enough for us to avoid making a mistake in identification. Now let's examine whether the papacy can be the fulfillment of the prophecy. In order to do this we'll look

---

* In fact, God chose the language of comparison, the language of symbols and images, not to confuse us but because it is probably the only way to describe events and phenomena that haven't happen yet. Until they take place, there are no words to describe them.

at its history and compare it with each of the characteristic traits of the antichrist.*

He will come after the fall of the Roman Empire (Daniel 7:23, 24)

Although Christianity became an official and recognized religion in the time of Constantine, the authority of the bishop of Rome existed only in conjunction with the power of the emperor and was rather limited. However, during this period a powerful foundation of the papal authority was established in Europe. Before Constantine, one caesar followed another. After Constantine, the succession of caesars was superseded by a succession of pontiffs. The Roman Empire still had emperors, but the throne in Rome was occupied by a bishop. This radically changed the influence of the church, but the pope's powers were still limited. That situation changed dramatically after the fall of the Empire. The pope became a new political power, combining both religious authority and the power of the state (see Daniel 7:24).

In A.D. 476, Romulus Augustus was forced to abdicate the throne, and the papacy quickly and firmly started to exert tremendous influence on history, becoming a new political power that owed its origin to the pagan empire of Rome.

He is both a real man and a kingdom (Daniel 7:17, 23)

As we have clearly shown in the previous chapter, we are to recognize that according to Daniel 7:17, 23, the antichrist is both a man and a kingdom over which he rules. Can these details of the prophecy be correctly applied to the papacy? Absolutely. The papacy is comprised of both the pope as its head and the institution of the

---

* We give here only a brief overview, assuming that the reader is familiar with the prophecy of Revelation 13 and its interpretation.

47

papacy. It is not only a religious power, but oftentimes a political power as well.

Nobody denies that the antichrist would be a man heading a "kingdom" and that the papacy is both a man and a kingdom. But this raises some pertinent questions. If the antichrist is a pope, then are all the popes the antichrist or just one of them? If the antichrist is only one of them, which one? Should we wait for a pope who will rule for three and a half years, as the book of Daniel predicts? Since the pope or antichrist is to come during the fall and fragmentation of the Roman Empire, has the antichrist already come and ruled? To understand these things, we need to study the other details of the prophecy since only the total of all the evidence can give us a trustworthy picture.

He will arise among the ten kings who follow Rome's fall, and will subdue three of these kings (Daniel 7:24)

It is surprising how precisely the prophecy has been fulfilled. After the fall of the powerful and united Roman Empire, there appeared in its place ten barbaric tribes, but only seven of them were able to survive after the sixth century. Today, the seven are known as the Alemans, Burgundians, Franks, Lombards, Saxons, Suevi, and Visigoths. All of these adopted Catholic Christianity and for centuries remained under the pope's great influence, and oftentimes completely dependent upon his will.* The other three tribes—the Heruli, Vandals, and Ostrogoths—didn't exist long. After crushing military defeats, their descendants were assimilated with the other tribes and disappeared forever in the melting pot of history. Each of these three tribes rejected the Catholic version of Christianity and

---

* In the context of Daniel 7, the little horn, or the eleventh horn, refers to the papacy. The prophet underlines that it would be different from the other horns (see Daniel 7:24), and the papal power was markedly different from the power of the kings of the barbaric tribes.

professed the Arian doctrine. Their defeat opened the way for the papacy to exercise sole control of the religious life of Europe—and soon its political life as well. This time period was later called the Dark Ages or the first half of the Middle Ages.

He will persecute God's saints (Daniel 7:25)

Modern man can hardly imagine the scope of the persecution and the degree of intolerance of dissent that were common in the Middle Ages. The papacy had control not only over religion but also over science, medicine, art, law, and therefore the entire state. If Gordano Bruno, more of a scientist and a freethinker than a heretic, was executed, what hope were there for those whose main conflict with the papacy was their religious ideas? Millions of people were burned at the stake, imprisoned, tortured, or forced to hide from persecution. As awful as this persecution was, it was ostensibly carried out for God and in His name! Through this time, the antichrist pursued two goals. First, he got rid of the saints of the Most High, who were able to expose his deceit. And second, by carrying out these atrocities under the guise of religion, the antichrist discredited God Himself. As a result, atheism emerged and started to spread.

Yet some people still make shocking attempts to justify the persecution. For example, John Allen, the chief Vatican analyst for CNN, states that the Inquisition is the atheist's beloved argument.[10] The conclusion being that if you don't want to be taken for an atheist, forget about the Inquisition and the other persecutions perpetrated by the Catholic Church. But this is only half of the problem. Allen gracefully offers the idea that this persecution was simply due to the world people lived in at that time—that it was just a matter of that time period and its morals. He also argues, it was the state agencies that carried out the inquisition, implying that the responsibility may be transferred to the secular authority.¹¹ We can see before our eyes that the rehabilitation of the Inquisition is gaining momentum.*

He will attempt to change God's law (Daniel 7:25)

The prophet Daniel was told that the antichrist would "intend to change times and law" (Daniel 7:25). If the prophecy is indeed speaking here of the papal power, we can determine how it fulfilled this detail. To do this we can compare the text of the Ten Commandments in the Bible with the text of the Ten Commandments as given by the Catholic Church. Even a child who has mastered reading and knows how to play the game Find Five Differences, should be able to see the discrepancies between the two. The Catholic Church has completely removed the second commandment, which forbids image worship, and has divided the tenth commandment into two parts in order to make up for the missing second commandment. It has also replaced the seventh-day Sabbath of the fourth commandment with a command to keep Sunday instead.¹² Thus, millions of adherents of the Catholic and Orthodox Churches† have become victims of a fundamental fraud. The church has sought to get rid of God's law and its Sabbath relationship with "time" by substituting human traditions in its place.

---

* Many of those who lived at that time would probably be surprised by such an interpretation of their history—that the papacy was held hostage by the time and could do nothing with monarchs eager to shed the blood of heretics.

† The Ten Commandments in the Orthodox Church are not different from the Ten Commandments of the Bible. However, only the letter of the law was kept; the spirit and the meaning of the law were changed. The end result of this approach is no different from that of the Catholic Church—Orthodox Christians use images in worship and emphasize Sunday as a new day of rest and worship.

The Ten Commandments in the Bible and in Catholicism, table 3

God's Ten Commandments (Exodus 20:3–17)	The Ten Commandments in the Church of Rome
1 "You shall have no other gods before Me" (verse 3).	1 "You shall worship the the Lord your God and him only shall you serve."[13]
2. "You shall not make for yourself a carved image" (verse 4).	2 "You shall not take the name of the Lord your God in vain."[14]
3. "You shall not take the name of the LORD your God in vain" (verse 7).	3 "Remember the sabbath day, [Sunday]to keep it holy."[15]
4. "Remember the Sabbath [Saturday] day, to keep it holy" (verse 8).	4. "Honor your father and mother."[16]
5. "Honor your father and your mother" (verse 12).	5. "You shall not kill."[17]
6. "You shall not murder" (verse 13).	6. "You shall not commit adultery."[18]
7. "You shall not commit adultery" (verse 14).	7. "You shall not steal."[19]
8. "You shall not steal" (verse 15).	8. "You shall not bear false witness against your neighbor."[20]
9. "You shall not bear false witness against your neighbor" (verse 16).	9. "You shall not covet your neighbor's house."[21]
10. "You shall not covet" (verse 17).	10. "You shall not covet...anything that is your neighbor's."[22]

He will have dominion for three and a half years (Daniel 7:25; Revelation 13:5)

From the book of Daniel, we learn that the power of the antichrist would last for three and a half years (Daniel 7:25). The book of Revelation refers to the same period as "forty-two months" (Revelation 13:5). We don't know if it was revealed to John that his future readers would use other calendars, but for some reason he considered it important to specify that this period also equals 1,260 days (Revelation 12:6)—that is, each month is to consist of exactly thirty days. The God of the Bible is rather precise.

As we learned in the previous chapter, during the early period of Christianity the church fathers were already writing based on Bible prophecy that the antichrist would have power for three and a half years. They also believed that his coming would take place after the fall of the Roman Empire. However, by the middle of the sixth century, there appeared to be a serious problem with this interpretation. Rome had fallen; ten kings had risen in its place, but intense efforts to identify the antichrist led to nothing. By the end of the sixth century, it was clear that something had gone wrong—that something was wrong with the prophetic interpretation—but what was wrong exactly no one could say for sure. Rome had fallen years before, and the antichrist's dominion for three and half years should have changed the world. Why, then, could no one identify this "man of sin"? Besides, it was a settled belief that soon after the coming of the antichrist the end of the world would occur. Why then, if the antichrist had already come without being recognized, had the end of the world not yet taken place, and why had Christ not come to consume His enemy with "the breath of His mouth"?

The only explanation that theologians were left with was that the prophecy would be fulfilled in the future. But if they were to expect his appearance in the future, what were they to do with the statement that the antichrist would come soon after the fall of the Roman Empire?

Each passing year, and each passing century, increasingly discredited their attempts to explain the dilemma. The theologians were at a crossroads. Should they link the coming of the antichrist and his three and a half years of dominion to the time of the fall of Rome or to the time of Christ's second coming? The first option was more biblically sound and consistent with the writings of the church fathers, but the second seemed to fit more correctly with the harsh reality of still not being able to identify the antichrist by name. The more time that passed and the further the church moved away from the time of the fall of Rome, the more popular the second view became.*

However, at the turn of the eighteenth and nineteenth centuries, events occurred that inspired new faith in the words of the prophets. What happened? In 1798, French General Berthier captured Pope Pius VI. This event produced a bombshell. The key figure of the Christian world, who had influenced the lives of millions for many centuries, had been checked as in a game of chess.† The papacy lost its power and was relegated to the margins of political life. These events led to an unprecedented interest in the biblical prophecies. Thanks to the Reformation, many people were convinced that the papacy was the antichrist, but the matter of his three and a half years of dominion had not been solved. And now, with the Reformation giving the people the opportunity to study and read the Bible in their native language, many sincere researchers, scientists, and ordinary people turned to the prophecies and made amazing discoveries.

One such discovery was the "year-day" principle.[23] According to this principle, one "day" in biblical prophecy equals one literal calendar year in history. In fact, this principle was known earlier as the Scripture often mentions it, and those who had studied the Bible were familiar with it (c.f. Leviticus 25:1–8; Numbers 14:34; Deuteronomy 32:7; Job 10:5; 15:20; 32:7; 36:11; Ezekiel 4:4–6; etc.).

---

* Some still consider that the coming of the antichrist is a future event. To solve the contradiction, they invent the term "revived" Roman Empire.

† Checked, but not yet placed in checkmate.

Nevertheless, this principle was not used in interpreting the three and a half years of the antichrist's dominion.* Everyone, or nearly everyone, was convinced that the prophecy was speaking of literal years. But now, many people started to pay attention to the fact that the Bible also refers to this the period as forty-two months or 1,260 days. Was this simply a casual clarification by the prophet John with no real significance? When the year-day principle was followed, and the 1,260 prophetic days were equated with literal years and subtracted from 1798, the year Pope Pius VI had been taken into captivity, the result was A.D. 538.† It turned out that this date, A.D. 538, not only brought one to the time of the "ten kings" when the papacy had taken a dominant position, but it also helped Bible students to see the history of the Middle Ages in the light of prophecy as the history of the antichrist. It became apparent that the antichrist was to be identified as the institution of the papacy, in which popes replaced each other, rather than as any pope specifically.

At this point, someone might ask, "Is it correct to interpret a prophecy, not before its fulfillment but afterwards, from the perspective of the time periods that have passed?"

It is not difficult to give an answer. Many times, Jesus Himself told His disciples that He would be crucified and then would be resurrected on the third day. Did they understand His words? No, they did not. Even after they found His tomb empty, they said to each other, "We were hoping that it was He who was going to redeem Israel" (Luke 24:21). If Jesus had to interpret the prophecy once again for them after its fulfillment, it only goes to show how

---

* Probably the eyes of the scholars "were restrained" (Luke 24:16), and they were not able to apply the familiar principle before the fulfillment of the prophecy. Modern Bible scholars keep studying this prophetic period (see http://boruh.info/khristianstvo/issledovaniya/977-538-god-i-ukaz-yustiniana).

† In this year the tribe of Ostrogoths was expelled from Rome and soon, together with the Heruli and Vandals, their mark in history was lost. Many researchers came to the conclusion that this year was the beginning of the period of rule by the antichrist.

difficult it was for them to understand it beforehand. This shows how hard it is for a person to see an erroneous, but commonly held, view for what it really is! Understanding this weakness, Jesus said, "And now I have told you before it comes, that when it does come to pass, you may believe" (John 14:29). According to these words, it is quite natural that prophecy becomes clear, not before, but after its fulfillment. This happens not only because of its difficulty but also because of our weakness.

As for Daniel's prophecy, there is one more reason why the church fathers and its first interpreters couldn't understand all the details of the prophecy. Daniel was told that his book would have to be "sealed" and that it would not be available for understanding until the end of time (see Daniel 12:9, 10). Many of the things taught by the church fathers were correct, but the three-and-a-half-year period apparently remained a riddle; it was "sealed," until the allotted time became a reality. Why? Probably because true Christianity always lived in the hope of the soon second coming of Jesus Christ. It is unlikely that it would have been wise to tell those who lived in the sixth century that the story of sin would last for so long. However, the Bible assures us that "the Lord is not slack concerning His promise, as some count slackness, but is longsuffering toward us, not willing that any should perish but that all should come to repentance" (2 Peter 3:9).

He will receive "a deadly wound" (Revelation 13:3)

Those who expect the antichrist to come in the future and believe that he will be a certain evildoer, who will exercise his dominion for three and a half years, ignore the "deadly wound" that he is to receive. In their mind, Jesus will come immediately after the antichrist arrives. Such an approach is understandable—why should one interpret a troublesome detail in the prophecy if one can just ignore it and hope that most people will read their biblical commentaries rather than the Bible itself. With such an attitude, you can just skip the uncomfortable passages, and soon nearly everyone will believe that there are no such words in the Bible.

However, it is the detail of the deadly wound that helps those who study to find an answer to the important question, "If the papacy is the antichrist who lost his power in A.D. 1798, and this loss was his deadly wound,* then why didn't Christ come soon afterwards as the church fathers taught He would?" Remember that Cyril of Jerusalem taught that "after perpetrating such things for three years and six months only, he [the antichrist] shall be destroyed by the glorious Second Advent from heaven of the only-begotten Son of God, our Lord and Saviour Jesus, the true Christ, who shall slay Antichrist *with the breath of His mouth*, and shall deliver him over to the fire of hell."[24] Where did Cyril learn of such a sequence of events? Remember that he was commenting on Daniel chapter 7. Right after Daniel saw the beast or antichrist, he said,

> "I watched till thrones were put in place,
> And the Ancient of Days was seated; . . .
> The court was seated,
> And the books were opened" (Daniel 7:9, 10).

What is Daniel describing here? Apparently, he is watching a scene of judgment in heaven. The prophet says nothing of the Second Coming. Instead, he tells us that he has seen a judgment going on in heaven. Cyril thought the judgment must be the end of the world, and that's why he allowed himself to depart from the

---

* Some theologians interpret the "wound" as the Protestant Reformation and its healing as the ecumenical movement, which tries to eliminate differences between Protestants and Rome. In this case, this prophetic period is a period of persecution and is not related to the wound and its healing. Despite the differences in understanding of the wound and its healing, both groups of theologians agree that the prophecy speaks about the papacy.

text and confuse the judgment with the Second Coming. However, the heavenly judgment was shown to the prophet because it is held in heaven and not on the earth, while on the earth the beast or antichrist was able to do nothing as a result of his deadly wound (see Daniel 7:11). These two events—the heavenly judgment and the Second Coming—do not take place simultaneously.

The subject of the judgment is not the main theme of this book,[25] and that is why we are not going to elaborate on it further except to note that the Second Coming is the execution of the sentence that was pronounced earlier in the judgment and that on the day of the Second Coming the destiny of everyone has been determined. This is the reason that the judgment in heaven starts prior to, rather than during, the Second Coming or the end of the world. The first angel of Revelation 14 (see Revelation 14:6, 7) warns those "living on the earth" about the judgment that is going on in heaven. This implies that people still live on earth and that the story of sin is still going on while the angel is being sent to warn the world about the beginning of the judgment in heaven. This helps us to recognize why Jesus didn't return to finish the story of sin right after the beast or antichrist received his deadly wound.

His deadly wound will be healed (Revelation 13:3)

Both Daniel and John indicated that the beast/antichrist will receive a deadly wound (Daniel 7:11; Revelation 13:3). But what is unexpected for many is the fact that in the book of Revelation the antichrist rises again, and his deadly wound is healed. "And I saw one of his heads as if it had been mortally wounded, and his deadly wound was healed. And all the world marveled and followed the beast" (Revelation 13:3). John underlines that the resurrection of the antichrist would be surprising. Everyone thinks that the antichrist has been done away with, but he revives for his last battle with

Christ and His people. This is why the prophet John continues to speak about the antichrist after Daniel has finished his story.

The resurrection of the antichrist is also a subject that is uncomfortable for those who expect the appearance of the antichrist during the last three and a half years of the world's history. They face a challenging question, How does one explain the healing of the deadly wound when Christ Himself is expected to defeat the antichrist and bring about the end of sin? However, if we identify the antichrist as the papacy, everything falls into place. In 1798, the pope, the head of the Roman Church was taken prisoner, after which he soon died. This was a devastating blow for the church, but it was a check, not a checkmate yet. The pope was removed from the world political stage for a time but not permanently. According to the words of the prophet, the deadly wound was to be healed. The process of healing is a sequence of events rather than one single event. While theologians have different interpretations about the healing of the wound, they all agree that the authority and influence of the head of the Roman Catholic Church keeps growing around the world today.

He will blaspheme (Daniel 7:8, 11, 20; Revelation 13:5, 6)

Why would the antichrist blaspheme? Wouldn't he expose himself by his blasphemies? That would be true if we understand blasphemy as uttering curses against God or His people. For this reason, some people tend to see the conflict between the Christian and Muslim civilizations as a conflict between Christ and the antichrist. But this approach is too simplistic. The real antichrist acts much more subtly. He is not going to utter curses against God, which would be abhorrent. However, it is still possible to detect his deceit. The truth is that the Bible defines blasphemy not so much as verbal curses against God, but rather actions and claims by a person who puts himself in God's place (John 10:33). Therefore, if a person assumes

God's name and claims to forgive sins (Mark 2:5–11), he puts himself in the place of God and commits blasphemy.

The prophet John draws our attention to the fact that he saw blasphemous words on the heads of the beast (Revelation 13:1). We are not told what names John saw written on the beast's heads, but we know for sure that the prophet considered it to be blasphemy to ascribe to one's self the names of God. The beast himself and his actions terrified the prophet, but the greatest tragedy was that everything was being done under a cloak, or mask, of piety and godliness. Claiming the names of God for himself, the beast acted as if he were God.

Why does the antichrist need to assume the names of God? We can begin to understand the answer to this question by thinking about identity theft, when someone hacks your email or your social media accounts or creates an account for you on social networks without your permission. Imagine what your enemies could do if they had the password to your email account? Or if they created a new account on a social network in your name and inserted your picture there to make it look credible. People would think they were communicating with you, while you're unaware. They could even distribute malware in your name and send out misinformation or resort to extortion, as so many hackers do. The higher your position, the more prominent you are, the more damage they could do if they cracked your password and impersonated you online.

But when someone dares to assume God's name and His identity, the opportunities to mislead grow in proportion to God's divine status. The literal translation of the word, *antichrist,* is not only "*against* Christ" but also "*instead of* Christ." To be able to impersonate Christ is just what the antichrist wants. Why should he be aggressive and expose himself by being so? Because he wants people to come to him, thinking that they are coming to God (or His representative) when they pray and receive instruction—even though God has nothing to do with this at all (Matthew 7:22, 23).

If the Reformers were correct about their view that the papacy is the antichrist, we should consider how blasphemy is related to the papacy. Today, the head of the Catholic Church is widely known as the pope of Rome or just the pope.* However, this is not the only name or title that the pope holds. If we consult Wikipedia, we will find a rather interesting list of names that are ascribed to the Pope. Among such titles include supreme pontiff, supreme high priest of the universal church, and servant of the servants of God, bishop of Rome, vicar of Christ, successor of the prince of apostles, the primate [archbishop] of Italy, and others.[26] While the names of the pope can be a separate and rather interesting subject for discussion, we are primarily interested in this book in the pope's title as the supreme high priest of the universal church.[27] Of all His titles, this one has a direct relationship to the temple and its services.

This is what the *Catholic Encyclopedia* says regarding the meaning of this title: "The terms Pontifex Maximus, Summus Pontifex, were doubtless originally employed with reference to the Jewish high-priest, whose place the Christian bishops were regarded as holding each in his own diocese (I Clem., XL).... After the eleventh century† it appears to be only used of the popes."[28] Therefore, according to the Roman Catholic view, the place of the Jewish high priest in the era of the New Testament was replaced, not by Jesus Christ but no less than by the pope himself. What a twist! Is this not a substitution

---

* Isn't this what Jesus had in mind when He taught us not to call anyone "father" (Matthew 23:9)?

† In A.D. 1054, the church split into Eastern and Western branches (i.e., the Roman Catholic and the Orthodox Church). In order that no one would think that the bishops of the Eastern Church were equal in their rank to the bishops of the Western Church, the rank of high priest was assigned to only one person—the pope of Rome. By analogy with the Old Testament institution of the priesthood, all the other bishops had to be content with the position of an ordinary priest. This put the Eastern Church in a subordinate position in relation to Rome. In response, the Orthodox patriarchs continued to call themselves priests in their dioceses, but never dared to call themselves priests of the universal church, as did the pope of Rome.

of concepts and a theft of Christ's title? However, millions and even billions of people take it at face value. And this happens even though Christ Himself did not dare to claim this title. The Scripture says,

> And no man takes this honor to himself, but he who is called by God, just as Aaron was.
> So also Christ did not glorify Himself to become High Priest, but it was He who said to Him:
> "You are My Son,
> Today I have begotten You" (Hebrews 5:4, 5).

According to the Bible, it is Jesus, and only Jesus, who is the High Priest. The Epistle to the Hebrews leaves no doubt that only Jesus is worthy to be our High Priest:

> Seeing then that we have a great High Priest who has passed through the heavens, Jesus the Son of God, let us hold fast our confession (Hebrews 4:14).

> For such a High Priest was fitting for us, who is holy, harmless, undefiled, separate from sinners, and has become higher than the heavens; who does not need daily, as those high priests, to offer up sacrifices, first for His own sins and then for the people's, for this He did once for all when He offered up Himself (Hebrews 7:26, 27).

Are the pope of Rome or those who call themselves priests in the Eastern church sinless? Don't they need to confess their own sins? Therefore, the High Priest of the New Testament is Jesus Christ, "separate from sinners," "higher than the heavens." All others cannot be called by that name, especially to claim its universal meaning.

Under the pressure of such clear and indisputable biblical evidence, the so-called high priests are forced reluctantly to lower their status from high priest to being representatives of Jesus Christ, our true High Priest. Trying to avoid this conclusion, they admit, "Yes, of course, we do not dispute that Jesus is our High Priest. But we are His representatives." This answer is a vivid example, however, of how easy it is to mislead by playing with words. After all, we must not forget that the pope's title is not *representative* of the High Priest, but pontifex maximus (high priest). No one would argue that there is a difference between the president and his representative. After all, the representative does not solve anything or make decisions—the president does.

Who says that the pope is even the "representative" of our heavenly High Priest? Did he not simply declare himself as such? That is like saying that a social media account that has been illegally created on your behalf is not you—but your representative. The fact that it was created illegally means that it cannot represent you. The fact that it bears your name does not mean that it legally represents you. Where does the Bible say that anyone on earth is to be the high priest or his representative? So there is not a huge difference whether the popes call themselves a high priest of God or His representative. In both cases, their credentials are only ones that have been issued by themselves.

In addition to assuming titles belonging to Jesus Christ, they have claimed prerogatives belonging only to Him as well. The popes claim that it is they—not our heavenly High Priest—who decides whether a person is forgiven, and that heaven must support the pope's decision![29] In such a situation, it doesn't matter even if a believer understands that our true High Priest is in heaven because, according to the teaching of the Roman Catholic Church, it is the pope, not Jesus, who makes the decision whether or not to forgive.

Finishing our reflections on the blasphemous names of the antichrist, we can come to the clear conclusion that he assigns God's name or title to himself. By stealing the title of "High Priest" and pretending to be Him, the antichrist can redirect our prayers of thanksgiving and confession in the wrong direction. In the time of Christ, there was neither email nor social networks, so Jesus used another illustration and called those who pretend to be someone other than who they are wolves in sheep's clothing (Matthew 7:15). Taking on a form of innocence and of being a servant of God, the antichrist tries to get us to trust him and give him our allegiance. Scripture predicts he will be successful in this and that the world's attention will be focused on the earthly priesthood, rather than on our heavenly High Priest, Jesus Christ. A blasphemous name allows the antichrist to counterfeit the "email" address of the heavenly High Priest and appear to act on His behalf.

He will sit in the temple of God, claiming to be God (2 Thessalonians 2:4)

Even though nine of the ten biblical characteristics of the antichrist have found their fulfillment in the papacy, it is too early to condemn the suspect. We should beware of the current widespread temptation to announce the identity of the antichrist based on only a single match. Yet sometimes twins differ only in the color of the eyes or only in their weight, but this one detail identifies who is who. The same is true in this case. We will be able to tell whether the papacy is the antichrist or his twin only after we study the very last detail—the prophecy that he will sit in God's temple, claiming to be God (2 Thessalonians 2:4).

Through the centuries, this prophecy has evoked great interest, but much in it remains unclear to this day. For example, the temple of Jerusalem was destroyed in A.D. 70, yet for this prophecy to be fulfilled it seems necessary for it to be rebuilt. If the pope is the antichrist, why has there been not one pope who has rebuilt the temple and established his throne there? Can it be that the points of overlap between the papacy and the antichrist, numerous as they are, are still insufficient to accurately identify him? Can the view that the papacy is the antichrist be just another delusion, although it has a lot more biblical evidence that supports it? How can we be sure we are not mistaken? These questions deserve our careful study, so we will devote the next two chapters to examining them.

Conclusion

If the Reformers were right in identifying the papacy as the antichrist, then we can understand why the prophecy says that many people would not recognize the antichrist.

First, they searched for him in the wrong time period. They paid attention to the future and to the present and completely ignored the past. Attempts to find and identify the antichrist began during the time of the apostles. These attempts continue today, with more and more opinions appearing every year. It's easy to get lost in this diversity. However, even in the nineteenth century there was more consensus on this issue than there is today. For example, among Protestant churches, especially on the American continent, there was no doubt that the papacy was the antichrist. This message was boldly preached; books were written; it was taught at home and in Sunday schools. Their separation from the Catholic Church was the very foundation of their existence. Protestants did not hesitate to continue to profess the faith of their Reformation predecessors. Today, however, many Protestants suffer from a loss of historical memory and can't give a definite answer to the question: Who is the antichrist? They are lost in a multitude of guesses because the newspaper headlines and the words of prominent politicians get more attention than the text of the ancient Scriptures. Before looking for the antichrist, it would be a good suggestion for twenty-first century Christians, especially those in Protestant churches in America, to recollect what the founders of their churches believed in, what price they paid for their beliefs, and why they had enough reason to do both.

The other reason why the antichrist has not been recognized is that his coming was expected to be from outside the church, rather than from within it. People looked elsewhere, while it was necessary to look inside the church. It is like looking around the house for your hat when it's on your head, or putting something in the most visible place when trying to hide it. The elephant in the room cannot see the elephant there. It's been said that French writer Guy de Maupassant didn't love the Eiffel tower but always dined in the restaurant located on its ground floor. When asked why, he said, "This is the only place in Paris where it is not visible."

Satan knew that only the church knows about the coming of the antichrist and expects it. He knew that the only place where we would not see the antichrist—and where he would be looked for least—would be the church itself. So he chose to have the antichrist rise from within it. Long before that, the Holy Spirit inspired the apostle Paul to write a warning for us: "For I know this, that after my departure savage wolves will come in among you, not sparing the flock. Also from among yourselves men will rise up, speaking perverse things, to draw away the disciples after themselves" (Acts 20:29, 30).

Not only the church, but every Christian personally, should always remember this lesson in order not to become a wolf in sheep's clothing.

Notes

1. Hippolytus, *"Treatise on Christ and Antichrist,"* *Hippolytus, Cyprian, Caius, Novatian,Appendix,* The Ante-Nicene Fathers, Translations of the Writings of the Fathers down to AD 325, vol. 5, eds. Alexander Roberts and James Donaldson (New York: Charles Scribner's Sons, 1903), 207.

2. Sunan Abi Dawud, 4285.

3. Joel Richardson, *The Islamic Antichrist* (Los Angeles: World Net Daily, 2009), 50.

4. Dorothy Gilliam, "A Superstitious View of Reagan's Victory," *Washington Post*, November 15, 1980, https://www.washingtonpost.com/archive/local/1980/11/15/a-superstitious-view-of-reagans-victory/b40adcaf-9005-40a3-92f7-8cc8c003369e/.

5. David Gardner, "Obama is the Antichrist, say one in four Republicans," *Daily Mail,* March 25, 2011.

6. "Newspaper Exegesis," *Pousto*, November 4, 2013, accessed February 7, 2020, https://pousto.wordpress.com/2013/11/04/newspaper-exegesis/.

7. Ron Rhodes, *Unmasking the Antichrist* (Eugene, OR: Harvest House, 2012), 41.

8. Ellen G. White, *Testimonies for the Church*, vol. 9 (Silver Spring, MD: Ellen G. White Estate, 2010), 243, https://text.egwwritings.org/publication.php?pubtype=Book&bookCode=9T&lang=en&collection=2&section=all&pagenumber=243&QUERY=9T+243.

9. Rhodes, *Unmasking the Antichrist*, 41.

10. John L. Allen, *The Catholic Church: What Everyone Needs to Know* (Oxford: Oxford University Press, 2014), 65.

11. Allen, 65.

12. "The Lord's Day," *Catechism of the Catholic Church* , 3.2.1.3.2, accessed February 9, 2020, https://www.vatican.va/archive/ENG0015/__P7O.HTM.

13. "The First Commandment," *Catechism of the Catholic Church* , 3.2.1.1, accessed February 6, 2020, https://www.vatican.va/archive/ENG0015/__P7B.HTM.

14. "The Second Commandment," *Catechism of the Catholic Church* , 3.2.1.2, accessed February 6, 2020, https://www.vatican.va/archive/ENG0015/__P7H.HTM.

15. "The Third Commandment," *Catechism of the Catholic Church*, 3.2.1.3, accessed February 6, 2020, https://www.vatican.va/archive/ENG0015/__P7M.HTM.

16. "The Fourth Commandment," *Catechism of the Catholic Church*, 3.2.2.4, accessed February 6, 2020, https://www.vatican.va/archive/ENG0015/__P7R.HTM.

17. "The Fifth Commandment," *Catechism of the Catholic Church*, 3.2.2.5, accessed February 6, 2020, https://www.vatican.va/archive/ENG0015/__P7Y.HTM.

18. "The Sixth Commandment," Catechism of the Catholic Church, 3.2.2.6, accessed February 6, 2020, https://www.vatican.va/archive/ENG0015/__P83.HTM.

19. "The Seventh Commandment," *Catechism of the Catholic Church*, 3.2.2.7, accessed February 6, 2020, https://www.vatican.va/archive/ENG0015/__P89.HTM.

20. "The Eighth Commandment," *Catechism of the Catholic Church*, 3.2.2.8, accessed February 6, 2020, https://www.vatican.va/archive/ENG0015/__P8H.HTM.

21. "The Ninth Commandment," Catechism of the Catholic Church, 3.2.2.9, accessed February 6, 2020, https://www.vatican.va/archive/ENG0015/__P8P.HTM.

22. "The Tenth Commandment," *Catechism of the Catholic Church* , 3.2.2.10, accessed February 6, 2020, https://www.vatican.va/archive/ENG0015/__P8T.HTM.

23. For a more detailed study of the "year-day" principle, see William Shea, *Selected Studies on Prophetic Interpretation* (N.P.: Biblical Research Institute, 1982), 56–93.

24. S. Cyril, *S. Cyril of Jerusalem: Catethetical Lectures*, A Select Library of Nicene and Post-Nicene Fathers of the Christian Church, vol 7, eds. Henry Wace and Philip Schaff (New York: Christian Literature Company, 1894), 107, 108.

25. For further details, see Clifford Goldstein, *1844 Made Simple* (Nampa, ID: Pacific Press', 1988) .

26. Wikipedia, s.v. "Pope," last modified February 8, 2020, https://en.wikipedia.org/wiki/Pope.

27. In Latin, *Summus Pontifex* or *Pontifex Maximus.*

28. *Catholic Encyclopedia*, vol. 12 (Robert Appleton Company, 1911), s.v. "Pope."

29. This is what the Catechism of the Catholic Church, says on this subject.

> In imparting to his apostles his own power to forgive sins the Lord also gives them the authority to reconcile sinners with the Church. This ecclesial dimension of their task is expressed most notably in Christ's solemn words to Simon Peter: 'I will give you the keys of the kingdom of heaven, and whatever you bind on earth shall be bound in heaven, and whatever you

loose on earth shall be loosed in heaven. (Matt. 16:19; 18:18; 28:16-20.) The office of binding and loosing which was given to Peter, was also assigned to the college of the apostles united to its head.

The words bind and loose mean: whomever you exclude from your communion, will be excluded from communion with God; whomever you receive anew into your communion, God will welcome back into his. Reconciliation with the Church is inseparable from reconciliation with God. ("The Sacrament of Penance and Reconciliation," *Catechism of the Catholic Church*, 2.2.2.4.6, accessed February 9, 2020, http://www.vatican.va/archive/ENG0015/_P4C.HTM)

Certain particularly grave sins incur excommunication, the most severe ecclesiastical penalty, which impedes the reception of the sacraments and the exercise of certain ecclesiastical acts, and for which absolution consequently cannot be granted, according to canon law, except by the Pope, the bishop of the place or priests authorized by them. ("The Minister of this Sacrament," *Catechism of the Catholic Church*, 2.2.2.4.8, accessed February 9, 2020, http://www.vatican.va/archive/ENG0015/_P4E.HTM)

Here we must pay tribute to the Eastern Church since they dared not usurp such power. They believe that it is God who forgives, but that forgiveness is possible only through His mediator and "representative"—that is, through a priest.

Chapter 3

Will the Temple Be Rebuilt?

The apostle Paul tells us that the antichrist is to sit in God's temple: "Let no one deceive you by any means; for that Day will not come unless the falling away comes first, and the man of sin is revealed, the son of perdition, who opposes and exalts himself above all that is called God or that is worshiped, so that he sits as God in the temple of God, showing himself that he is God" (2 Thessalonians 2:3, 4).

The fact that we learn this from the apostle Paul, rather than from Daniel or John, makes this prophecy unique. Repeated attempts to explain how this prophecy is to be fulfilled have not yet led to a common understanding of the key issues. What kind of temple is spoken of here? What is the meaning of the phrase, "the temple of God"? Will the Jerusalem temple ever be rebuilt?

1. What do the Jews believe?

Until about the middle of the twentieth century, the dominant view was that this text is not referring to the literal temple in Jerusalem. However, when the state of Israel was formed and many Jews returned to their historical homeland, some saw this event as a sign of the literal fulfillment of Paul's prophecy about the temple. In 1987, the Jews opened the Temple Institute, the main task of which was the restoration of the temple. Since then, the number of supporters of the idea of a literal temple has continued to increase. In this context, it would be interesting to study and try to understand what is behind the desire of some Jews to rebuild the temple and what this has to do with the prophecy.

It would probably be difficult to find a better source of information regarding the goals and objectives of this organization than the Temple Institute's official website. On the website, the leaders of the Institute explain that it was founded with the purpose of fulfilling a divine command to Israel to build a house of God or the temple. Toward this end, the Institute carries out all the necessary studies, teaches people about the functions of the priests, makes the clothes and items for the sanctuary, and prepares for its construction. These Jews consider the construction of the temple as a matter of faithfulness to God; without it, they feel they can't obey His commandments.[1] The Pentateuch of Moses, or the Torah, consists of 613 commandments, 202 of which are impossible to fulfill without a temple because they are associated with temple worship.[2] These Jews expect the coming Messiah but do not think they need to wait until He will help them build the temple. The temple must be built to give believers the opportunity to serve God as He has commanded. In their view, Judaism without a temple is only nostalgia—a memory of what this religion should be. They derive their confidence that God approves of their intentions from the prophecies of the Old Testament speaking about the temple.

It is interesting to note here, that among the prophecies of the Old Testament about the restoration of the temple the prophecy of Ezekiel is not only the most extensive, but it is also the only prophecy that detailed the size of the new building. It would seem natural to assume that the Jews should plan to construct the temple according to the specifications set forth through this prophet. However, the Temple Institute, for some reason, does not intend to build such a temple. Let's see why.

First, we need to consult the prophecy itself. It was given as a promise to the Jews taken into captivity to Babylon that the city of Jerusalem and the destroyed temple would be restored. Why, then, did the restoration of the temple not happen according to the plan described by the prophet? There can be only one answer to this question: "Prophecies respecting a future glory of Israel and Jerusalem were primarily conditional on obedience.... They would have met a literal fulfillment in the centuries following had Israel fully accepted God's purposes concerning them. The failure of Israel made impossible the fulfillment of these prophecies in their original intent."[3] Only a few returned, and these fell far short of God's purpose for them.

A contemporary of Ezekiel, the prophet Jeremiah, best explains the principle of conditional prophesies: "The instant I speak concerning a nation and concerning a kingdom, to pluck up, to pull down, and to destroy it, if that nation against whom I have spoken turns from its evil, I will relent of the disaster that I thought to bring upon it. And the instant I speak concerning a nation and concerning a kingdom, to build and to plant it, if it does evil in My sight so that it does not obey My voice, then I will relent concerning the good with which I said I would benefit it" (Jeremiah 18:7–10).

The conditional character of some prophecies helps us understand why they have not been fulfilled, but it doesn't answer the question, "What stops the Jews from rebuilding the temple today, using Ezekiel's plans and specifications?"

First, today there is a mosque—the Dome on the Rock—sitting on the traditional site of the Jerusalem temple. And there are different opinions as to where the temple should be erected. Some believe that it must be built on the place where the mosque stands today. Others believe that it could fit beside the mosque.

To destroy the mosque, which is the third holiest site in the Muslim world, in order to build a Jewish temple on that site would cause such conflict that many believe it would be the beginning of

World War III. No one in their sound mind would venture to take such a step. The only option is to build the temple near the mosque. However, the size of Ezekiel's temple is much bigger than the space next to the mosque. This means that it would be impossible to build a temple the same size as the one shown to the prophet Ezekiel in vision without removing the mosque.

Second, Ezekiel's temple is so large that its construction would not only require the destruction of the mosque, but it would also require the space of the entire Temple Mount. This raises another unsolvable problem—the Eastern Wall of old Jerusalem. This wall sits on a Muslim cemetery. In the wall itself there is an inactive gate—the Golden Gate. Jews believe the Messiah will enter through this gate. Christians say that this already took place during Jesus' triumphal entry into the city prior to His crucifixion. When the Turks conquered Jerusalem, Süleyman the Magnificent ordered the Golden Gate sealed shut so that the prophecy of the Messiah's entry through it would never be fulfilled. Some mosques were built right next to the gate, and the sultan organized a cemetery for Islamic soldiers just outside the wall, so that on the day of judgment when the dead are resurrected, they could prevent the Messiah from entering the city through the Golden Gate. It would be impossible to use this area for rebuilding the temple because God, through Moses, prohibited building His house on human bones or even touching a dead body before visiting the temple. No ritual cleansing of any kind would purify the earth from the defilement caused by the cemetery and make it suitable for the construction of the temple. It is inappropriate for an ordinary Jew to even go through a cemetery to get to the temple, so it would be even more inappropriate for the High Priest to do so. For all of these reasons, it appears impossible to begin the construction of Ezekiel's temple or even Solomon's smaller temple. However, the Temple Institute continues to collect generous donations from gullible people who could have saved their money if they have studied the books of Moses and the prophecies. As sad as it is, we must tell them that they are mistaken.

2. What do Evangelicals believe?

Oddly enough, nobody knows whether there are more Jews who wish to rebuild the temple or Christians. It seems that Christians would have nothing to do with the Jewish temple, wouldn't it? Don't Christians believe that the Messiah has already come? Don't they believe that the sacrifices in the temple lost their significance when Jesus became the sacrifice for our sins on the cross? Then why are there so many Christians donating millions of dollars and encouraging the Jews to rebuild the temple?[4]

The point here is that many Christians also believe that the Scriptures predict the restoration of the temple. But unlike the Jews, they quote both the Old Testament and the New Testament as support for this idea—especially 2 Thessalonians 2. For several decades, influential Christian pastors and theologians have been writing books[5] and preaching sermons from their pulpits about the restoration of the temple. There is an entire generation of Christians who cannot even imagine that the temple would not be rebuilt, yet it was not long ago when not one Christian believed the temple should be restored. A relatively short time has passed since this teaching started to become quite popular among evangelical Christians. The main difference here is that these Christians believe that it is the antichrist who will come to a rebuilt temple, while Jews look for the Messiah to do so.

Let's give the floor again to Jimmy DeYoung, who is one of the brightest representatives of this position. He explains on *The John Ankerberg Show*,

> Let me just remind everybody of the Scriptures. Daniel nine, twenty-seven, "And in the midst of the week he

[the antichrist] will put an end to the sacrifice and offering. . . . He will set up abomination that causes desolation" [NIV]. Jesus confirmed that in Matthew chapter twenty-four verse fifteen: "When you see standing in the holy place 'the abomination that causes desolation,' spoken of through the prophet Daniel" [NIV]. The apostle Paul confirms the same thing in the Second Epistle to the Thessalonians chapter two verse four: "He [the antichrist] sets himself up in God's temple, proclaiming himself to be God." And in Revelation chapter eleven verse one the prophet John was told to measure the space for the temple of God. "Go and measure the temple of God"[NIV]. So we have four proof texts that there will be a temple on the temple mount.[6]

According to DeYoung's view, all these prophecies speak about the rebuilding of the temple in Jerusalem and about the coming of the antichrist, who in some way defiles this temple. Though the prophecies themselves do not say a word of the rebuilding, his logic is simple—the temple is mentioned and the "abomination of desolation" is in it. This is enough for him to conclude that the temple will be rebuilt. When we compare the position of the Jews and that of the Evangelicals, we have something like the following:

Differences Between Jewish and Evangelical Views Regarding the Third Temple, table 4

Jews	Evangelicals
The Old Testament predicts the rebuilding of the temple.	Both the Old and the New Testaments predict the rebuilding of the temple.
The temple is necessary in order to obey God and keep His commandments.	The temple is necessary for the prophecy about the antichrist to be fulfilled.
The system of sacrifices will be restored in the temple.	"The abomination of desolation" will be set up in the temple by the antichrist.
The Messiah will come to the temple.	The antichrist will come to the temple.

In this comparative analysis, we should pay attention to the fact that the motives that drive the Jews are much more noble than those of the Evangelicals. For the Jews, it is a matter of their loyalty to God; for the Evangelicals, it is a reality show in which the antichrist will deceive the Jews and persecute them while Christians will observe these events from a safe distance.

The only clear way to understand who is right is to study the Bible for ourselves. That means that if we want to know the truth, we should examine each of the prophecies cited. There are not many*— only four.† *If these prophecies are, indeed, talking about the rebuilding*

---

* In this book we are not going to elaborate on each of the prophecies that are cited by the Jews. We have already explained the most detailed of them—the prophecy of Ezekiel. This prophecy was conditional in nature. We'll speak briefly of the other Old Testament prophecies later.

† Evangelicals do not mention other texts confirming their position. They sometimes say that there is other scriptural evidence (i.e., Daniel 11:45), but since these texts are even less convincing, they speak of them rarely and reluctantly.

of the temple, then we also must believe that it will be rebuilt. However, if they refer to something else, then we have no biblical grounds to say that the temple will be restored. In that case, the hopes of both Jews and Christians, although unobjectionable at face value, still have nothing to do with the prophecies.

So what prophecies are readily cited as a proof that the temple of Jerusalem will be rebuilt?

1. Daniel 9:27
2. Mathew 24:15
3. 2 Thessalonians 2:3, 4
4. Revelation 11:1

3. The prophecy of Daniel 9:27

In this chapter, we are going to pay attention only to the first two texts. The words of Paul about the man of sin in the temple of God (2 Thessalonians 2:3, 4) will be examined in the next chapter, and the study of the prophecy in Revelation 11 will conclude our research.

Let's read the whole passage of Daniel.

> "Know therefore and understand,
> That from the going forth of the command
> To restore and build Jerusalem
> Until Messiah the Prince,
> There shall be seven weeks and sixty-two weeks;
> The street shall be built again, and the wall,
> Even in troublesome times.
> "And after the sixty-two weeks
> Messiah shall be cut off, but not for Himself;
> And the people of the prince who is to come
> Shall destroy the city and the sanctuary.

The end of it shall be with a flood,
And till the end of the war desolations are determined.
Then he shall confirm a covenant with many for one week;
But in the middle of the week
He shall bring an end to sacrifice and offering.
And on the wing of abominations shall be one who makes desolate,
Even until the consummation, which is determined,
Is poured out on the desolate" (Daniel 9:25–27).

Frankly speaking, it is not clear how anyone can conclude that verse 27 says that it will be the antichrist who brings sacrifice and offering to an end, but let's do everything in order. First, we must say that Daniel uses the familiar "year-day" principle here.* When he is speaking of "seven weeks and sixty-two weeks," he is speaking respectively of 49 years and 434 years, which together comprise 483 years. That means that 483 years should pass from the command to restore Jerusalem† (457 B.C.) to Christ, the Prince. The Messiah is the main person here in this prophecy. This is the first, the simplest, and the most important conclusion that can come from any unbiased research. Let's state all the points.

The antichrist is not mentioned in the first part of verse 27

We can find only two characters in the context of verses 25–27—Christ and a "prince who is to come." There are no other persons

---

* For some reason, all agree that prophetic weeks are meant here, not literal weeks. However, when Daniel and John tell us about 1,260 days or three and a half years, some argue that these periods should be considered literal and not prophetic. This resembles a double standard.

† There were four different decrees, but the decree of Artaxerxes is the only one of which the angel is speaking. For details see Frank Holbrook, ed., *70 Weeks, Leviticus, Nature of prophecy*, Daniel & Revelation Committee Series, vol. 3 (Silvers Spring, MD: Biblical Research Institute, 1986) 64–74; Clifford Goldstein, *1844 Made Simple* (Nampa, ID: Pacific Press', 1988), 47–50.

acting in this passage. We know who Christ is, and, as for the prince whose people destroy the city and the temple, it was the Roman General Titus who led the battle against Jerusalem in A.D. 70. Some translations contain the word, "he," in verse 27—"he shall bring an end to sacrifice and offering." This pronoun, "he," refers to someone mentioned earlier. The events happening in verse 27 happen as a result of the acts of either the Messiah or Titus. To ascribe these acts to some unmentioned third person is to ignore the context of the passage.

We were taught even in elementary school that the number seventy follows the number sixty-nine. Both basic arithmetic and the text itself forbid us to insert hundreds of years between the end of the sixty-ninth week and the beginning of the seventieth week. This means that the last prophetic week should extend to the end of A.D. 34 and complete the prophetic period of 490 years. If the covenant is to be confirmed during this last week, it is Christ who must do it simply because Titus was not yet born at that time.

An analysis of the literary structure of the passage shows us that a technique of Jewish poetry is employed here in which ideas or themes are paired together in a distinct pattern. This means that the first part of verse 26 is paired with (speaks to the same idea as) the first part of verse 27, and the second part of verse 26 is paired with the second part of verse 27. We can represent it with symbols as follows:

    A (verse 26)   A' (verse 27)
    B (verse 26)   B' (verse 27)[7].

An understanding of how Jewish poetry functions makes it very clear that both the beginning of verse 27 and the beginning of verse 26 speak about Christ. Moreover, it becomes clear that the sacrifice will end because Christ is put to death (verse 26).

Parallelism in Daniel 9:26, 27, table 5

Verse 26	Verse 27
A "And after the sixty-two weeks / Messiah shall be cut off, but not for Himself."	A' "Then he shall confirm a covenant with many for one week; / But in the middle of the week / He shall bring an end to sacrifice and offering."
B "And the people of the prince who is to come / Shall destroy the city and the sanctuary. / The end of it shall be with a flood, / And till the end of the war desolations are determined."	B' "And on the wing of abominations shall be one who makes desolate, / Even until the consummation, which is determined, / Is poured out on the desolate."

This is fully consistent with Christian theology. When Christ brought Himself as a sacrifice, the service in the temple that pointed symbolically to this event was ended by God Himself, as evidenced by the fact that the veil of the temple was torn from the top to the bottom. Thus, it is Christ, not antichrist, who ended the sacrifices. It remains only to wonder why those who claim to be Christians are willing to sponsor the rebuilding of the temple and restore the sacrificial system.

The prophecy says, "He shall confirm a covenant with many for one week" (verse 27). The angel also explained that this would happen in the middle of the week. How was this prophecy of the confirmed covenant fulfilled? As we know, the earthly ministry of Christ lasted for three and a half years. The day before His death, He gathered His disciples for the Passover supper where He declared, "This cup is the new covenant in My blood. This do, as often as you drink it, in remembrance of Me" (1 Corinthians 11:25). These words of Jesus explain how the covenant was confirmed. Jesus brought Himself as a sacrifice for sin and established the rite of the Lord's

Supper as a reminder of this event. "This cup is the new covenant in My blood." We should not be confused by the word "new," as if Jesus was ratifying a brand-new covenant. It is a common misconception that God had two covenants, one for Jews and another for Gentiles. The apostle Paul clearly says that the blessings of the covenant God made with Abraham belong not only to the Jews but also to the Gentiles (see Galatians 3:14). This means that through Abraham God made a covenant with both the Jews and the Gentiles (see Galatians 3:8, 26–29). It's also wrong to consider that before Christ, people were justified by works, and then after the cross we are justified by faith. Paul gives the Galatians an example, which shows that Abraham was justified by faith and not by works of the law (see Galatians 3:6). He reminds them that they have received the Holy Spirit by faith and not by works of the law. Thus, always and in all nations, God has set forth the same terms of salvation. Jesus only confirmed this covenant by dying on the cross; He did not institute a new covenant.

But, then, what is the meaning of the word "new"? The Epistle to the Hebrews says, "The first covenant had ordinances of divine service and the earthly sanctuary" (Hebrews 9:1). Since the earthly sanctuary and its ceremonies lost their meaning after the crucifixion of Christ, there are no such ordinances in the new covenant. That's why Jesus calls it "new" (see Hebrews 8:13). Apart from this fact, everything about the covenant remains the same—the conditions of salvation and the parties that entered the covenant and the promised blessings—all remained in effect in the renewed covenant, which Christ confirmed by His death.

The second part of the Daniel 9:27 does not speak of the antichrist

The second part of verse 26 speaks about "the people of the prince" who will destroy the city and the temple. This prophecy was fulfilled when the Romans destroyed Jerusalem and the sanctuary in A.D.

70. As we have seen, according to the principle of Hebrew poetry, the second part of verse 27 refers to the same event and the same persons. Any argument that a new character is introduced in verse 27—especially such an important one as the antichrist—cannot be upheld by the text itself.

Issues with mathematics

Attempts to explain the prophecy of Daniel 9 as referring to the antichrist often lead to insoluble problems with the sixty-nine weeks or 483 years. Most of these charts suggest counting the sixty-nine weeks as beginning in 444 B.C. or 445 B.C. or even 446 B.C. But at this point, their problems are not over but just beginning. Counting 483 years (excluding year "zero") from these dates, they come to 40, 39, or 38 B.C. But none of these years ever appear in their calculations or charts. They use A.D. 30, 32, or 33. We would like to ask, "Where do these dates come from?" However, it seems that most of these interpreters fail to notice this new development in the science of mathematics, this startling discovery in the theory of numbers! Sometimes they try to explain this discrepancy by the fact that the Jewish year was shorter than modern years, but this is just another attempt to exploit the ignorance of some people. The Jewish calendar is a lunar/solar one. This means that the months are determined by the cycle of the moon and the years by the cycle of the sun. To synchronize the twelve lunar cycles into one solar cycle, it is necessary to add an additional month periodically (seven times every 19 years). Doing this made their year match the solar cycle, and it also made it possible for the Jews to always keep the Passover in the spring.

Below we list some of these charts that perform miracles in the science of mathematics.

ANTICHRIST AND HIS TEMPLE

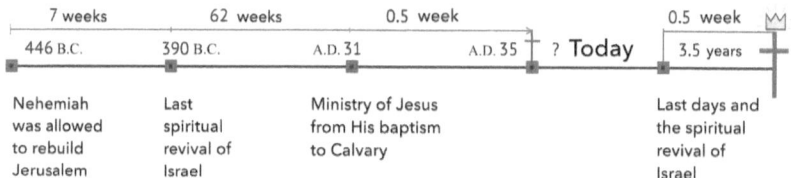

Chart 1

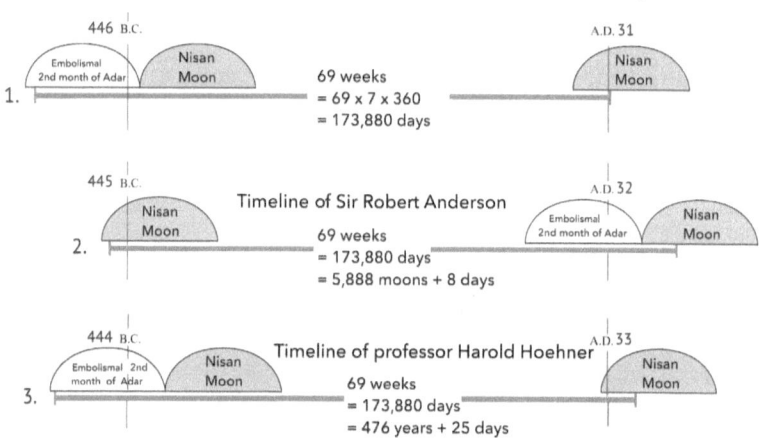

The testimony of the Nisan moons in the establishing the timespan of the 69 weeks

Chart 2

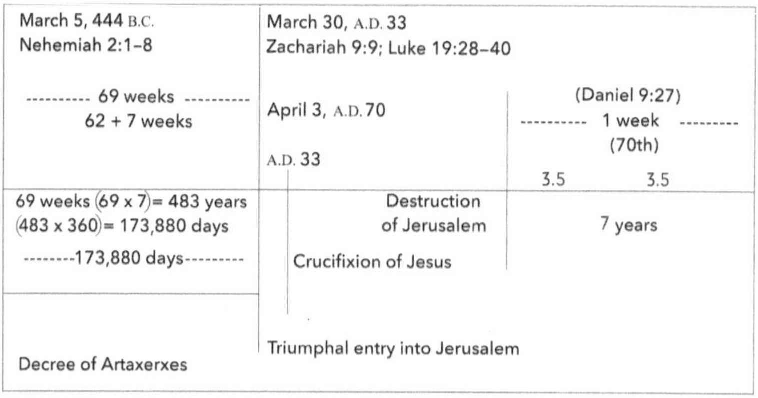

March 5, 444 B.C. Nehemiah 2:1–8	March 30, A.D. 33 Zachariah 9:9; Luke 19:28–40	
--------- 69 weeks --------- 62 + 7 weeks	April 3, A.D. 70 A.D. 33	(Daniel 9:27) --------- 1 week --------- (70th) 3.5 3.5
69 weeks (69 x 7) = 483 years (483 x 360) = 173,880 days --------173,880 days--------	Destruction of Jerusalem Crucifixion of Jesus	7 years
Decree of Artaxerxes	Triumphal entry into Jerusalem	

Chart 3

So we can conclude that the first of four so-called temple prophecies does not promise to rebuild the temple. How are we to properly understand the prophecy of Daniel 9:27? The next chart answers this question.

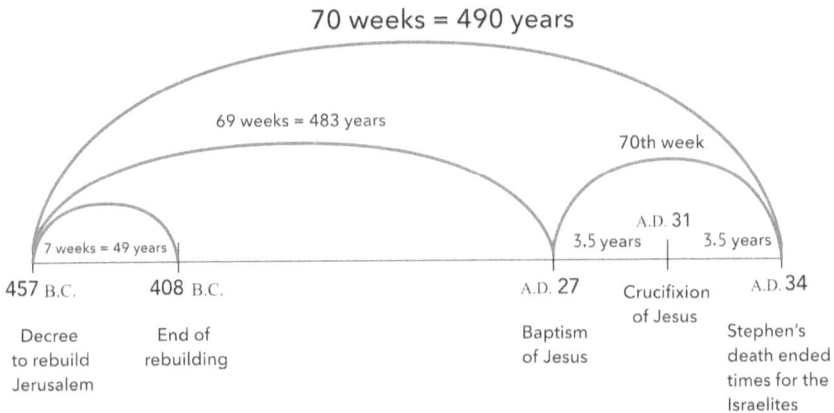

Chart 4

First, it is necessary to take the decree of Artaxerxes (457 B.C.) as marking the beginning of the sixty-nine prophetic weeks. The decrees of Cyrus and Darius issued in 538/537 B.C. and 520 B.C. applied only to the temple and not to Jerusalem as a whole. The decree of 445/444 B.C. gave Nehemiah permission to only make repairs to the walls and gates of the city. All this work was completed in just 52 days (Nehemiah 6:15). That short time period could be enough to only repair and not to rebuild the city.

Second, the phrase "until Messiah the Prince," means the time before Christ's *ministry* began—not before His *birth*. The word, *Christ*, means "the anointed one," and we read of the anointing of Jesus Christ by the Holy Spirit in Luke 3. The story refers to His baptism. At the beginning of this chapter, Luke states that this occurred "in the fifteenth year of the reign of Tiberius Caesar" (Luke 3:1). Historians agree that the fifteenth year of Tiberius equates to A.D. 27. "Some have been puzzled as to how Christ could begin His work in A.D. 27 when the record says that He was about 30 years of age when He started His public ministry (Luke 3:23). This is because when the Christian Era was first computed, an error of about four years occurred. That Christ was not born in A.D. 1., is evident from the fact that when He was born Herod the Great was still alive, and Herod died in 4 B.C. (see Matt. 2:13-20)."[8]

Third, the last week immediately follows the sixty-ninth since it is needed to complete the time allotted for Israel (see Daniel 9:24), which is followed by the "times of the Gentiles" (Luke 21:24; Revelation 11:2) when the gospel was preached to the Gentiles. To tear the last prophetic week off from the previous one is possible only if one pulls the text out of its context.

Fourth, in the middle of the last week—or after three and a half years of ministry—Christ was sacrificed, and this event confirmed the covenant and put an end to offerings.

Fifth, the 490 years of probation for the Jews ended with the stoning of Stephen, the first martyr for Christ. A witness to this event was Saul, whom God later made to be the apostle Paul and sent him to preach to the Gentiles.

In this prophecy there is no indication that the temple must be rebuilt.

5. Jesus' words about "the 'abomination of desolation' " in Matthew 24:15

According to the view of some interpreters, the other prophecy that presumably speaks of the rebuilding of the temple is the one expressed by the words of Jesus, " 'Therefore when you see the "abomination of desolation," spoken of by Daniel the prophet, standing in the holy place' (whoever reads, let him understand), 'then let those who are in Judea flee to the mountains' " (Matthew 24:15, 16). The logic behind this is the same as their interpretation in Daniel 9—the abomination of desolation can refer only to the temple and consequently it must be rebuilt. Therefore, even if the

Bible text doesn't mention the temple in this context, the proponents of this interpretation do not see the need to put forth additional arguments in favor of their position.

However, in our opinion, it is not the text's reference to the abomination of desolation that is crucial, but rather it is the reference to the prophecy of Daniel. In other words, Jesus' words in Matthew 24 are nothing more than His explanation of the second part of Daniel 9:27. Remember that we learned earlier that verse 27 was referring to Titus and not to the antichrist. If the conclusions we set out above are true, then this prophecy speaks of the events of A.D. 70 and has nothing to do with the restoration of the temple. Let's check whether this is correct.

First, we need to make an observation. In some translations of Daniel 9:27, the word *temple* or *sanctuary* appears.* This makes some people believe that the temple is implied here. However, these words are not present in the original Hebrew text but reflect the opinion of the translators that it should be there. Thus, it is not a matter of translation but one of interpretation, and we cannot agree with such an interpretation. Also the word *wing* has caused many people to believe that the scripture is speaking here about the temple. However, the Hebrew word כָּנָף (*kanaph*) can be also translated as "edge," "border," or "corner" (of the earth), (i.e., Job 37:3; 38:13; Isaiah 11:12; 24:16; Ezekiel 7:2) and the translators used this meaning in more than ten instances in the Old Testament. Does this mean that one is not able to learn the truth concerning key matters of the Bible without a knowledge of the original languages of Scripture? Certainly not. Anytime there is a need for an explanation, the Bible explains itself. So it is this time. To understand the prophecy it is enough for us to understand how Jesus explained it.

---

* The word *temple* is used in NIV, GNT, ICB, NIVUK, and NIRV. The word *sanctuary* is used in TLB, and it appears as "place of worship" in *The Message*. We do not find either of those terms in most of the English translations of Daniel 9:27 or in the Hebrew text.

Let's read again Matthew 24:15, 16. " 'Therefore when you see the "abomination of desolation," spoken of by Daniel the prophet, standing in the holy place' (whoever reads, let him understand), 'then let those who are in Judea flee to the mountains.' "

First, note that Jesus advised the disciples to flee when they saw the abomination. If Jesus was talking here about the destruction of the temple by the Romans, there is a big problem with the usefulness of His counsel. The fact is that when the Romans rushed into Jerusalem, their anger was so strong that even Titus was not able to control them. At this point it was too late for the inhabitants of Jerusalem to flee for their lives.

Second, Jesus did not say that the "abomination of desolation" would be in the temple, but in the "holy place." What does that mean? Again, the Bible explains itself. "But when you see Jerusalem surrounded by armies, then know that its desolation is near. Then let those who are in Judea flee to the mountains, let those who are in the midst of her depart, and let not those who are in the country enter her" (Luke 21:20, 21).

Luke repeats Jesus' words, but he quotes Jesus as saying, "Jerusalem surrounded by armies" instead of the " 'abomination of desolation,' spoken of by Daniel the prophet, standing in the holy place." *This means that these are interchangeable concepts.* That is why we believe that the words of Daniel would be better translated as "on the edge [of the earth] will be the abomination of desolation." Inhabitants of Jerusalem standing on her walls could see armies surrounding them on the horizon (on the edge of the earth). This wording makes Jesus' counsel of practical value and doable. But how could people escape from the surrounded city? Historians say that the first siege of the city in A.D. 66 was interrupted. But in A.D. 70, the Romans came back, and this time they destroyed the city. This short respite was enough for all who trusted the words of Christ to be saved.

Probably the only issue that requires further explanations is the question, "Why are the Roman troops called 'the abomination of desolation' standing in the 'holy place'?" If we understand that the Holy Land was not limited to the borders of the city of Jerusalem, and if we also recognize the attitude of the Jews toward the pagan idols and their images on the Roman banners, then everything falls into place. The Christians who lived in Jerusalem at that time were Jews, and they could easily understand that "when the idolatrous standards of the Romans should be set up in the holy ground, which extended some furlongs outside the city walls, then the followers of Christ were to find safety in flight."[9] In any case, whether we understand the "abomination of desolation" to be the idols around Jerusalem or the destruction of the temple, we must agree that this prophecy was fulfilled by Titus and not by the antichrist. The prophecy referred to, and was fulfilled through, Herod's temple, not the temple which some people hope to rebuild today.* This means that neither Daniel 9:27 nor Matthew 24:15 contain a single word about the temple being rebuilt!

Conclusion

As we have seen, the reference to the "abomination of desolation" in Daniel 9:27 and Matthew 24:15 does not give us a basis for stating that the temple will be rebuilt. When individuals come to such a conclusion, it is difficult to understand what principles of interpretation are guiding them. But what is even harder to understand is the motivations of those Christians who want the temple to be

---

* Sometimes we can say that prophecy can have a double fulfillment, but in this case only the first fulfillment is the literal one; the second is symbolic. For example, Jesus said, "But as the days of Noah were, so also will the coming of the Son of Man be" (Matthew 24:37). Noah built a literal ark but that does not give us the right to say that the ark will be built again. A second and literal fulfillment of the "abomination of desolation" is contrary to this principle of a dual fulfillment of the prophecies.

restored and to begin functioning. Jews want to build the temple to worship God, but why then do Christians, who believe the antichrist will come to this temple, donate funds for its restoration? The Jews do not believe Jesus Christ to be the promised Messiah and do not embrace His death on the cross as a sacrifice for sin. So they don't see any reason for the temple service and sacrifices to end. In other words, those who wish to rebuild the temple and offer sacrifices there do so because they deny that Jesus is the Messiah. John warned us about this when he said that the antichrist (in the broad sense of the word) would deny that Jesus is the Messiah (1 John 2:22). Therefore, whenever we hear that the sacrifice of Jesus did not accomplish enough (and thus it is necessary to compensate this lack through other sacrifices) or that He did not do anything at all (since He was not the Messiah), we must recognize this as the handwriting of the antichrist. What an amazing thing to see Christians sponsoring and inspiring the Jews to build the temple! The temple is useless without a sacrifice, and why does the God of the Bible need an earthly temple and its sacrifices if the Lamb of God has already been slain?

Summing up the results of our research in this chapter, we can state the following points:

1. Ezekiel's prophecy about the restoration of the temple was conditional; it depended on the loyalty of Israel to God. The refusal of many Jews to return from the Babylonian captivity made the fulfillment of this prophecy impossible.
2. Other Old Testament prophecies about the Lord coming to the temple (such as Haggai 2:7–9) were fulfilled when Jesus was on the earth (John 2:13–16).
3. Other prophecies of the Old Testament speak about the rebuilding of the temple after the Babylonian captivity. They are also conditional, and the condition is "if you diligently obey the voice of the LORD your God" (Zechariah 6:15). These

prophecies can have a second fulfillment in the Christian church (1 Corinthians 3:16, 17; Ephesians 2:19–22; 1 Peter 2:3–5) as the church is called the body of Christ (Ephesians 1:22, 23, John 2:19–22).

4. The context of Daniel 9:27 speaks about the Messiah, who will confirm the covenant and put an end to the sacrifices. The New Testament shows how exactly this was fulfilled (see Matthew 27:50, 51). The word *he* can refer only to the Messiah and not to the antichrist, since the latter never appears in the context of the passage.

5. The seventy prophetic weeks started in 457 B.C. and ended in A.D. 34, completing the determined time for Israel. The last prophetic week followed the sixty-ninth week and lasted from A.D. 27 to A.D. 34.

6. Jesus warned that the "abomination of desolation" in the "holy place" would be a sign for the Christians to flee for their lives. When the standards (pagan images, flags, and banners) of the Roman army surrounded Jerusalem, the believers understood that the prophecy had been fulfilled.

7. Not long before His crucifixion Jesus spoke words that could be understood as meaning that the temple would not be rebuilt. He said, "See! Your house is left to you desolate" (Matthew 23:38). When the veil in the temple was torn apart, the services conducted there lost their meaning, and the temple literally became "desolate." Probably only an antichrist (in the broad sense of the word as one who does not believe that Jesus is the Lamb of God) could inspire and promote the rebuilding of the temple.

If our conclusions are correct, then the temple will never be rebuilt. Or at least, if it is rebuilt, this will have nothing to do with the prophecies.* But even if we assume that the temple is to be rebuilt, then why has no pope shown any inclination to participate in this project? If the Protestants are correct in their conclusions, then the pope is the man of sin who must sit in the temple, but he does not seem to be in a hurry to fulfill this prophecy, which should put his opponents in a quandary. Maybe the reformers rushed ahead too quickly and were mistaken in claiming the pope to be the antichrist. In addition, we have a simple but natural question. Where in this temple can you find anything on which the antichrist is able to sit? Anyone who is familiar with the structure of the temple knows that there is not a single piece of furniture upon which it would be possible for a man to sit. If the temple were to be rebuilt, could we expect the antichrist to bring a chair or a throne to the temple? Or maybe he would sit on the floor? So where would the antichrist sit? To answer these questions, we shall continue to examine 2 Thessalonians 2:3, 4 in the next chapter.

Notes

1. "About the Temple Institute," The Temple Institute, accessed February 10, 2020, www.templeinstitute.org.
2. "Statement of Principles," Temple institute, accessed February 21, 2020, www.templeinstitute.org/statement.
3. Francis D. Nichol, ed., *The Seventh-day Adventist Bible Commentary*, vol. 4, (Hagerstown, MD: Review and Herald', 1977), 703.
4. "The World Is Growing Brighter," Temple institute, accessed February 21, 2020, https://www.templeinstitute.org/world_membership.htm.
5. Thomas Ice and Randall Price, *Ready to Rebuild* (Oregon: Harvest House Publishing, 1992), and Ron Rhodes, *Unmasking the Antichrist* (Eugene, OR: Harvest House, 2012).

---

* For example, a copy of Solomon's temple with increased dimensions was built in Brazil. This building and buildings like it have nothing to do with biblical prophecies.

6. You can listen to the full version of the opinion expressed here at The John Ankerberg Show, accessed February 10, 2020, https://www.youtube.com/watch?v=fTEvVRpOFxM.

7. For further study, see the Daniel and Revelation Committee, "70 Weeks," 75–118.

8. Nichol, *The Seventh-day Adventist Bible Commentary,* vol. 4, 853.

9. Ellen G. White, *The Great Controversy* (Nampa, ID: Pacific Press®, 2005), 25.

Chapter 4

Where Will the Antichrist Sit?

The apostle Paul predicted that the "man of sin" (the antichrist) would sit in God's temple, claiming to be God: "Let no one deceive you by any means; for that Day will not come unless the falling away comes first, and the man of sin is revealed, the son of perdition, who opposes and exalts himself above all that is called God or that is worshiped, so that he sits as God in the temple of God, showing himself that he is God" (2 Thessalonians 2:3, 4).

For many centuries, theologians and ordinary believers have tried to find the answer to the question, "In what temple will the antichrist sit?" When the apostle Paul wrote his second epistle to the Thessalonians, the temple of Jerusalem was not yet destroyed, and one might think that the apostle was talking about it. However, the Romans destroyed that temple in A.D. 70, and since that time, no one has been able to answer this question definitively. Since then many centuries have passed, and during this time many theories have appeared offering a solution to this problem. Because the temple had been destroyed many centuries ago, and there was no hope for its restoration, Paul's reference to the antichrist sitting in "the temple of God" was most often interpreted symbolically. However, the formation of the state of Israel in the middle of the last century led some people to argue that the prophecy would be fulfilled literally and that the temple would be rebuilt soon. Therefore, we can divide all possible interpretations into

Literal
- The antichrist will sit in the temple in Jerusalem, which is to be rebuilt.

- The antichrist will sit in the heavenly temple. The principle of literal interpretation requires such an option but to accept it means to recognize that the antichrist is more powerful than Christ.

Symbolic
- We are to understand the temple as the church or the gathering of the believers rather than as a literal building or a structure. In such a case, "to sit in the temple" means that the antichrist will establish his own rules and laws for a church organization. Since the temple is a symbol of the Christian believers, the throne of the antichrist should be understood as his power rather than any actual "chair" or church office.

- We are to understand the temple as we understand our body to be the temple of the Holy Spirit (see 1 Corinthians 6:19, 20). In this case, it is even more difficult to identify a literal throne, and the "man of sin" is a collective image symbolizing pride and rebellion against God. In this view, the antichrist cannot be a specific person; he can only be a certain force or system that makes everyone obey it and submit their minds to its control.

In each of these proposed interpretations, the key is to understand the meaning of "the temple of God" in 2 Thessalonians 2:4. Bible students immediately notice the "temple" in this prophecy and spend a lot of effort trying to explain it. However, this approach often renders them a disservice. And as a result they come to different and sometimes opposite conclusions. At first glance, Paul's prophecy has nothing to do with other prophecies about the antichrist. Still, it is hard to imagine that this passage exists completely on its own. We need to understand that it does not "hang in the air" and that it is closely related to other prophecies about the antichrist—sometimes with only subtle connections. So instead of focusing on the word *temple* we are going to focus on seemingly minor details, specifically to the fact that the antichrist, first, will "sit" in the temple; second, that he will be "showing himself that he is God"; and, third, this will happen after the "apostasy." In this chapter, we will discuss the question of where the antichrist will "sit" "showing himself that he is God." The question of "apostasy" will be explored in the following chapter.

1. Other prophecies on this subject

If Paul's prophecy is part of a larger mosaic, then we should be able to find the other parts of it and see how it fits into the overall picture. The other Scripture texts that will help us understand this question are

- Revelation 13:2;
- Revelation 2:12, 13;
- Isaiah 14:13, 14;
- Daniel 8:9–12.

The first three of these passages refer to the throne of Satan. What kind of throne is this? How is it related to the throne of the antichrist? In a situation where information must be gathered bit by bit and every passage, every detail of the prophecy is significant, it is sometimes surprising that those who study 2 Thessalonians 2:4 pay no attention to these texts. If the antichrist is to sit on a throne in the temple, we need to understand what these prophecies are talking about. In the fourth passage, Daniel 8:9–12, the throne of Satan and the antichrist are not mentioned; the texts' connection with the prophecy of Paul is more subtle, but it will be impossible to fully understand 2 Thessalonians 2:4 without it. We can understand Paul only in the light of Daniel's words; failure to recognize this connection leads any interpretation to internal and/or external contradictions.

However, a careful reader may suspect us of willfully misinterpreting these passages. Aren't they speaking about Satan? Why do we say that they are about the antichrist? To answer this question, let's read the first passage—Revelation 13:2. "Now the beast which I saw was like a leopard, his feet were like the feet of a bear, and his mouth like the mouth of a lion. The dragon gave him his power, his throne, and great authority."

We know from previous chapters that the beast here is the antichrist and that the dragon represents Satan. John was shown that the throne of the antichrist was once the throne of Satan, so we have the right to say that these are not two separate thrones but the same one. This means that if we can understand where the throne of Satan is located, we will be able to understand where the throne of the antichrist is! Since this first passage says nothing about where the throne is located, let's see what John writes on this topic in the second passage—Revelation 2:12, 13. "And to the angel of the church in Pergamos write, 'These things says He who has the sharp two-edged sword: "I know your works, and where you dwell, where Satan's throne is. And you hold fast to My name, and did not deny My faith even in the days in which Antipas was My faithful martyr, who was killed among you, where Satan dwells."'"

First, John specifies Pergamos and the church there as those to whom the message is addressed. Second, he mentions twice that this is where Satan dwells and where his throne is. Third, he specifies that Satan lives where God's faithful martyr, Antipas, was put to death. What does it all mean?

Perhaps we should start with the Pergamos church. In Revelation 2; 3, John writes letters to the seven churches located in Asia Minor (modern Turkey). If we are to believe the words of John, the throne of Satan and the antichrist are to be found in the city of Pergamos. The problem with this literal approach to the interpretation of John's letter is that today we can hardly call what is left of Pergamos, a "town," much less a city. Today, it is just a heap of ruins. The city is a desert, and we are not able to find a throne or "the man of sin" sitting on it. Where, then, are we to seek Satan's throne?

Many Bible students agree that the messages to the seven churches are not only appeals to the Christians living in these cities in John's day, but that they also apply to different generations of the Christian church. *The seven churches of Revelation represent seven successive periods in the history of the Christian church from its formation until the second coming of Christ.* Revelation is a prophetic book that speaks of "which must shortly take place" (Revelation 1:1) using examples of famous historical realities. Since Pergamos was destroyed long ago, and since the antichrist will continue his fight against God and His people until the Second Coming, we believe it is necessary to agree with the interpretation of Pergamos as a specific period in the history of the Christian church. If so, then we need to examine what happened during this period in order to find the throne of Satan and the antichrist. The Pergamos church is the third in the sequence of the seven churches, following the churches in Ephesus and Smyrna. Historians and theologians suggest identifying the seven churches with the following periods in the development of the Christian church as a whole:

1. Ephesus (A.D. 27–100)
2. Smyrna (A.D. 100–323)
3. Pergamos (A.D. 323–538)

4. Thyatira (A.D. 538–1565)
5. Sardis (A.D. 1565–1740)
6. Philadelphia (A.D. 1740–1844)
7. Laodicea (A.D. 1844–present time)[1]

If our conclusions are correct, it is the historical period of the Pergamos church that explains the mystery of the antichrist and his throne. What happened during that time—A.D. 323–538?

It is probably no exaggeration to see Emperor Constantine's conversion to Christianity as the most striking event of this period. Constantine began to take an active part in the affairs of the church, and many of his decisions permanently determined the direction of its development. One of these was his decision to move the capital of the empire from Rome to Byzantium, later called Constantinople and New Rome. But the old Rome remained the empire's largest center of public and cultural life. With Constantine's move to Byzantium, a vacuum appeared in Rome that needed to be filled. Then Constantine decided to place Rome under the control, not of a secular force, but a religious one—the bishops of Rome. When we study historians' evaluations of these events, our attention is drawn to the fact that this was not only about the transfer of power from the emperor to the bishops but also about the transfer of the emperor's residence itself. Historian Philip Schaff believes that was a heavenly ordained move: "Constantine, by divine command as he supposed, in the year 330, transferred the seat of his government to Byzantium."[2] What are these historians talking about? What exactly happened? How did it take place?

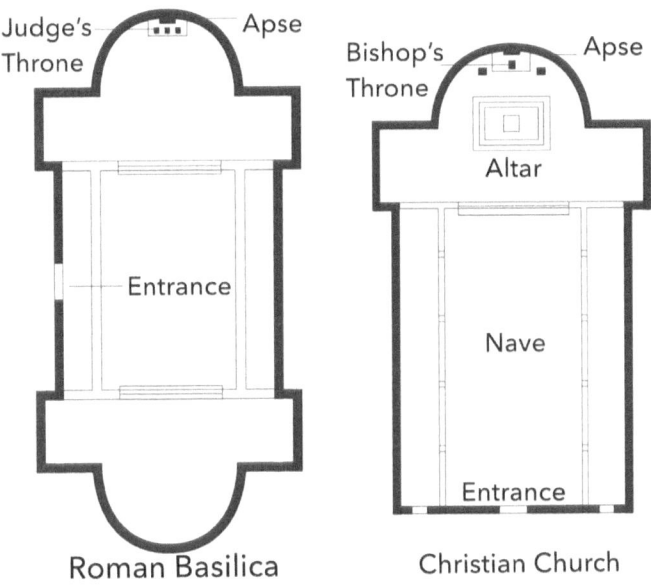

Roman Basilica was rebuilt and the Roman bishop sat on the throne of the Roman Emperor.

In order to understand, we need to take a closer look at these events. When Constantine left Rome, he gave the Lateran Palace (Basilica) to the bishop of Rome and began the construction of St. Peter's Basilica. This probably happened during the time of Pope Miltiades, the predecessor of Sylvester, who began to use the palace as his residence. The Lateran Palace was reconstructed and became the residence of Sylvester and later the cathedral of Rome containing the chair of the bishop of Rome and the papal throne. When we study the history and architecture of the basilica, we conclude that the Christian priest "now sat in the basilica where the Roman Emperor had previously sat."[3] In our opinion, this is an interesting observation. It means that the pope inherited not only power in Rome but also the throne of the emperor. With minor changes to the architecture of the building, any basilica easily became a temple of the Catholic Church in which the priest took the place of the presiding judge.

Another building that draws our attention is St. Peter's Basilica in Rome. The old St. Peter's Basilica stood from the fourth to the sixteenth centuries on the spot where the new St. Peter's Basilica stands today in Vatican City. Construction of the basilica began during the reign of Emperor Constantine. This building, from which the pope today addresses the whole world, stands where the circus of Nero was once located! And the circus of Nero was known for being a place of public execution and martyrdom of Christians. Thus the two main buildings from which the pope operates were both given to him as a legacy of the empire—both are located in Rome, both have their own throne (the throne of the bishop of Rome)—and one of them (the Basilica of St. Peter) was built on the very spot where Christians were martyred.

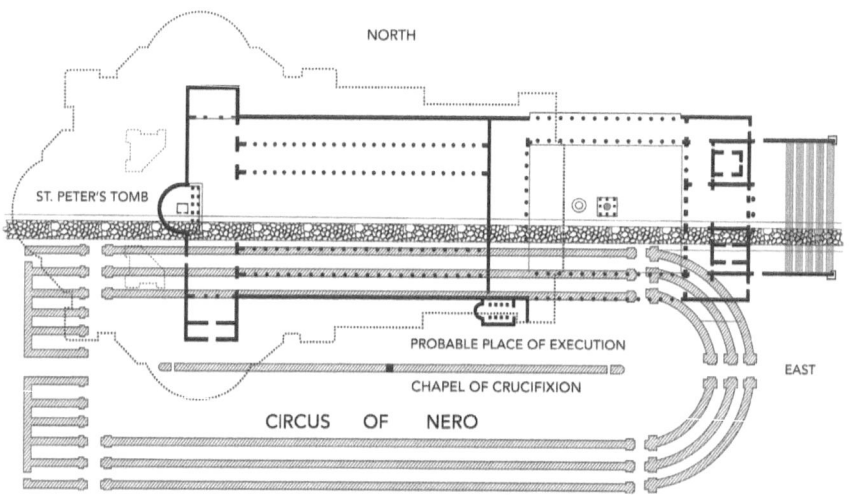

St. Peter's Basilica stands where the circus of Nero was once located.

What is the relation of these buildings to the throne of the antichrist and his temple? Based on the previous chapters, we can assume that the pope has something to do with the antichrist, but what is the relationship between the Roman Empire and Satan or his throne?

Remember, the antichrist received his throne from the dragon, that is Satan (Revelation 13:2). Satan has never tried to kill Christ personally; it was the people who were moved by his spirit who put Him to death. So we can consider the dragon to be not only Satan himself but also a real historical figure inspired by Satan to perform deadly actions against Christ.* Who can this figure be? Through whom did Satan act this time? John points us to the answer by saying that it is the dragon who will try to kill Jesus and inflict persecution on His people (see Revelation 12:3–13). Who did this?

Jesus was born and lived during the time of the Roman Empire. Pontius Pilate was the Roman governor in Palestine and was the one who sentenced Jesus to death by crucifixion. The soldiers of Rome executed the sentence, and they were sent to guard His tomb to prevent His resurrection. When the Christian church began to grow rapidly, the emperors of Rome were the first to institute large-scale persecutions against the church, and it was the emperors who continued this persecution until the beginning of the fourth century. John said that Satan's throne was where "Antipas . . . My faithful martyr" (Revelation 2:13) was put to death. In this connection, it is interesting to recall that in the year A.D. 65, the Roman circus was where Christians were publicly executed. If Antipas is to be the symbol of the Christian martyrs, we have every reason to assume that the throne of the emperor of Rome is the seat of Satan spoken of in this prophecy (see Revelation 13:2). Therefore, Rome and its emperors were used as instruments in the hands of the dragon to oppose God and His people on earth. So when we want to understand how the dragon gave his throne to the antichrist, we

---

* Satan acted the same way in the Garden of Eden when he was deceiving Eve. He did not come to her as an angel who had rebelled against God. He used the serpent under whose appearance he could hide himself. His favorite method is to hide himself and his actions, using benign masks and changing them depending on time and circumstances.

must pay attention to whom and how pagan Rome handed over its throne.

Finishing our study of the first two (Revelation 2:12, 13 and Revelation 13:2) of the four texts of Scripture concerning the antichrist and his throne, we can formulate our main conclusions as follows:

1. The letter to the church of Pergamos (Revelation 2:12, 13) is a prophecy related to a certain period in the history of the Christian church. It is intended to help us to find answers to questions concerning the throne of Satan and the antichrist.
2. The dragon of Revelation 12:3–5 is Satan himself (see Revelation 12:9), who in this period of world history acted through the power of the pagan Roman Empire and its emperors.
3. Just as the dragon gave his throne to the antichrist (see Revelation 13:2) so pagan Rome gave its throne to the bishop of Rome.
4. According to Revelation 2:12, 13, the throne of Satan—and later, the throne of the antichrist—would be where Christians were martyred. The Circus of Nero in Rome, the site upon which St. Peter's Basilica with the seat of the bishop of Rome stands today, was once the place of public execution of Christians. Another residence of the pope with his throne, the Basilica of Saint John Lateran, given to the pope by the emperor, is also in Rome.
5. What was once the throne of an emperor or a judge in a pagan basilica now became the throne of the high priest or a priest in a Christian basilica.

On the one hand, these conclusions give us extra "evidence" that the pope is the antichrist. The physical evidence—the throne received from Rome and still standing on the place where for many centuries Christians were martyred—is a tacit witness to that identification, but it is inconvenient for Rome. It seems we can say that the throne upon which the antichrist sits has been found.

On the other hand, we have a problem. This high throne is not in the Jerusalem temple, but in a Christian basilica. But what does a basilica have to do with the temple in Jerusalem? Isn't it obvious that these are different buildings? Is it reasonable to say that Paul's prophecy concerning the temple does not refer to the temple in Jerusalem? To examine this question, we turn to the next of our four passages—Daniel 8.

Daniel 8:11 and the prophecy of Paul (2 Thessalonians 2:4)

The temple has always been the center of religious life for the Jewish people. However, the death of Jesus Christ on Calvary abolished the temple sacrifices, and soon after Christ's resurrection and ascension, the author of Hebrews drew the attention of his readers, not to the earthly temple but to the heavenly one, "For Christ has not entered the holy places made with hands, which are copies of the true, but into heaven itself, now to appear in the presence of God for us" (Hebrews 9:24). This was addressed primarily to the Jews because they regarded the service in the temple as their top priority. In the new reality following Jesus' sacrifice, it was necessary to draw their attention to Jesus as the heavenly High Priest and to the heavenly sanctuary as the new center of their religious life (Hebrews 4:16; 6:18–20; 12:22–24). The destruction of the temple in A.D. 70 caused the Jews to give even more credence to the Christian message and led them to make the heavenly sanctuary, not the earthly one, the center of their worship.

However, the destruction of the temple had a dual effect. On the one hand, it pointed to the true temple of God and the heavenly High Priest. But on the other hand, it put the prophecies about the antichrist in a complete deadlock. If the antichrist is to sit in the temple of God, yet the earthly temple no longer exists, is it possible that the prophecy means that the "man of sin" or even Satan himself, would sit in the temple of heaven?

Today, solutions to this problem are being proposed by the interpretations mentioned at the beginning of the chapter; among these, the view that the temple in Jerusalem will be restored is gaining popularity. So where will this temple appear? Will the antichrist rise to heaven to sit in the temple there, or will he build a temple on the earth?

The answer is simple. The temple will come down from heaven! And this answer is not an unrestrained fiction; it is an answer written in the Bible, but for some reason little attention is paid to it. We are doomed to merely guess, until we see the connection of Paul's prophecy to Daniel 8. Here is what Daniel says: "He [the "little horn" power] even exalted himself as high as the Prince of the host; and by him the daily sacrifices were taken away, and the place of His sanctuary was cast down" (Daniel 8:11).

The expression, "cast down,"* could be (and we are convinced, *should* be) also translated as "overthrown" or "thrown." In verses 10–12, all that was "cast down" was thrown from heaven "to the ground," and verse 11 states that even "the place of His sanctuary"† would not avoid this fate. In other words, the prophet Daniel says that the heavenly sanctuary will be thrown down from heaven to earth! So we do not need to guess from where the temple of the antichrist is to appear; the Bible itself tells us. All these actions will be accomplished by the "little horn." This little horn is none other than the antichrist.‡ Incredible! Is this even possible? Isn't that the

---

* Hebrew: שָׁלַךְ. The same word is used in verses 7 and 12 where it is translated as "cast down."

† Hebrew: מִקְדָּשׁ is also translated as "sanctuary" in Daniel 9:17 and 11:31.

‡ Daniel also speaks about the little horn in Daniel 7:8, which refers to the antichrist. We omit further evidence here, assuming that the reader is familiar with the prophecies of Daniel 7 and 8.

craziest idea you have ever heard? Even after we have read about it from the Bible itself, our mind refuses to believe it, does it not? And yet it is so.

In order to explain this difficult text of scripture and explain how the antichrist casts the heavenly sanctuary down to the earth, we need to look at some simple examples from everyday life. Remember in the second chapter of this book we examined the blasphemous names connected with the beast or the antichrist and the example we used regarding identity theft? This time, let's take it a little further.

If someone creates a social network account in your name, it can severely damage your reputation, of course, but the identity thief will still be limited in his capabilities. The more a scammer knows about you, the longer he can remain unexposed, and the more harm he can cause. After your name, the next most important part of your personal data is probably your address. Knowing your address and having access to your email address, the scammer can redirect all your correspondence to himself. He can visit the post office, introduce himself using your name, and tell the clerk he has moved and needs all his (your) mail forwarded to a new address. If he gets access to your email account, he can send the same notification to the contacts in your address book and receive the emails which were intended only for you. In both cases, he will be able to get more information about you, including those things that are strictly confidential.

If the antichrist illegally appropriates the title of Christ (as does the priest), then his next step would be hacking His address. And what is God's address? Of course—it is His temple. Can the antichrist throw the heavenly temple from heaven to the earth? Of course not, if we are speaking literally. But does that mean he cannot do with an earthly temple what he did with the title of priest—namely, to call it the "temple of God?"

Two arguments speak in favor of this. First, the idea of blasphemy as identity theft can be traced to 2 Thessalonians 2:3, 4 when Paul says that this "man of sin" will be "showing himself that he is God." If the antichrist is going to take over the title of Christ, then why couldn't he do the same with the place of Christ's ministry?

Second, Daniel himself explained how the antichrist would cast down the sanctuary to the ground: "And he cast truth down to the ground" (Daniel 8:12). He did all this and prospered. Note that it is the *truth* that would be cast down. Here the same verb is used as in verse 11, which speaks of what would happen with the sanctuary. This indicates a connection between verse 12 and the previous verses. In verses 9–12, the antichrist commits unimaginable actions. He casts to the ground what belongs to God, including the heavenly sanctuary. How is this even possible? We understand that the antichrist is not stronger than God, so the only way to overthrow the sanctuary, as Daniel explained, is to "cast truth down to the ground" (Daniel 8:12). Daniel's phrase points to a subtle link between his prophecy and that of Paul. Both are writing about the same thing but using different wording. Daniel says that the antichrist will "cast truth down to the ground"—the truth concerning the heavenly High Priest and His sanctuary. Paul says that the man of sin will show "himself that he is God" and defile God's temple. Both prophecies talk about apostasy; both speak of the antichrist; both speak about the sanctuary; both speak about blasphemy. This means that these two prophecies are inseparably linked.

Parallels Between Daniel 8:9–12 and 2 Thessalonians 2:3, 4, table 6

Motif	Daniel 8:9–12	2 Thessalonians 2:3, 4
Antichrist	"little horn" (verse 9)	"the man of sin" (verse 3)
Blasphemy	"He even exalted himself as high as the Prince of the host" (verse 11)	"who opposes and exalts himself above all that is called God" (verse 4)
Apostasy	"Because of transgression" (verse 12)	"the falling away comes first" (verse 3)
Sanctuary	"and the place of His sanctuary was cast down" (verse 11)	"so that he sits as God in the temple of God" (verse 4)

Why would the antichrist declare his residence to be the temple of God? The answer is simple—to steal the address of the heavenly High Priest. In other words, one good turn deserves another, or in for a penny, in for a pound. After the antichrist calls himself the High Priest, assigning himself the High Priest's "address" is the next natural, logical, and inevitable step. One who has called himself a priest must have a temple because what would a priest be without a temple? The antichrist blasphemes not only when appropriating the title of the priest; he goes further than that. To make his deception credible, he declares his residence to be the temple of God. Thus, the high priest and his temple on earth oppose the heavenly High Priest and His temple.

Now, let's get back to the question of what the Basilica of St. Peter has to do with the Jerusalem temple. As we have seen, the throne of the pope, both in the Lateran Palace and in the Basilica of St. Peter, was given to the church as a legacy from Emperor Constantine and the Roman Empire. In addition, St. Peter's Basilica was built where the Circus of Nero once was and where the Christians were martyred. Therefore, based on the prophecies of Revelation 2:12, 13 and Revelation 13:2, we have concluded that the throne of the pope in Rome is the throne of the antichrist. But if Revelation 2:12, 13 and Revelation 13:2 help us to find the throne, then Daniel 8:11 and 2 Thessalonians 2:4 help us to understand why the basilica can be understood as the temple of God. The antichrist is blaspheming not only against Christ as the heavenly High Priest but also against the heavenly sanctuary, pretending to be the high priest or His representative and making the basilica to be the temple of God or its earthly copy.

2. Are the "representatives" truly representatives?

The Bible calls the devil a "liar and the father of it" (John 8:44). Lying is his main and most powerful weapon. It's the same weapon that Daniel predicted would be used successfully against the heavenly High Priest and His sanctuary (Daniel 8:12). The main conflict between God and Satan, between Christ and the antichrist, occurs at the level of words. We can call the substitution of concepts and plays on words to be the favorite techniques of the antichrist. With the help of these tools, one can turn white into black and vice versa. So when we are talking about the high priest and his temple, it is very important to define the concepts and to give the definitions.

Usually the ministers of the Orthodox or the Roman Catholic[*] Church are called priests, and the place of their service is called a temple. If you ask ordinary people, millions and hundreds of millions of them will answer that a priest performs the service in the temple. Note that no one will use the words a *representative of the Priest* or a *copy of the temple*. And it is here that the play on words begins. Why? Because under the pressure of truth and biblical evidence, the priests would have to admit that they are only the representatives of the true Priest, Jesus Christ, and that their buildings are only a representation of the heavenly reality.[†] Then why have millions of Christians been taught to call priests not representatives of the Priest but priests? It is because the Catholic Church or the Orthodox Church does not see a big difference between the first and the latter. This approach leads to the fact that many people neither realize that there is a heavenly temple nor know anything about the High-Priestly ministry of Jesus. That is, the heavenly realities fade into the background or are even forgotten.

It is sometimes said that it is not good to cling to words. Arguably, it's not a big deal whether we call a person a priest or a representative of a priest. As the saying goes, call me a pot but heat me not. But in this case, two questions arise. First, which term is more correct—*priest* or *representative of a priest*? The answer is unambiguous. The correct term is *representative of a priest*. Then is it not a paradox that the Catholic Church has chosen the less correct term?

---

[*] From here on we will not make a clear distinction between the Catholic and the Orthodox churches, between Catholic and Orthodox church buildings, or between the title of a high priest and that of a priest. There are more common traits between them than differences. Moreover, when speaking of temples and priests, we shall use the plural. The reasons for this approach will be presented in the next chapter.

[†] Those who are extremely curious can read about it in the books often read exclusively by the priests themselves, and that is why many people remain uneducated in this matter.

Second, if the choice of the term is not actually important, then why not be called a representative—that is, by the correct term—if it makes no difference? When the issue is presented like that, then it suddenly turns out that after all, it really is better to be called a priest and the preference is not inconsequential or random. It's like when someone says, "It doesn't matter what church you go to; the crucial thing is that you believe in Jesus." However, as soon as you ask that person to leave his church and join another, the "unimportant" thing suddenly becomes "important"—even very important—and you realize that you have been misled or simply cheated. You've been told that something doesn't matter, only to find out that it matters a great deal and the person is not going to change. Likewise we are told that it doesn't matter what name we use for the one who ministers in the church, yet at the same time no one is going to change the term which has become familiar for the laity.

This is how the "father of lies," or the antichrist, operates. First, he uses one word and then another. When it is convenient, he can differentiate between these words, but if it is inconvenient, he prefers to forget about this distinction and say that you have misunderstood his point. As the saying goes, idle folks lack no excuses. In doing so, he completely confuses his prey, who begins to think that this well-known expert must know better. Because common sense fails to understand these verbal intricacies, a person thinks the "holy" church knows for sure what is right, and therefore it is better not to argue and just believe.

But let's assume that tomorrow we'll wake up in the morning to find out that the Catholic and Orthodox priests have decided that they have not been explaining to their followers well enough that they are only representatives rather than the actual priests and that their temples only bear the name of temples but are not temples in reality. Does this change the basic question of who gave them the authority to make these claims? How do we know that such statements are legitimate? How can they prove that they are not costumed impostors? Do they really represent the heavenly High Priest and His temple?

Let me give you one more example. I once returned home and saw I had a phone message on the answering machine. Wondering where the call was from, I checked and found out that the call was from Washington, DC.* I became distracted and didn't listen to the message. About a week later when I returned home, I again noticed that I had gotten another call from Washington and had been left a message. This time I decided I could not afford to forget about it and turned on the answering machine. The person speaking said he was an inspector of the tax service and asked me to call him back immediately. Since it had been nearly a week since the first call, I decided not to wait and dialed his number. The conversation went like this:

"Good afternoon, you have left a message asking me to call back..."

"Hello, thank you for calling. How are you?"

"I'm well, thank you. What can I do for you?"

"My name is Inspector David. I represent the IRS, department of financial crimes. My identification number is four three, five six seven. I need to warn you that our conversation is being recorded. Sir, tell us how we can contact your lawyer."

"My lawyer? Why?"

"Sir, you'll need a lawyer; do you have his contact information?"

I understood that the conversation would be a serious one, and although I speak English, I decided to be sure I understood everything.

"Sir, English is my second language, so I need an interpreter."

"Well, what is your native language?"

"Russian."

"Okay, when we find a translator, we will call you back. Goodbye."

---

* The location of many federal agencies.

"Goodbye."

This was on Monday. All week I was waiting for him to call back. Finally, on Friday, I decided to call him myself.

"Hello. I spoke with you on Monday. Have you found a Russian interpreter?"

"Yeah, he'll be able to proceed with the case but not today."

"Is it possible to somehow speed up this process and clarify the situation?"

"Yes, you can call the general number, one eight hundred, eight two nine, one zero four zero. They have translators on staff."

So I opened the official website of the IRS, and after making sure that the phone number matched the one specified on the website, I called. After long conversations with a computerized answering machine, I was told that the approximate wait time for a reply was about twenty-nine minutes. I hung up and again dialed the first number.

"Tell me, can we communicate without a translator?"

"Yes, of course. At any time, if you do not understand something, you can stop us, and we will spend as much time as needed to explain everything."

"Okay, what's the matter?"

"Sir, our calculations show that you did not declare part of your income, and we have passed your case to the court."

"I'm sorry, but professionals do my tax return. I gave them all the necessary documents."

"Sir, they have just filled in papers for you, but all the responsibility lies with you."

After a few more questions, I realized that this person knew the tax system of the United States better than I did. After all, even Einstein had found the US tax code hard to understand.

"Well," I asked, "besides the court, what are my other options?"

"The case will not be brought to court only if you meet three conditions. First, you must pay a fine of two thousand nine hundred and fifty dollars. Second, it must be done today. Third, you must agree that during the time the money transfer is being sent to us that you will be in touch with us and that our conversation will be recorded. If you refuse to cooperate with us, we will forward your case to the court today and notify the local police department."

At the time of this conversation, I had studied the IRS website backwards and forwards. On one of the sections of the website I had found tips on how to recognize fraud on the phone. The first item in this list said, "Representatives of the IRS will never call you to discuss your tax debt without sending you first an official notice by mail." This statement completely contradicted what I had been dealing with. So when I was asked for my cell phone number in case the conversation was cut off, I gently and politely refused. It didn't take long to wait for the reaction. A heretofore polite "representative" of the IRS turned into a monster and promised to immediately forward my case to the court and to put me and people like me in jail behind bars—and then hung up.

Two minutes later, there was a new call on the display of my answering machine, and this time it was not a call from Washington. The display read "IRS." I picked up the phone and a pleasant, but unfamiliar, voice informed me that my case was being sent to the court and that I would spend the next five years in prison. I thanked the speaker and wished him a good day.

Three minutes later, the phone display showed me that the sheriff of the local police wanted to talk to me. A new voice offered me a choice—appear immediately at the police station and surrender to the authorities or remain at home until the sheriff arrived with an arrest warrant.

I replied that I would come to the police station myself, but that I would need some time to pack. "When is the end of the sheriff's working day?" I asked. At that point, the caller hung up!

As you can probably fathom, no one bothered me further—neither that day nor the next week nor even a month later. Interestingly, the IRS website also stated, "Representatives of the IRS won't threaten you that they will appeal to the local police or other law enforcement agencies with the requirement to arrest you for the nonpayment."

This example shows us how to distinguish between a real and a false representative. If the official IRS website says that its representatives do not call, but write letters, we are stupid if we continue to communicate with an "IRS representative" on the phone. If the Bible says that the true High Priest and the true temple are in heaven, and if it also warns that there are scammers pretending to be Him and presenting their buildings as His temples, then it is foolish to think that they can be His representatives. In this case, the Bible is like a website with tips on how to recognize a fraud—a fraud that is not carried out by phone but rather by the Church priesthood. Someone is wanting to speak with us, not as an IRS agent, but rather as one speaking on behalf of God, or more precisely, in the name of Jesus as the High Priest. To make all this more credible, this person tries to usurp Jesus' address and convince us that he speaks to us, not from Washington, DC or an IRS office but from the "office" of God or from the temple. If the IRS checks whether or not we have paid all our debts to the state, Jesus pleads for the forgiveness of all our "debts" before God. *The Bible itself (God's only "official website") says that there is not, and cannot be, any other representative before whom we should confess our sins.* "For there is one God and one Mediator between God and men, the Man Christ Jesus" (1 Timothy 2:5). Scammers use one's ignorance of the Bible, but this is not some dubious source or legend or tradition; this is the Word of God Himself.

Daniel clearly says that the truth about the High Priest and His temple will be cast down. That is, he clearly indicates in what area the fraudsters are going to concentrate their efforts. But unfortunately, millions of people become victims of frauds carried out both by telephone and in the church. They continue to communicate with such representatives, thinking that they are paying their "debts," but in fact, their transactions or confessions do not reach the person for whom they are intended. The antichrist acts the same way. The appropriation of God's name and His address allows him to convince the world of his legitimacy and to receive the worship that belongs only to God. Sincere and gullible people think that they come to worship God, but in fact they go to the scammer who has taken His place.

The antichrist is not ordinary Catholic or Orthodox believers, but those who occupy the place of Christ, which belongs only to Him. Many people have been taught that by confessing their sins to a priest or by praying to an icon they are addressing God through them as through windows, but the fact is that God doesn't have any other priest or representative except Jesus Christ and no other sanctuary but the one in heaven. All these so-called representatives or windows act as mediators between us and God, and in doing this they take the place of Christ. When we overcome the deception of the swindler by the word of truth, he increases the power of his deception through false miracles, so-called contacts with the "spirits" of the dead, and false healings. And when even these tools do not deceive, he becomes angry and furious.

There is only one function of the priests, which can be performed by sinful men in the era of the New Testament, and it is not associated with the service in the temple. This function doesn't belong only to the ministers of the church, rather it belongs to *every* Christian. This function is the proclamation of the gospel. The apostle Peter calls all who believe "a chosen generation, a royal priesthood, a holy nation, His [God's] own special people, that you may proclaim the praises of Him who called you out of darkness into His marvelous light" (1 Peter 2:9). It is evident that everyone who becomes a Christian also becomes a priest so that he or she "may proclaim" the gospel. But this has nothing to do with the service in the temple. This function of the priesthood needs no temple; it does not divide believers into those who can offer sacrifices to God and those who can't, because all can "continually offer the sacrifice of praise to God, that is, the fruit of our lips, giving thanks to His name" (Hebrews 13:15).

3. *In persona Christi* or the art of impersonation

The term, *in persona Christi,* which literally means "in the person of Christ," is an important term in Roman Catholic theology. It is used to convey the idea that any time a priest performs a sacrament, he acts on behalf of Christ or even as Christ Himself. In other words, we can say that any time a priest conducts Mass, he steps into the place of Christ. Henri de Lubac, a Catholic cardinal and theologian whose works had a tremendous influence on the Second Vatican Council, wrote, "It is through our ordination to a priestly ministry that we become as Jesus Christ, we speak, act, sanctify as if we were Him."[4]

The Orthodox Church speaks about this issue more carefully. The Orthodox Church understands that "in the person of Christ" sounds too provocative and reminds people of the antichrist. That is why the Orthodox Church says that a bishop or priest acts not *instead of* Christ but *with* Christ. They assure us that during the Eucharist, Christ Himself acts and sanctifies the bread and wine. Some may think that this point of view makes Orthodox theology different from that of the Roman Catholic. But it only seems so. In fact, in Orthodox theology the priest is as if he is Christ's icon; he is Christ's image. Without a priest, no sacrament is valid or legitimate. This means that even if Christ has granted His forgiveness to a sinner, he neither can know about it nor receive it without a priest. *De jure,* it is an act of Christ, but *de facto,* it is the act of a priest. Like an icon, the priest is supposed to be a "window" to God, but in fact he becomes a wall between man and God, "For there is one God and one Mediator between God and men, the Man Christ Jesus" (1 Timothy 2:5).

But how is this amazing transformation even possible? How does this transformation of a common person into a priest occur? Henri de Lubac has already answered that question: "It is through our ordination to a priestly ministry."[5] Speaking of one who becomes a priest, Gregory of Nyssa is translated as writing, "It was not a long time ago, just yesterday, when he was one of many, one in a crowd. And now, suddenly he becomes a leader, a head, a teacher of godliness, committing secrecies. And all this happens without any change in outward appearance. On the outside he remains the same, but his soul is transformed into a better one by invisible power and grace."[6] Dionysius the Areopagite believed in the "holy power of priesthood,"[7] which places a man in special ministry. That is why a priest, having access to the grace of God, can "be made sacred and pass on to those who are under him . . . this sacredness, which he received from God."[8]

Does it really work that way? No doubt that with the help of persistent efforts to spread these ideas, many have started to believe that this mysterious transformation takes place. However, we think that these ideas have nothing to do with the Bible and that in their essence they remind one of a child's faith in Santa Claus. Sometimes it's enough to put a coat, beard, and hat on an everyday man to make a child believe that this person is a superman who will make his wishes come true.

This faith in the mysterious transformation of a common man into a priest is like the faith of a child. Even though we grow older, we still want to believe in miracles and magic. And someone has studied us as well as a good psychologist. Priestly garments, as well as any other uniform, can have an almost bewitching influence upon many people. Any man who wears it becomes like an icon, and people are ready to confess their sins to this man and ask for forgiveness. A policeman, who wears a uniform, has a real power, which is limited by the laws of the state. But the power of a priest is intangible and is limited only by our imagination. Sacraments, indeed, remain a secret. Has a priest received the "holy power of priesthood" or not? We don't know because we cannot see it. Priestly garments, on the other hand, are an objective reality; we can see them, and they remind us of the priestly status of a man, especially if he wears a beard.* Whether we should believe someone only because he claims to act *in persona Christi* and wears priestly garments is a question everyone will have to answer for himself. But we would like to suggest to our reader not to rely on his or her imagination but rather on the Word of God, which says, "Do not look at his appearance or at his physical stature, because I have refused him. For the Lord does not see as man sees; for man looks at the outward appearance, but the Lord looks at the heart" (1 Samuel 16:7).

Yet we would like to give priests credit. They are not selected to be priests simply at random. No one was born a priest. Each of them had his own growth in the knowledge of God and wanted to serve Him wholeheartedly. But at some point in that process, they were convinced that it was their honor to serve *instead* of Christ or *with* Christ. They probably did not have enough time to figure out all the subtleties involved, and thus they became victims of delusions. Despite this, they never ceased to serve God faithfully and sincerely according to the instruction they were given. They do charitable work, teach the law of God, and sometimes even sacrifice their lives for the cause of God. All this evokes deep respect and even admiration. And that is why we are far from passing judgment on anyone. God is the judge, and only He can judge fairly. But unfortunately, the sincerity of our motives does not mean that our beliefs are true. The apostle Peter was a faithful disciple of Jesus, but one day he had to hear tough words from his beloved Teacher: "Get behind Me, Satan!" (Matthew 16:23). Such words are painful. They hurt, but they are true. Jesus called black things black and white things white;

---

* Catholic priests usually do not have beards. They considered it a custom of barbarians. Orthodox priests, on the other hand, typically wear beards because they believe it helps them to reflect an image of Christ.

in other words, He called things by their right names, and in this case He was truthful to Peter and Himself. Peter had to know that, at that moment, without realizing it, he had become an instrument in the hands of Satan. At that moment, Peter acted as Satan himself would act. Peter spoke on Satan's behalf, just like the serpent did in the Garden of Eden. It was an "in the person of Satan" moment.

It is here where many people make a mistake. We are not to put labels on people and paint them only in black or white. Peter's desire to follow Christ did not stop Jesus from telling Peter the truth and calling him Satan. Jesus realized that, at that moment, the enemy of human souls was speaking with Him through Peter. Peter was acting and talking on Satan's behalf. In fact, it was Satan himself, who approached Jesus in the person of Peter. In the same way, the godly lives of priests and the sincerity of their hearts do not abolish the fact that the moment they act *in persona Christi* or take His priestly title consciously or unconsciously, willingly or otherwise, they overshadow Christ, put themselves in His place, and become the antichrist.

We want to believe that many of those who call themselves priests were simply unable to understand the essence of what was happening, just as was the case with Peter. As we suppose, they were all ordinary people, desiring to serve God. At one time, when they received the appropriate education, it was explained to them what it means to be a priest. How well they understood this, we do not know, but one thing is obvious: it was difficult for them to resist authority, system, and tradition.

4. Old Testament examples

In one of his epistles, the apostle Paul wrote, "Now all these things happened to them as examples, and they were written for our admonition, upon whom the ends of the ages have come" (1 Corinthians 10:11). The apostle was talking about the journey of the people of

Israel through the wilderness into the Promised Land. Paul considered the events that happened to Moses and his people not only as instructive examples but also as examples of future events that are especially important for those "upon whom the ends of the ages have come." The book of Revelation, like no other book, confirms these words. It is full of symbols and images; the Exodus of the Jews from Egypt becomes an image of how God will deliver His people from the persecution of this world in the last days of its history. But the Exodus story is only one of many examples. The conflict between Christ and the antichrist is complex and multifaceted. In order to describe this conflict, it is not a single image that is needed, but many of them. Therefore, in order to help us understand better what is happening today, Paul offers to examine them carefully in all their diversity, since everything was "written for our admonition." In this sense, the appearance of the antichrist and his temple is no exception.

There is a story in the Old Testament that helps us understand what happens when there is not one but two or more centers of worship. It also shows us why it was so important for the antichrist to create his own worship and what consequences that had. This is the story of King Jeroboam.

Immediately after the division of Israel into the northern and southern kingdoms, Jeroboam, king in the north, realized that his citizens had too many links with those living in the south, now known as Judah. It was like the division of Germany into west and east, or the partition of Korea into North and South sections, or the division of Russia and Ukraine.* People living in those countries have their own characteristics, but by and large they have always been one nation. They also have shared a long history; they have experienced many victories and defeats together. They are inextricably

---

* Jesus was probably thinking of such cases when He said that a brother would rise up against a brother (see Matthew 10:21; 24:7).

linked by family ties, have common traditions and culture, and do not need an interpreter in order to communicate. For centuries they used to be one state, had a single political and economic system, and most importantly, shared a single religion. They worshiped one God. To divide such a nation into two and to count on its loyalty is as though you're dividing a family and think the children won't miss the second parent. Nature abhors a vacuum. Jeroboam understood this well enough, and he was going to fill the vacuum. Like in the modern countries mentioned above, different currencies were introduced, monuments were demolished, streets were renamed, and history was rewritten. Jeroboam tried to erase everything Israel and Judah had in common in order to make two nations out of one. "There is nothing new under the sun" (Ecclesiastes 1:9).

"Jeroboam's greatest fear was that at some future time the hearts of his subjects might be won over by the ruler occupying the throne of David. He reasoned that if the ten tribes should be permitted to visit often the ancient seat of the Jewish monarchy, where the services of the temple were still conducted as in the years of Solomon's reign, many might feel inclined to renew their allegiance to the government centering at Jerusalem."[9] "And Jeroboam said in his heart, 'Now the kingdom may return to the house of David: If these people go up to offer sacrifices in the house of the Lord at Jerusalem, then the heart of this people will turn back to their lord, Rehoboam king of Judah, and they will kill me and go back to Rehoboam king of Judah' " (1 Kings 12:26, 27).

The motives of Jeroboam were clear and simple. If the people kept the same culture, religion, and traditions, if they continued to gather on family and religious holidays around the same table and in one and the same temple, it would lead to only one question: How long was the northern kingdom going to exist? The dissolution of the northern kingdom would be inevitable, and then Why would one nation need two kings? In other words, the northern kingdom would again team up with the southern one. It was only a matter of time. Jeroboam could not allow "the heart of this people" to turn back to the one and same center of worship in Jerusalem. All means were justified, including idolatry, as he tried to save his own life and power. Therefore, the king asked advice, made two calves of gold, and said to the people, "It is too much for you to go up to Jerusalem. 'Here are your gods, O Israel, which brought you up from the land of Egypt!' And he set up one in Bethel, and the other he put in Dan. Now this thing became a sin, for the people went to worship before the one as far as Dan" (1 Kings 12:28–30). "Taking counsel with his advisers, Jeroboam determined by one bold stroke to lessen, so far as possible, the probability of a revolt from his rule. He would bring this about by creating within the borders of his newly formed kingdom two centers of worship, one at Bethel and the other at Dan. In these places the ten tribes should be invited to assemble, instead of at Jerusalem, to worship God."[10]

Note the difference between the words Jeroboam said in his heart and those he said to his people. He cared about his own fate when thinking in his heart, but made it look as if he cared for his people when addressing his audience. "Why bother going to Jerusalem?" he was saying. "Your king has taken good care of you. Now you do not need to go so far. Pray to God here." And for even greater convenience, he established not one center of worship, but two. "In arranging this transfer, Jeroboam thought to appeal to the imagination of the Israelites by setting before them some visible representation to symbolize the presence of the invisible God. Accordingly, he caused to be made two calves of gold, and these were placed within shrines at the appointed centers of worship. In this effort to represent the Deity, Jeroboam violated the plain command of Jehovah: 'Thou shalt not make unto thee any graven image.... Thou shalt not bow down thyself to them, nor serve them.' Exodus 20:4, 5."[11] New centers of worship required new priests, altars, sacrifices, and holidays.

> He made shrines on the high places, and made priests from every class of people, who were not of the sons of Levi.
>
> Jeroboam ordained a feast on the fifteenth day of the eighth month, like the feast that was in Judah, and offered sacrifices on the altar. So he did at Bethel, sacrificing to the calves that he had made. And at Bethel he installed the priests of the high places, which he had made. So he made offerings on the altar which he had made at Bethel on the fifteenth day of the eighth month, in the month which he had devised in his own heart. And he ordained a feast for the children of Israel, and offered sacrifices on the altar and burned incense (1 Kings 12:31–33).

"So strong was Jeroboam's desire to keep the ten tribes away from Jerusalem that he lost sight of the fundamental weakness of his plan."[12] He believed that if Jerusalem was the dwelling place of the God who had brought Israel out of Egypt, so the same God must be in the northern country as well. If there was the altar in Jerusalem, so there should be an altar in his land also. If there were priests in Jerusalem, there must be priests in his land. If there were holidays and religious feasts in Jerusalem, his people should have them also. If there was the temple in Jerusalem as the center of religious life in Judea, he should have even more—two religious centers, one at Bethel and another in Dan. Making copies and imitating the original was the key to the success of this project. Absence of a worship center would make people go straight to Jerusalem. Thus, the worship at Bethel and Dan was not just filling a vacuum; it was not just a substitution of the worship in Jerusalem—but was the antithesis, or contradistinction, of it. What were the results? The ten tribes were plunged into idolatry and never returned to their brothers in the south.

Satan learned the lessons of these events and decided to do the same in the era of the Christian church. The story of how Jeroboam copied and imitated Jerusalem reminds us of the antichrist, who in Revelation chapter 13 copies and imitates Christ. Christ is our true High Priest in heaven. He is doing intercessory ministry in the heavenly sanctuary. We have no other mediator before God. No matter what titles and names people call themselves or what garments they wear, no matter how they try to copy the temple and its service, it's just a fake that turns "the heart of the people" from the heavenly Jerusalem and forever binds their loyalty to the earthly priests and their temples. And the better the counterfeit, the less the need of the original. That is, the counterfeit's high quality is designed not to help one find the original but to make him forget it.

Therefore, by establishing this ministry on the earth, the antichrist does not lead people to Christ but opposes Christ and His ministry in heaven. He tries to convince us that we serve the same God, that it is only for our convenience, and that we need visible images—priests, temples, icons, and holidays. The antichrist is trying to cause us to believe that we need mediators or priests on the earth because it is supposedly from them, or through them, that we get our sins forgiven or learn that our sins are forgiven. In fact, just as the priests in Bethel and Dan were mere costumed impostors and were not appointed by God for their ministry, so also today the priests who offer sacrifices were appointed by themselves to do so in defiance of the Bible. The absence of shrines at Bethel and in Dan would have encouraged the people to go to Jerusalem. In the same way, it is not the presence, but the absence of self-proclaimed priests and their temples that would teach us to appeal directly to the heavenly High Priest who is faithful and true. To replicate the ministry of Christ as close as possible and to pretend to be Him—this is the power of the antichrist's deception and the secret of the devotion of his followers.

5. How has the antichrist pretended that the basilica is the sanctuary?

The father of lies realized that it was not enough simply to call a basilica the sanctuary. The architecture of these two buildings is different, and this drawback had to be eliminated. It did not appear to be too difficult. After the destruction of the Jerusalem temple in A.D. 70, Christians suffered persecution for nearly two centuries. The construction of churches at that time was not even a point under discussion. But when persecution ceased in the beginning of the fourth century, questions concerning the shape of church buildings arose. It turned out that most Christians were not from a Jewish background but from a Gentile one. They didn't remember, and couldn't remember, what the temple's structure had been. Additionally, the Christians wanted to be different from the Jews. As you remember, Hippolytus of Rome taught that the antichrist would owe his origin to the Jewish nation. Given these circumstances, prevailing opinion was that an exact copy of each part of the temple was not necessary, but the decision was made to keep its main "features of character." Leonid Ouspensky, a Russian Orthodox theologian, put it this way: "They built Christian sanctuaries, and they did so in strict accord with the revealed character of the place of worship, with the very principle according to which the tabernacle and the Jerusalem temple had been built."[13] Please note that we are talking about both the tabernacle of Moses and the Jerusalem temple. From the point of view of architecture, these constructions have a different design. One could notice similarities between them, not in the materials used or even in their dimensions, but in the common "principles" or "features of character" of the buildings.

What were these main features of character? First, both the tabernacle of Moses and the Jerusalem temple were to be built along an east-west axis, with the entrance facing east. Second, there should be three compartments: the outer court, the Holy Place, and the Most

Holy Place. And third, the interior of the temple and its structure were supposed to be a reminder of the Garden of Eden. In order to convince people that a basilica can be called the "temple," both Roman Catholic and Orthodox churches were built in accordance with these principles. Let's look at them more closely.

Orientation along an east-west axis

Tertullian and Origen, who lived in the late second and early third century, said that when Christians prayed, they turned to face the east. Later, probably in the early fourth century, it was written in the Apostolic Constitutions that "Church edifices should be erected with their 'heads' towards the East."[14] "Thus from the earliest period, the custom of locating the apse and altar in the eastern extremity of the church was the rule."[15] This rule was followed for many centuries. For example, almost twelve centuries later Leonardo da Vinci in his famous painting, "The Last Supper," featured all the apostles and Christ Himself on one side of the table. This was done not by accident. The artist wasn't trying to show how the supper had happened in reality; otherwise, he would have drawn the apostles recumbent around the table, rather than sitting on chairs. Why did da Vinci make such a free interpretation? Not only in order that the audience could see the faces of the apostles and Jesus but also because that was the way the Eucharist was served in the churches. All believers, including the priests, turned their faces in one direction—to the east.

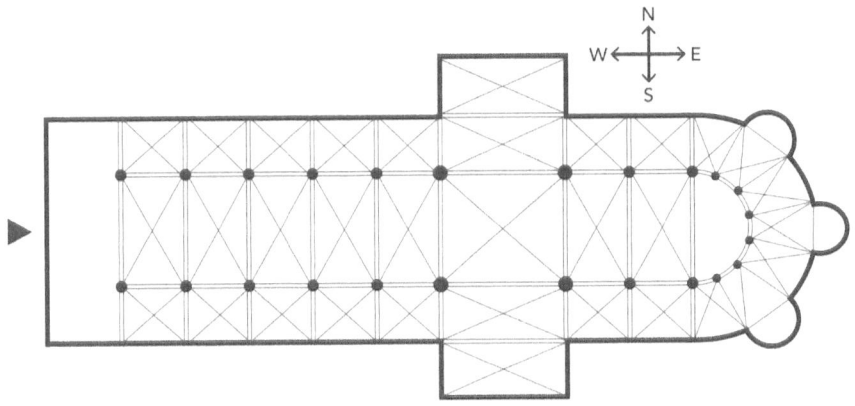

Typical church plan

Even though the Church explains today that prayers are offered towards the east because Jesus will come again from the east, things are not so simple. Catholics themselves admit that "the practice of praying while turned towards the rising sun is older than Christianity."[16] In other words, this practice started even before the birth of Christ and was a practice of pagans worshiping the sun. How God views this is evident from the book of the prophet Ezekiel:

> So He brought me into the inner court of the Lord's house; and there, at the door of the temple of the Lord, between the porch and the altar, were about twenty-five men with their backs toward the temple of the Lord and their faces toward the east, and they were worshiping the sun toward the east.
>
> And He said to me, "Have you seen this, O son of man? Is it a trivial thing to the house of Judah to commit the abominations which they commit here? For they have filled the land with violence; then they have returned to provoke Me to anger. Indeed they put the branch to their nose. Therefore I also will act in fury. My eye will not spare nor will I have pity;

and though they cry in My ears with a loud voice, I will not hear them" (Ezekiel 8:16–18).

God calls such a ministry an "abomination," so it's hard to say which religion—paganism or Christianity—was reflected more in the orientation of Christian churches to the east. Although the Orthodox Church is more scrupulous in the observance of *The Apostolic Constitutions*, the Catholic Church sometimes allows exceptions. For example, the "heads" of the Lateran Basilica and Basilica of St. Peter, in Rome, are directed toward the west, as is the temple in Jerusalem. Despite these and a few other exceptions, the orientation along an east-west axis is a basic principle in the construction of a new church edifice in both the Roman Catholic and Orthodox churches.

Division into the outer court, the Holy Place, and the Most Holy Place

Both the basilica and the temple were rectangular in shape, which provided an excellent opportunity of making a basilica in the likeness of the temple and to reproduce in it the temple's division into the outer court, the Holy Place, and the Most Holy Place. But before we see how this was done, let's recall the prophecy of Daniel: "And the place of His sanctuary was cast down" (Daniel 8:11). A more accurate translation would read something such as this: "And the foundation of His sanctuary was thrown down" (author's translation). We have already explained the meaning of the word translated "cast down" or "overthrown" but have deliberately refrained from commenting on the word *foundation*. Interestingly, it was not the sanctuary itself but rather its *foundation* that was to be cast down. Of what foundation does the prophecy speak?

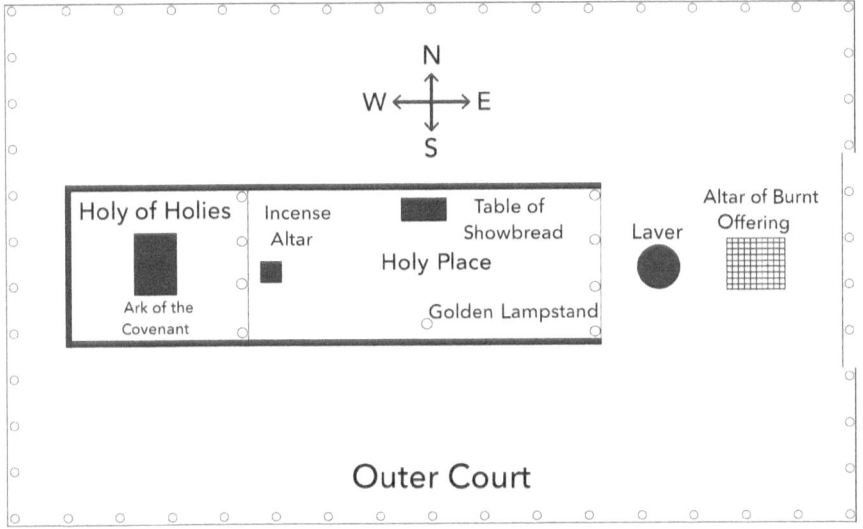

If we are to answer this question traditionally, we have to say that the prophecy is speaking about "righteousness and justice" (Psalms 89:14; 97:2), which are the foundation of God's throne. This conclusion can be made if we know that this throne is the one in the temple in heaven. It is partly acceptable, since, later in Daniel 8:12, Daniel himself says that even the "truth" would be cast down. But at any rate, in verse 11 he says that it is not the foundation of the *throne* that would be cast down, but rather the foundation or "place" of the *sanctuary*. Does it make any significant difference?

Today, when archaeologists find the remains of ancient buildings, they can draw conclusions just based on the shape of the foundation about what the building was and how it was divided into rooms. If we approach the question from this angle and assume that the word *foundation* has something to do with the compartments of the sanctuary, then the prophecy would seem to indicate that the antichrist would attempt to cast down the heavenly sanctuary to the earth by copying the compartments of the heavenly temple, its Holy Place and Most Holy Place, and trying to reproduce them on the earth. This is exactly what is involved in the second principle of construction of any Catholic and Orthodox church. Each temple is divided into an outer court, a Holy Place, and a Most Holy place. Sometimes not even all the laity are aware of this fact, but the priests understand clearly the relationship between the structure of an earthly temple and the heavenly one.

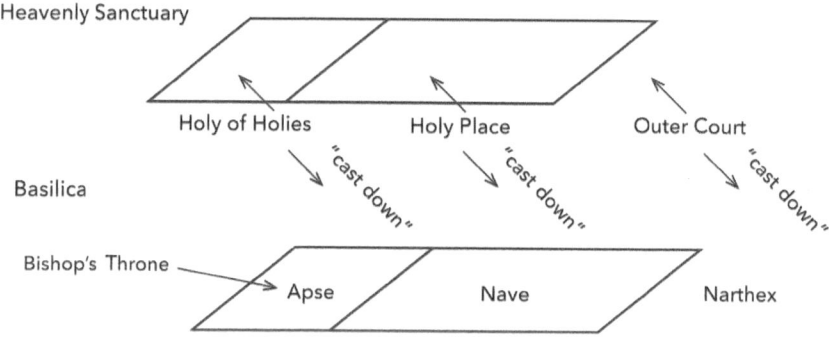

One of the extant documents describes in detail how the ceremony of laying the foundation of a church is to be conducted. The document dates to the beginning of the eighth century and is translated as, "Laying the Foundation."* The author is thought to be John of the city Odzun in Armenia. According to the elaborately prescribed order of worship, the ceremony of laying the foundation of a church was to end with the "proclamation 'FROM ON HIGH.' "[17] Is it not amazing how these words resonate with the words of Daniel that the foundation of His sanctuary† will be cast down to the ground?

In order to convince their parishioners, Catholic and Orthodox priests must explain the structure of the temple and its significance. For example, this is how it is explained in the Russian Orthodox Church:

> As the Old Testament temple (in the beginning—the tabernacle) was divided into three parts: the Most Holy, sanctuary, and courtyard, so an Orthodox

---

* Literally, "Laying Foundation."
† Daniel used Hebrew *mow-kone*, which is translated as "place" or "foundation." See Psalm 89:14; 97:2.

Christian church is divided into three parts: the altar, the middle part of the temple, and the porch. As the Most Holy signified the kingdom of heaven, the altar now also means the kingdom of heaven.

In the Old Testament no one could enter the Most Holy. Only the high priest could enter it once a year and only with the blood of a purifying sacrifice. After all, the kingdom of heaven has been restricted to humans after the fall. The high priest was a prototype of Christ, and this action of his signified to the people that the time would come when Christ would open the kingdom of heaven to all, by the shedding of His blood through His suffering on the cross. That's why when Christ died on the cross the veil of the temple that had covered the Most Holy was torn in two parts. From this moment on, Christ opened the gates of the kingdom of heaven for all who come to Him by faith.

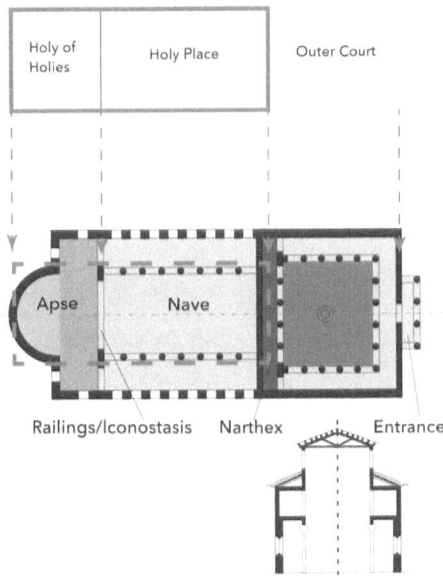

Division into the outer court, the Holy Place, and the Most Holy Place in Christian basilica.

The middle part of the temple in the Orthodox Church corresponds to the Holy Place of the biblical sanctuary. None of the people but the priests had a right to enter the sanctuary of the Old Testament temple, but in the Orthodox Church all Christian believers enter because now the kingdom of God is opened to everyone.

The courtyard of the Old Testament temple, where all the people freely came, corresponds to the porch in an Orthodox church, which is now of insignificant value. Previously, it was for the catechumens who were preparing to become Christians and who had not yet been baptized though the sacrament of baptism. Now, sometimes those who have sinned grievously and backslidden from the church are temporarily sent to stand in the porch for correction.[18]

The Catholic Church uses other names for the different compartments of the temple. The outer court corresponds to the narthex, the Holy Place to the nave, and the Most Holy Place corresponds to the apse.* The names differ, but the liturgical function of these compartments of the temple are the same in both the Orthodox and Catholic Churches. In both, the throne for the priest is in the Most Holy Place, but it is often not seen in Orthodox churches because it is hidden by the iconostasis. This is the main external difference between a Catholic and an Orthodox church. Catholics believe that since the veil in the temple was torn, consequently there is no need to hide the Most Holy Place from the people. The Orthodox Church agrees with this position only partially.

---

* The same names are used in the Orthodox Church sometimes.

Despite these minor differences, both the Catholic and the Orthodox Churches convey the same message to their visitors—this building is the temple of God. Their churches are structured to copy the temple of Solomon where the bread and wine of the Eucharist are stored in the new "Holy of Holies." That is why they do not pay any attention to the possible reconstruction of the temple in Jerusalem.

It is interesting to note that without realizing it, many Protestant churches not only copy the arrangement of a Catholic church but even teach that their churches should also be regarded as temples. They call their places of worship, sanctuaries; their churches, temples; the pulpit, the Most Holy; and the communion table, the altar. Often at the beginning of worship they sing, "The Lord is in His holy temple. Let all the earth keep silence before Him" (Habakkuk 2:20). Those singing urge all the worshipers to silence and reverence. This is certainly commendable, but at the same time it presupposes that this place is the temple. They need only to call their pastors, priests, and the difference from the Catholic view would be minimal and purely symbolic.

This example shows how successful the Catholics and the Orthodox have been in teaching their congregations to view the church building as the temple situated on earth. If the descendants of those who left the Catholic Church five centuries ago still believe this, what can be said of those who are practicing Catholics today? Even five hundred years have been unable to finally erase these beliefs from their heritage. Without realizing it, they use Catholic theology and pass it on from generation to generation, not in the form of doctrine but rather in their church buildings and oral traditions. Once again, this confirms that the antichrist has chosen a very effective method of brainwashing in relation to the sanctuary and has successfully persuaded millions of believers.

In conclusion of this subsection, and in order to be fair, we must say that lately, especially after the Second Vatican Council, the Catholic Church has changed. Sometimes these changes may seem radical. For example, a temple can now be round. The question arises, "Has the division of the temple into three compartments been abolished?" Not at all. In fact, these are cosmetic changes, but the essence remains the same. The fact is that in the "round" configuration, the outer circle still corresponds to the narthex, the inner circle to the nave, and the center to the Holy of Holies. The same principle was used in Exodus when Moses was commanded to draw a line around the mountain where the Israelites were supposed to be (the outer court). Only the priests could cross this line (the Holy Place). But even they could not climb to the top of the mountain where God dwelt (the Most Holy Place).

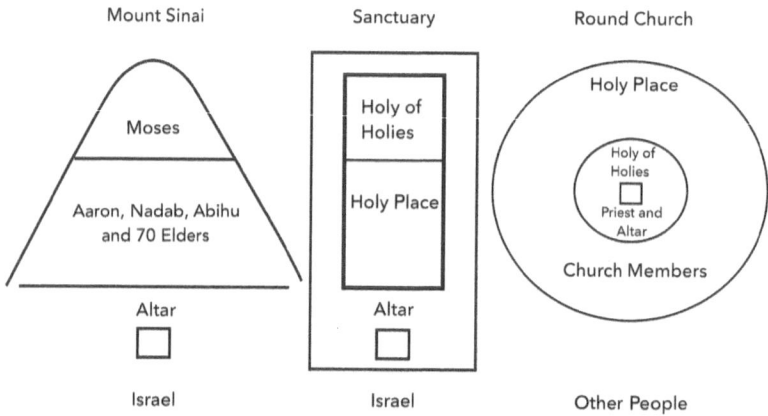

Division of a round church into the outer court, the Holy Place, and the Most Holy Place.

Therefore, we agree with Michael Davies, a British teacher and writer who has devoted many of his works to the Second Vatican Council. He posed a question to himself and answered it: "What precisely does the Liturgy [The teaching of the Second Vatican Council on liturgical reform] Constitution mandate regarding changes in our sanctuaries? The answer is brief and simple: Nothing!" [19]

Reminder of the Garden of Eden

Many Bible scholars have noticed for a long time that there is much in common between the sanctuary and the Garden of Eden.[20] When we read the description of the creation of the Earth where God placed Adam and Eve and compare it with the description of the creation of the sanctuary we can see many parallels.

> Are these merely occasional coincidences? Not at all! For the modern reader it may be difficult to grasp the parallel structure of these descriptions. However, for Semitic thinking it was quite obvious and clearly testified to the fact that the construction of the sanctuary was the embodiment of God's plan just as the creation of the world was the work of His hands.
>
> As the Garden of Eden was located in the east so the entrance of the sanctuary is also in the east. Adam and his family brought their first sacrifice to the gates of the Garden of Eden. Now the gates of Eden are the entrance to the tent of meeting. When a person came here it was as if he was in contact with the future new earth. In the vast sun-scorched desert, the eyes of the Israelites turned to the sparkling splendor of the tabernacle, decorated with bright and exquisite images of various plants. Bunches of grapes, pomegranates, palm trees, abundance of gold and precious stones—all this created a special mood, evoked memories of a lost Paradise, and guided the souls of the wanderers of the desert to another land, the earth created again.
>
> Later when Solomon built the temple of the Lord, he decorated it with unprecedented pomp and splendor. In his temple there were even more

pictures of plants although the ark, lamp, and other ritual objects remained the same. The decoration of Solomon's temple, again and again, is reminiscent of the Garden of Eden, causing not only a nostalgia for the lost, but also a hope for the return of God's Kingdom in all its glory and beauty.[21]

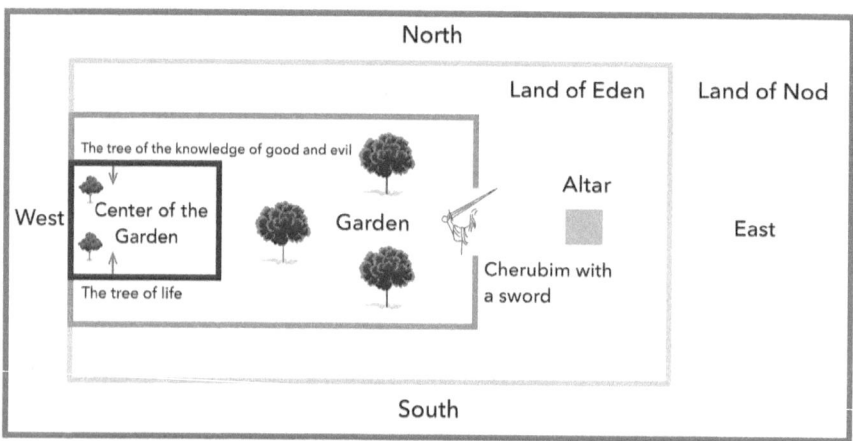

It was not only Moses and Solomon who used these images. Imitating the Garden of Eden is another principle, which guides the construction and decoration of Catholic churches today.

> One of the great temple images is that of the garden....
> The *hekal*, or Holy Place, serves as a memory of the original Garden of Eden in which God "walked" with Adam and Eve without the necessity of a temple, since the garden itself was already the place where humanity and God met.[22]

Modern churches abound not only with images of saints but also of plants, trying to convince us that it is here where God meets man, as He once did in Eden.

6. Original or fake?

Constructing church buildings in accordance with the above principles, the papacy has managed to convince believers to refer to the basilica as the temple of God. Twice assigning sacred titles—for the priest and for the sanctuary—the antichrist sits in the "temple of God showing himself as God" (2 Thessalonians 2:4). However, if you are still in doubt, you can ask, "But isn't Paul speaking about the antichrist sitting in the *real* temple of God? After all, we understand that the basilica is not really God's temple. It's just a fake."

Let's answer the question. Daniel explained that the place of the sanctuary would be "cast down,"* and it was only because of this that the antichrist gained the chance to call earthly buildings the temple of God. We understand that the "man of sin" cannot truly be God but can only pretend to be Him. Similarly, he cannot sit in the real temple of God, since according to the Bible, the only real temple of God is in heaven. The only thing the antichrist can do is to pretend that his temple is the temple of God. Even if he built it in Jerusalem, the house would be "left desolate," as Jesus said (see Matthew 23:38). Whatever temple and wherever it is built—in Jerusalem or in Rome, Constantinople or Moscow—any earthly temple is doomed to be desolate because the true High Priest ascended into heaven.† Therefore, there is really no difference either in the case of a basilica or in the case of someone building a temple in Jerusalem—both would only be a fake.

In both cases, the antichrist cannot sit in the real temple, which is and will remain in heaven, but only in its counterfeit. Why

---

* We want to remind readers that it is better to understand this attack of the antichrist as blasphemy, that is, to "cast down" means to assign heavenly titles to earthly realities.
† Jesus said, "But the hour is coming, and now is, when the true worshipers will worship the Father in spirit and truth" (John 4:23). In other words, He was trying to tell us the time is coming when any earthly temple will have no meaning.

would the antichrist build another temple in Jerusalem when he has already got enough of them? Moreover, some people are just waiting to discover the antichrist in the Jerusalem temple, while no one pays attention to the other fakes. The important thing is not whether these temples are real from the point of view of God and His Word but what the antichrist says about them. They call themselves priests, and they call the place where they conduct their service a temple. God's Word pronounces a verdict upon them based on their own testimony about themselves: "But I say to you that for every idle word men may speak, they will give account of it in the day of judgment. For by your words you will be justified, and by your words you will be condemned" (Matthew 12:36, 37). Therefore, their temple is as much the true temple of God as the man of sin pretending to be God can be the real God.

7. Architectural theology

Architectural theology is a term little known, or totally unknown, to most Protestant theologians. Many people have heard about the doctrines, legends, and traditions of the Church and have discussed the decrees of its ecumenical councils. These things are explored, books are written about them, and they are taught in seminaries whether Catholic, Orthodox, or Protestant. These areas of theology are known and developed well enough. Several branches are even distinguished by specific titles. For example, the doctrine of salvation is known as *soteriology*, the doctrine of the church as *ecclesiology*, the study of the end-time as *eschatology*, and so forth. At the same time, it is practically impossible to find even the smallest article about the theology of architecture. Protestants do not talk about it at all, either because they do not know about it or because they do not understand its true value. Even Orthodox theologians, who understand the role of architectural theology, rarely explore this topic or make it a subject of theological debate.

So what is *architectural theology*? It is a theology that tells us what we can learn about God from the architecture of a church building. It comes not from the Bible or from tradition, but specifically from architecture. According to this idea, the architecture of a church should intentionally carry a message; it needs to embody this message. It tells people something about God. In other words, architecture is a continuation of the theology of the church, of what the church believes, expressed in how a church building is constructed. Since Catholic scholars explain architectural theology better and in more detail, we are going to hear from them.

> Just as words have meaning and grow from an accepted lexicon of connotations, architecture bears meaning as well. The Church holds to the principle *lex orandi-lex credendi*, that is, "the law of prayer is the law of belief. We pray as we believe and we also believe as we pray. As an immediate response to an encounter with God, prayer is primary. We then try to articulate this belief in theology books, rituals, and liturgical art and architecture. . . . A properly built church is the faith of the Church in built form. . . .
>
> Art and architecture are therefore never purely neutral.[23]

According to the principle, *lex orandi-lex credendi*, the architecture of the Church is never separated from its theology. In this case, architecture is only a continuation of theology or a good example of what the Church believes. For this reason, "today's pastor, committees, and church architects are to realize first of all that all architectural decisions are theological decisions. Then it must be understood that liturgical architecture is indeed *liturgical*, designed according to not only physical requirements of the ritual action, but to the very theology of the liturgy in all of its many dimensions.

By definition, then, church architecture is intimately bound to the teaching of the Church and the traditions handed on from generation to generation."[24]

Hence the natural conclusion that *"there are right things to believe, and therefore right ways to pray and right ways to build. These three ideas [theology, liturgy, architecture] can never be separated. Belief finds its liturgical expression in language, both the language of the spoken word and in the language of liturgical art and architecture."*[25]

Summing up the basic statements of architectural theology, we can identify its four basic principles: "First, in thinking this way about the revelatory nature of liturgical art and architecture, the law of building is the law of belief: *lex aedificandi-lex credendi*. Second, this principle is true because church architecture can rightly be understood as the *built form of ideas*, with *church architecture the built form of theology*. Third, proper church architecture is *sacramental* in that it signifies in material form an invisible theological reality. Lastly, because there are right beliefs, there is in fact a right way of building."[26]

What is the message carried by a temple? What invisible reality does it make visible? What theology does the Church refer us to in the architecture of its buildings?

We have already learned the answer—the heavenly temple was to be "cast down" to the ground and presented to the people. In his letter to artists, John Paul II encouraged them to fill the temples with images, "because it makes the otherwise invisible things of heaven knowable to the eye."[27] Paul Evdokimov, a famous Russian Orthodox thinker, puts it even stronger: "The Church's liturgy is not simply a copy of heavenly liturgy but is the eruption of the heavenly into history."[28] An interesting observation, isn't it? It means that a temple is not just a copy of reality; it is itself the reality erupted into earthly history. According to Evdokimov, who quotes Patriarch

Germanus, "The church is earthly heaven; in these heavenly spaces, God lives and walks about."[29]

The Protestants were called protestants because they did not agree with the doctrines of the Roman Catholic Church. They have revised and formulated a different soteriology, eschatology, and so on, but they have never tackled the subject of architectural theology. As a result, some of them have begun to teach that the temple of the antichrist will be built in Jerusalem, while others believe that the temple of the antichrist is to be found in the body, or rather in the mind, of the man possessed by him. However, they often do not notice that they haven't gotten rid of their Catholic heritage and that even five centuries after the Reformation they continue to teach that their church buildings should be treated as temples of God. One of the most influential Catholic scholars in the area of church architecture, Richard Vosko, said, "Human bodies have a way of remembering things that are not often clear in the mind. That is why people who grow up Catholic have liturgy in their bones. Some may leave the Church, but few shake the memory out of their bodies."[30] That may explain why at the beginning of the worship service some Protestants today continue to sing, "The Lord is in His Holy Temple," urging all participants to behave accordingly. They continue to build their churches almost completely in compliance with the architectural theology of the Catholic Church's "memory . . . of their bodies."[31] They retain the Catholic theology of the temple in their teaching, which according to the principle of *lex aedificandi-lex credendi*, means that the architecture of the building is only a continuation of theology of the Church and therefore cannot be neutral.

It was the misunderstanding of the architectural theology of the Catholic Church in the mid-nineteenth century that led Protestants into confusion. They didn't know what to call the sanctuary; their opinions were divided. Even today this Catholic baggage dominates Protestants, and they cannot understand what was written by Daniel. While some of them call their churches temples, others continue to expect the rebuilding of the temple in Jerusalem. They can hardly help Catholic and Orthodox Christians to get rid of misconceptions about the temple of God when they are confused themselves. It is difficult to pull the speck out of your brother's eye when you need the assistance of an ophthalmologist yourself.

8. The development of architectural theology

Extant documents show that from the beginning of the construction of church buildings, the attitude towards them was not that of a synagogue but of a temple. Nobody was bothered by the fact that there could be many synagogues but that there was only one temple in Israel. From the fourth century, church buildings began to grow like mushrooms in the darkness. Jeroboam built only two centers of worship in opposition to Jerusalem, but the Church built hundreds and thousands of temples. Despite their number, they were all constructed according to the above-mentioned principles, and therefore believers were taught to regard them accordingly.

As was rightly pointed out by Richard Vosko, "In the New Testament we learn that early Christians celebrated the 'breaking of bread' in their homes. The biblical texts provide no description of exactly how these houses may have been arranged for such gatherings. The architectural style of these places would have been indigenous to the region."[32] For three centuries, Christians hadn't been building churches. That is why this period of church history has not left us evidence explaining the causes of the changes.

One of the first comparisons of the church and the tabernacle, that is, the sanctuary built by Moses, comes from Methodius of Patara (A.D. 260–311). In his work, *The Church and the Tabernacle*, he says, "The Jews have prophesied the things which belong to us, but we prophesy the things of heaven. So therefore the Tabernacle was a symbol of the Church, and the Church is a symbol of the heavens."[33] Methodius wasn't writing about a church building;

he meant the Christians when he was speaking of the Church. He further explains: "But we ought to liken that Golden Altar within the Holy of Holies . . . to those who live in the state of chastity. They have protected their bodies with pure gold, unadulterated by carnal intercourse."[34] Though Methodius says nothing here about the church as a building, we want to draw attention to his allegorical interpretation of the Bible. He allows himself to go beyond the comparisons we find in the Bible and says that the golden altar was a symbol of Christian virgins. Perhaps this approach to the Scriptures is the main cause of all that happened later with the teaching about the temple.

Just a few years after the death of Methodius, in A.D. 323 there appeared another document known as "The Dedication at Tyre." In it, Eusebius of Caesarea writes a very interesting message to the bishop of Tyre: "I speak to you, Bishop Paulinus, to whom God has granted the signal honour of building and restoring this house on earth for Christ. . . . Maybe we should call you a new Bezaleel, the architect of the holy Tabernacle, or Solomon, King of a new and far better Jerusalem, or maybe a new Zerubbabel, who added to the Temple a new glory, far greater than the glory of a former one."[35]

Eusebius wrote these words to Bishop Paulinus in connection with the construction of a new basilica. Note how he, as a historian, evaluates the event. There is no doubt that his attitude to the construction of the basilica was the same as the attitude of the people in Solomon's time to the building of the temple.

Eusebius also gives us some interesting details. "When the Bishop finished the Temple, he placed at its head a seat to honour the presidents, and on either side of it other benches in strict order. In the centre he added the place of the altar, the Holy of holies."[36] As we remember, a basilica typically had a place for the throne, where a judge or other person in authority sat. It was decided to keep the throne in the basilica for a bishop. Benches were placed on both sides of the throne; such benches can be observed even today in some Catholic churches. Next to the throne of the bishop, an altar was erected, which replaced the altar of burnt offering. But unlike the Jewish temple, it was moved from the outer court into the Most Holy Place—or rather to a place that was called the Most Holy Place.

Eusebius goes on to say that just as in the temple not everyone could enter the Most Holy Place, so the architecture of the basilica was designed to block the way into the Most Holy Place of the church building. "To make this inaccessible to the congregation he [Paulinus] surrounded it with wooden rails."³⁷ And today such fencing is present in the Catholic Church in the form of a railing, and in the Orthodox Church in the form of the iconostasis.

These principles of constructing temples very quickly became compulsory for everyone. In the *Testamentum Domini** its author already uses the imperative mood. "I will tell you then how the House-Of-Holiness ought to be. . . . Let there be a throne by the altar. On the right and on the left let there be places of the presbyters, so that those who are more exalted and honoured, and those who labour in the Word, may sit on the right, but those who are of the middle age on the left."³⁸ This requirement has undergone various transformations. Sometimes these places were given to the priests and ministers of the church and sometimes to the choir. In one form or another, this tradition continues in modern churches.

It is possible to explain these strict rules of constructing temples only by their connection with the theology of the Church. A violation meant a change in the most important Christian teachings. Thus, architectural theology started to develop.

Continuing to study the documents, we find in the writings of Maximus the Confessor (A.D. 580–662) not only how a temple should be built, but what message it needs to communicate to

---

* This is translated as "The Testimony of our Lord." The document is dated to the fifth or even the fourth century and belongs to a genre of church ordinances. The author is unknown.

those who come into it. "The first Entry of the Bishop for the holy Church's Assembly is a figure and image of the first appearance of the incarnate Christ in this world. . . . And after this appearance, his ascension and the fact that he sat on the throne which is in the heaven of heavens is symbolised by the Bishop's entry into the sanctuary and his ascent to the priestly throne."[39]

In other words, a bishop designating himself an "image" or a "representative" of Christ on earth does this because he copies the ministry of Christ in the heavenly sanctuary. Maximus the Confessor confirms once again that the architecture of a church building, the order of worship, and the theology of the Church are a single whole and that they cannot exist without each other. Every action of the priest and every element of the building were to carry a theological meaning. Even the familiar three steps leading to the altar area of the temple* were to be a part of this "sermon." "The three steps which are in front of *bema*,† are the third heaven, to which the blessed Apostle Paul was taken up."[40]

With each passing century, this "sermon" of the Church became even stronger. Soon the iconoclastic controversy broke out. In order to complement the "sermon" preached by the architecture, icons, according to the viewpoint of some people, were to become a part of the interior of a church. Perhaps that is why new documents about the symbolism of the temple appeared at this time.

> The church is a Temple of God, a holy precinct, a House of Prayer, the Body of Christ. . . . The church is heaven upon earth, in which the heavenly God dwells and moves, and it bears the mark of the crucifixion, the grave and resurrection of Christ. It has a glory greater than that of Moses' Tabernacle of

---

* An element of the interior of a church kept in many church buildings.
† A platform elevated over the rest of the floor in the eastern part of a temple. Another name for it is *bima*.

Witness, which contained the mercy-seat and Holy of holies....

... The Holy Table is the place of the Tomb.... It is also the throne of God on which He is seated, who is "the God that rideth upon the cherubim,"...

... Indeed the Son of God and Judge of All has ordained earthly things according to the pattern of the heavenly....

... The rails* indicate in which place one should pray. Outside them is the place for the laity, and inside is the Holy of holies, only accessible to the priests....

... The prophets said (that God or Christ was in the east) in order to prevent us being disappointed, for we hope to receive once again "the Garden of Eden toward the East," and it is from the east that we are expecting the bright dawn of Christ's second appearance.[41]

These are the words of Germanus, patriarch of Constantinople (A.D. 715–730). On the one hand, he's not talking about something new, something that had never been said by anybody before. On the other hand, of course he develops and emphasizes the architectural theology of the temple. He perceives a sense of the sacred in every detail. *In fact*, for Germanus, as a supporter of the veneration of icons, *the temple is nothing but a huge icon*. It is the image of the heavenly, and therefore worthy of appropriate reverence. It is the symbolism of the temple that inspired the patriarch to let the icons take their place in the church.

With the Reformation the time had come for rethinking the theology of the church. However, Protestants did not always understand

---

* The iconostasis in the Orthodox Church.

the indivisibility of these three types of preaching: through theology, liturgy, and architecture. They gave almost all of their attention to the first—theology. For this purpose, Luther translated the Bible into German and gave people the opportunity to explore the Scriptures and get rid of error. As a result, there was a realization that the liturgy needed to be changed, but here the reform was not as radical as in theology. The third form of preaching—that of architecture—remained unchanged. Luther wrote: "The Antichrist took his seat in the church, yet not to govern it with divine laws, promises, and grace."[42] "He sits in the temple of God and rules with human commandments."[43] For Luther, as the historian Jaroslav Pelikan has said, "Although the pope was the Antichrist 'seated in the temple of God,' the church in which he was seated was still the temple of God."[44] In other words, for the reformers the content of faith (theology) was more important than its form (liturgy), and this was true even more for the theology of architecture. For Luther, the church building remained the temple.

The next event that influenced the form of faith, and the liturgy, was the Second Vatican Council. As a result, there were heard the voices of those who saw no need for strict adherence to tradition in the construction of temples. However, in reality any change is impossible. Even if the Church wanted to abandon architectural theology and begin to build temples without observing these traditions, what is to be done with those that are already built? For nearly seventeen centuries the Church has been building one temple after another, and the construction of each one spoke of its similarity to the temple in heaven. Even if the Church abandoned its teaching, it could not afford to reject what has been already built and begin demolishing church buildings. To do this would mean to recognize not only its spiritual, but also its financial, bankruptcy. Therefore, even though there is a rethinking of the liturgy within the Church, it is most likely that architectural theology awaits its Renaissance (see Daniel 11:45; Revelation 13:14). Then it will be when with great false signs and miracles that the prophecy of Paul will find its final and full fulfillment.

Conclusion

As we have seen, the answer to the question, "Where will the antichrist sit?" depends on a correct understanding of the prophecies of Daniel and John. Revelation 2:12, 13 and 13:2 point to the time and place where the dragon will give his throne to the beast. And Daniel 8:11 helps us to understand that the temple would appear "from heaven." Helen Dietz, a professor at Wayne University in Detroit, was able to summarize in several sentences the fulfillment of these prophesies in history.

> In this Christian replication of the Temple, however, the sanctuary now stood not merely for the earthly sanctuary at Jerusalem, but above all for the prototypal heavenly sanctuary extolled in the Epistle to the Hebrews as having been the model given to Moses for the Jerusalem sanctuary. This heavenly sanctuary was the eternal realm of the risen and glorified high priest Jesus who sits at the right hand of the throne of God the Father. . . .
> . . . To mention that the Christian priest "now sat in the basilica where the Roman emperor had previously sat" and other tangential similarities to the pagan basilica but fail to mention the deliberate continuities [in the architecture of the Church] with Judaic temple tradition is to distort history.[45]

Thus, we conclude that the temple, where according to the prophecy of Paul, the antichrist is to sit, is a church building, constructed in accord with some of the principles given to Moses by God.

While Protestants await the rebuilding of the temple in Jerusalem, the Catholics and Orthodox do not give any value to this event. Despite minor differences between the Catholic and the Orthodox Churches, they give the same message to their visitors—the church building is the temple of God. Their church buildings are designed to copy Solomon's Temple where the bread and wine of the Eucharist are stored in the new "Holy of Holies." That is why they do not attach any value to the potential rebuilding of the temple in Jerusalem.

The Catholic and the Orthodox Churches may well be proud of their temples, of their splendor and decoration. For them "a church building can be compared to a homily"[46] which tacitly testifies to their faith. However, according to the plan of God set forth through the prophets, this homily will be self-exposing in the concluding events of the history of sin. God has prepared a surprise for the antichrist. These "stones will cry out," and the things that today the antichrist is so proud of will testify against him.

But still several questions arise. For example, "Why are there many temples, yet Paul wrote of only one?" The apostle said that his prophecy would not be fulfilled until the "falling away" was revealed, so what kind of "falling away" is in question here? If the pope is the antichrist and his temple and throne are in Rome, what relation do Orthodox priests and their temples have to Paul's prophecy about the antichrist? What throne of Satan does the prophet speak about in Isaiah 14:13, 14? And, perhaps, the most important question: "How are we to understand the prophecy about the "abomination of desolation"?

Why is the question about the "abomination of desolation" so important? You probably remember that in the beginning of this chapter, we were talking about four different interpretations of the word, *temple*, in Paul's prophecy. We have shown that we have no biblical reason to understand the word, "temple," literally.

It is also difficult to agree that when he spoke of the temple, Paul was referring to the human body. First, because if it were that simple, then perhaps wouldn't it have been easier for Paul to simply name the body, the "body," rather than refer to a "temple"? Second, understanding that the temple refers to the body excludes the possibility that the "man of sin" will actually be a "man" who will sit in the temple. This interpretation would mean that the antichrist is only a system or a power imposed on a person, and consequently you would then need to exclude any interpretation in which the antichrist is a specific person. However, Daniel says that the antichrist will be both a "king" and his "kingdom" (Daniel 7:17, 23).

Understanding the temple as an assembly of believers does not encounter such contradictions and therefore can be preferred to other interpretations. However, interpreting the temple as either the body or as the assembly of believers comes to a standstill when we come to the question of the "abomination of desolation." That is why it is so important for us to understand what Daniel was talking about when he warned us of the "abomination of desolation." What is it? Where should we look for such an "abomination"? In the human body? Among the community of Christians? If the conclusions to which we have come in this chapter are correct, then the "abomination of desolation" is something that will appear and have to do with a church building. Is it possible that the "abomination of desolation" will be seen again—this time not around Jerusalem, but rather in the Christian church? We'll answer all these questions in the next chapter.

Notes

1. Ranko Stefanovic, *The Book of Revelation*, Adult Sabbath School Bible Study Guide, ed. Clifford Goldstein, January–March 2019, 17, 21–24.

2. Philip Schaff, *History of the Christian Church,* Nicene and Post-Nicene Christianity, vol. 3 (New York: Charles Scribner's Sons, 1891), 33.

3. Helen Dietz, "The Eschatological Dimension of Church Architecture: The Biblical roots of Church Orientation," *Sacred Architectural Journal* (October 2005): 12–14.

4. Henri de Lubac, *Thoughts on the Church, Russian edition* (Moscow: Christian Russia, 1994), 121, author's translation. Source information translated from Russian.

5. Lubac, 121, author's translation.

6. Gregory of Nyssa, quoted in *Creations*, vol. 8 (Moscow: Torletsky house, 1872) 6, 7. Original quote and source translated from Russian to English.

7. Dionysius the Areopagite, quoted in *Works,* (Saint Petersburg: Aletheia, 2002), 571. Original quote and source translated from Russian to English.

8. Dionysius, 571.

9. Ellen G. White, *Prophets and Kings* (Nampa, ID: Pacific Press˙, 2005), 99.

10. White, 99, 100.

11. White, 100.

12. White, 100.

13. Leonid Ouspensky, *The Theology of the Icon* (Crestwood, NY: St. Vladimir's Seminary Press, 1978), 23.

14. *Catholic Encyclopedia,* s.v. "Orientation of Churches," accessed February 23, 2020, http://www.newadvent.org/cathen/11305a.htm.

15. "Orientation of Churches" Catholic Answers Encyclopedia, Catholic.com, accessed February 23, 2020, https://www.catholic.com/encyclopedia/orientation-of-churches.

16. *Catholic Encyclopedia*, s.v. "Orientation of Churches," accessed February 23, 2020, http://www.newadvent.org/cathen/11305a.htm.

17. John Wilkinson, *From Synagogue to Church the Traditional Design:Its Beginning, its Definition, its End* (New York: Routledge, 2002), 201–205.

18. Original Russian source, http://www.bogoslovy.ru/zb05.htm, translated from Russian to English. "Bogoslovy" means "theologians" and ".ru" stans for Russian segment of internet. The website is posting articles, books, and other writings that explain theology of the Russian Orthodox Church.

19. Michael Davies, "The Catholic Sanctuary and the Second Vatican Council," Catholic Tradition, http://www.catholictradition.org/Eucharist/sanctuary4.htm.

20. For more details see Angel Rodriguez, "Genesis 1 and the Building of the Israelite Sanctionary," *Ministry*, (February 2002), https://www.ministrymagazine.org/archive/2002/02/genesis-1-and-the-building-of-the-israelite-sanctuary.html.

21. Alexander Bolotnikov, Gospel in the Old Testament Sanctuary, (n.p.: Source of Life Books, 2001), 60. Quote and source information translated from Russian to English.

22. Denis R. McNamara, *Catholic Church Architecture and the Spirit of Liturgy* (Chicago: Hillenbrand Books, 2009), 48, 49.

23. McNamara, 7.

24. McNamara, 8; emphasis in original.

25. McNamara; 8; emphasis in original.

26. McNamara, 9.

27. McNamara, 16.

28. Paul Evdokimov, *The Art of the Icon: A Theology of Beauty* (Redondo Beach, CA: Oakwood Publications, 1990), 120.

29. Patriarch Germanus, 98:384, quoted in Evdokimov, *The Art of the Icon*, 143.

30. Richard Vosko, *God's House Is Our House* (Collegeville, MN: Liturgical Press, 2006), 5.

31. Vosko, 5.

32. Vosko, 21.

33. Methodius of Patara, quoted in John Wilkinson, *From Synagogue to Church*, 189.

34. Methodius, quoted in Wilkinson, 190.

35. Eusebius of Caesarea to the Bishop Paulinus, "Dedication at Tyre," quoted in John Wilkinson, *From Synagogue to Church*, 190.

36. Eusebius quoted in Wilkinson, 191.

37. Eusebius quoted in Wilkinson, 191.

38. *Testamentum Domini*, quoted in John Wilkinson, *From Synagogue to Church*, 192, 193.

39. Maximus the Confessor quoted in John Wilkinson, *From Synagogue to Church,* 197.

40. Thomas of Marga, "Book of Martyrs," quoted in Wilkinson, *From Synagogue to Church*, 205. See also 2 Corinthians 12:1, 2.

41. Germanus, "Church Symbolism," quoted in Wilkinson, *From Synagogue to Church*, 198–200.

42. Jaroslav Pelikan, Helmut T. Lehmann, Hilton C. Oswald, eds., *Lectures on Genesis: Chapters 45–50,* Luther Works (St. Louis, MO: Concordia Publishing House, 1966), 8:283.

43. Jaroslav Pelikan, Helmut T. Lehmann, Hilton C. Oswald, eds., *Word and Sacrament III,* Luther Works (St. Louis, MO: Concordia Publishing House, 1966), 37:367.

44. Jaroslav Pelikan, *Reformation of Church and Dogma (1300–1700),* The Christian Tradition: A History of the Development of Doctrine, vol. 4 (Chicago: University of Chicago Press, 1984), 173.

45. Dietz, "Eschatological Dimensions of Church Architecture."

46. Vosko, *God's House Is Our House,* 19.

Chapter 5

What Is the "Abomination of Desolation"?

Among researchers of Bible prophecies today, there is no shortage of those who want to tell us what the "abomination of desolation" is. Most of them, however, believe that since the coming of the antichrist will happen in our day or in the near future, the "abomination of desolation" is either a present reality or something that will occur soon. For example, some believe that former US president Barack Obama is the antichrist, and therefore they are closely monitoring all his actions. According to them, the "abomination of desolation" already took place on March 22, 2013, when Obama visited the Basilica of the Nativity in Bethlehem. Instead of kneeling for prayer, he simply stood and stared, which was interpreted by some as an expression of disrespect to the temple that defiled it. They say that the appearance of the president interrupted prayer and worship, and that is enough to identify him as the antichrist who would put an end to the sacrifice.

With someone's creative hand and the help of the Internet, such misconceptions enter people's minds and increase the confusion and disarray clustered around this subject. In these kinds of interpretations, finding even one sign that is vaguely reminiscent of the antichrist is enough to declare someone to be the "man of sin." Unfortunately, the saying, "One heard the song, but got it wrong," is often the best description of what is happening in discussions about the antichrist.

1. All that glitters is not gold

Another example of reaching premature conclusions is attempting to compare the conclusions of the third and fourth chapters of this book without studying them further. For example, if we say that the banners of the Roman army surrounding Jerusalem equals the abomination of desolation "standing in the holy place" (Matthew 24:15), and if we then say that the temple equals a church building, we may then jump to the conclusion that placing national flags or other "pagan" symbols in a church is the setting up of the abomination, standing where it ought not be. This conclusion is particularly tempting to those familiar with the worship practices and interior decoration of the churches in North America, especially those in the United States. In the US, the national flag has become not only an integral part of the interior furnishings of church buildings, but sometimes* even a part of the worship service. This tradition began during World War II and became so dear to American Christians that it soon became commonplace and an unwritten rule. Today in most churches in the United States, the flag of the country is displayed in an honorable place, and from time to time, parishioners are united in pledging allegiance to their country and this symbol.

Considering what Jesus said about the "abomination of desolation" and what Paul said about the temple, it may seem that the Christian church in the United States is fulfilling the prophecy. However, although it may appear plausible, this interpretation is not correct. Let's explain why.

First, oddly enough, it is Protestant churches rather than Catholic churches that have given support to this tradition. Even

---

* For example, on Memorial Day or on Independence Day.

WHAT IS THE "ABOMINATION OF DESOLATION"?

more so, the Catholic Church has considered the issue serious enough to release an official statement on the matter. Here is what it says:

> The Bishops' Committee on the Liturgy has in the past encouraged pastors not to place the flag within the sanctuary itself, in order to reserve that space for the altar, the ambo, the presidential chair and the tabernacle. Instead, the suggestion has been made that the American flag be placed outside the sanctuary, or in the vestibule of the Church together with a book of prayer requests. It remains, however, for the diocesan bishop to determine regulations in this matter.[1]
>
> Our churches are places where everyone is welcomed, not just American citizens, but people of other countries, a place in which a gospel message that challenges the values of a country may be heard. Such a tradition is compromised by the presence of civil symbols. The Eucharistic Prayer for Reconciliation II says that through the Holy Spirit in this place, "enemies begin to speak to one another, those who were estranged join hands in friendship, and nations seek the way of peace together." ...
> Our standard as Catholics is the Cross of Christ, and it is to that we owe our allegiance. It leads us into the church to hear the Gospel, to celebrate Eucharist, and back out into the world to live it out.[2]

In our opinion, these are instructive statements. As we know, the Catholics consider a church building to be the sanctuary on earth. For them, setting a state flag in the sanctuary of God would mean not only violating the principle of separation of church and state, that is, "render therefore to Caesar the things that are Caesar's, and to God the things that are God's" (Matthew 22:21), but it would also be challenging God by defiling His sanctuary. However, by arguing in favor of their tradition they draw our attention to something else. First, the Catholic Church is a global church, and setting the symbols of any state in the church makes it more of a national church than a universal one and thus divides people. Second, state laws and God's laws are not always compatible with each other. Third, a faithful Catholic must first give his loyalty to God and then to the state; the state power cannot be compared to, let alone be put above, the authority of God. For Catholics, placing the symbols of the state in a temple of God means that the power of God and the power of the state are put on the same level. And that is unacceptable because God is above all. Today, when Christians pledge allegiance to their country, sometimes several times a week, but refuse even once to renew their covenant with God by promising to be faithful to their baptismal vows, this issue becomes especially relevant and raises the question, who is it that actually owns their allegiance?

Thus, Catholic churches have a clear directive not to set state flags inside the sanctuary, and that is why it is incorrect to consider such a practice as a fulfillment of the prophecy about the "abomination of desolation" (Matthew 24:15).

Second, this interpretation, though seemingly plausible is still incorrect, because placing the national flag in churches is largely a local phenomenon. In other words, this is a tradition of one country—the United States. Even churches in Canada, which differ very little from churches in the United States, do not place state symbols in their church buildings. It is hardly possible to compare this local practice with the abomination of desolation described in the prophecy, which certainly has a global application.

Third, this interpretation does not take into account other details of the prophecy that we are going to study below.

WHAT IS THE "ABOMINATION OF DESOLATION"?

2. What have we missed?

In chapter 3, "Will the Temple Be Rebuilt?" we have already studied the question of the "abomination of desolation." In that chapter, we learned that those who believe that the temple in Jerusalem is to be rebuilt refer to Daniel 9:27 and Matthew 24:15 as two of the prophecies giving them reason to believe that the temple will be restored. The logic of their argument is simple. Both Daniel and Jesus speak of the "abomination of desolation." Since this is the expression most often used in relation to the defilement of the sanctuary, they feel that the prophecy needs to be understood in this way, despite the fact that the words, *sanctuary* or *temple* do not appear in these passages. And since it is impossible to defile a ruined temple or a sanctuary that does not exist, they conclude that the temple must first be rebuilt and then defiled in order for Daniel's prophecy to be fulfilled. That is why some have come to the conclusion that one day a house of God will again be built in Jerusalem.

However, a detailed analysis of the text of the prophecy of Daniel 9:27, as well as the study of history, shows that the prophecy has already been fulfilled and that the "abomination of desolation" referred not to the destruction of the temple, but rather to the appearance of the pagan symbols on the banners of the Roman army in the holy land around Jerusalem. Those in Jerusalem who kept the prophecy in mind were able to flee, while it was too late to flee when the Romans attacked the temple.

Thus, we could say that we already know what the "abomination of desolation" is. It would seem that the question is settled, and we can make a point and move on. On the other hand, those who quote Daniel 9:27 and Matthew 24:15 as evidence that the temple will be rebuilt in Jerusalem are careful for some reason not to draw our attention to the fact that Daniel 9:27 is not the only prophecy Daniel recorded about the "abomination of desolation." This expression is found at least twice in subsequent chapters, and in these instances is truly related to a defilement of the temple occurring much later than the first century. Thus, it becomes obvious that we have not studied the question to its end, so we need to continue our research.

3. Daniel's prophecies about the "abomination of desolation"

In the book of Daniel, the prophecy of the abomination of desolation is found not once, but four times. Despite this fact, for some reason only one of these passages—Daniel 9:27—has become the subject of research and debate. The other three are most often surrounded by a mysterious silence. So where does Daniel speak of the abomination of desolation? Let's identify where these prophecies occur in his book.

1. Daniel 9:27 (cf. Matthew 24:15; Mark 13:14; Luke 21:20)
2. Daniel 8:9–14 (2,300 days)*
3. Daniel 11:31
4. Daniel 12:9–13

Of these four passages, only the first is widely known; it is cited whenever there are arguments in favor of the restoration of the temple in Jerusalem. This passage is also mentioned by Jesus Himself in the Gospels of Matthew, Mark, and Luke. But, contrary to popular belief, this prophecy has nothing to do with the construction of a

---

* In the NKJV, the connection of this passage with the others is not obvious, since the phrase "abomination of desolation" is not used here. However, analysis of the passages in the original language shows the overlap of both the subject as a whole and the specific words used by Daniel. As we read chapters 8 and 11, we find in both of them a casting down of the sanctuary, a taking away of the daily sacrifice, an apostasy (transgression or forsaking the covenant), and the host or the forces and desolation. The parallels in these passages are obvious and give us grounds to say that the "transgression of desolation" and the "abomination of desolation" are interchangeable concepts.

new temple because the prophecy was already fulfilled in the year A.D. 70 when Jerusalem was subjected to siege and destruction by the Romans.

However, there is another "abomination of desolation" in the book of Daniel. It is described in the second, third, and fourth of the passages listed above. Unlike the abomination of desolation mentioned in the first passage, this one has nothing to do with the destruction of Jerusalem. But that is not the most interesting thing to note. The interesting thing is that these passages actually speak about the defilement or the "casting down" of God's sanctuary and the termination of the sacrifice. In addition, it becomes clear after a close examination that these prophecies must be fulfilled *after* A.D. 70. After all, if the seventy weeks of Daniel 9 symbolize 490 literal years, then the references to 2,300; 1,290; and 1,335 days (see Daniel 8:14; 12:11, 12) must also refer to years and not days. And Daniel 12 clearly tells us that the vision refers to the time of the end. This means that these prophetic periods should come to an end, not in the first century but rather much later. The question arises: If the temple is destroyed and is not to be rebuilt, then how will the prophecy be fulfilled and how will the sanctuary be defiled? How will the Antichrist set up the "abomination of desolation"?

4. How will the antichrist set up the "abomination of desolation"?

Let's read what Daniel says of the way in which the Antichrist will set up the "abomination of desolation." The first and the most detailed passage is in Daniel 8:

> And out of one of them came a little horn which grew exceedingly great toward the south, toward the east, and toward the Glorious Land. And it grew up to the host of heaven; and it cast down some of

the host and some of the stars to the ground, and trampled them. He even exalted himself as high as the Prince of the host; and by him the daily sacrifices were taken away, and the place of His sanctuary was cast down. Because of transgression, an army was given over to the horn to oppose the daily sacrifices; and he cast truth down to the ground. He did all this and prospered.

Then I heard a holy one speaking; and another holy one said to that certain one who was speaking, "How long will the vision be, concerning the daily sacrifices and the transgression of desolation, the giving of both the sanctuary and the host to be trampled underfoot?"

And he said, to me, "For two thousand three hundred days; then the sanctuary shall be cleansed" (verses 9–14).

We find the next passage in Daniel 11:

For ships from Cyprus shall come against him; therefore he shall be grieved, and return in rage against the holy covenant, and do damage.

So he shall return and show regard for those who forsake the holy covenant. And forces shall be mustered by him; and they shall defile the sanctuary fortress; then they shall take away the daily sacrifice, and place there the abomination of desolation (verses 30, 31).

The last passage is found at the very end of the book of Daniel, in chapter 12:

WHAT IS THE "ABOMINATION OF DESOLATION"?

And he said, "Go your way, Daniel, for the words are closed up and sealed till the time of the end. Many shall be purified, made white, and refined, but the wicked shall do wickedly; and none of the wicked shall understand, but the wise shall understand.

"And from the time that the daily sacrifice is taken away, and the abomination of desolation is set up, there shall be one thousand two hundred and ninety days. Blessed is he who waits, and comes to the one thousand three hundred and thirty-five days.

"But you, go your way till the end; for you shall rest, and will arise to your inheritance at the end of the days" (verses 9–13).

To make our research easier, we will try to summarize everything Daniel says in these verses. It will give us a road map of exactly how the antichrist will defile the sanctuary.

1. He will cast down some of the host of heaven (Daniel 8:10).
2. He will cast down some stars (Daniel 8:10).
3. He will mount an attack on the Prince of the host (Daniel 8:11).
4. The daily sacrifice is taken away (Daniel 8:11).
5. He will cast down the place of the sanctuary (Daniel 8:11).
6. The covenant is forsaken (Daniel 11:30).
7. The antichrist will set his whole army against God (Daniel 8:12; 11:31).
8. The abomination of desolation is set up (Daniel 8:13; 11:31; 12:11).
9. The timeline of the 1,290 and 1,335 days are significant. (Daniel 12:11, 12).

In order to understand what all these actions mean, let's examine them in detail. *

The attack on the host of heaven (actions no. 1 and no. 2)

Before we can understand how the antichrist has cast down and trampled a part of the heavenly host and of the stars, we need to explain these symbols. To do this, let's ask a question: "Whom does the Bible call the host and the stars?" and read the answer in the Scripture.

The Scripture answers,

> And suddenly there was with the angel a multitude of the heavenly host praising God and saying:
> "Glory to God in the highest,
> And on earth peace, goodwill toward men!"
> (Luke 2:13, 14).

Here, the evangelist Luke tells us of the birth of Christ the Savior. When the shepherds were in the field at night, they saw an angel with the "heavenly host" announcing to them the coming of the Savior. We can easily determine that the host that accompanied the angel proclaiming the good news was nothing else but a multitude of angels who came to earth and appeared to the shepherds with the angel-evangelist. They heralded the birth of Jesus and glorified God.

However, the Bible refers to the angels of God, not only as "the host," but also as "the stars." For example, in the book of Revelation, the apostle John writes,

> And another sign appeared in heaven: behold, a great, fiery red dragon having seven heads and ten

---

* Actions 1, 2, 3, and 5 are also described in Revelation 13:6.

horns, and seven diadems on his heads. His tail drew a third of the stars of heaven and threw them to the earth. And the dragon stood before the woman who was ready to give birth, to devour her Child as soon as it was born. . . .

. . . So the great dragon was cast out, that serpent of old, called the Devil and Satan, who deceives the whole world; he was cast to the earth, and his angels were cast out with him (Revelation 12:3, 4, 9).

As we have already learned, the dragon who throws a third of the stars to the earth, is the devil. Verse 4 says that the stars were thrown down to the earth together with the dragon, and in the ninth verse John explains that these stars actually represented the angels. At first glance, this picture reminds us of what we have read in Daniel 8:10. In both cases, the devil cast down the angels from heaven. However, a closer reading shows the difference. In the book of Revelation, the fallen angels are "his" angels; i.e., the angels of Satan. The book of Daniel is not speaking about Satan, but about the "little horn," that is, the antichrist. And these angels whom he attacks are not "his" angels, but the "heavenly host." In other words, the prophets tell us that because Satan and his angels lost the war in heaven and were overcome by God and His angels, they were cast down to the earth. They continued this war on the earth through the antichrist, who wants to overthrow God and His angels from heaven.

But it would be incomplete to stop there. The fact is that the biblical symbol of "stars" does not always mean only angels. For example, in this same chapter where John writes about the dragon he says, "Now a great sign appeared in heaven: a woman clothed with the sun, with the moon under her feet, and on her head a garland of twelve stars" (Revelation 12:1). Who are these stars, and why are there twelve? Many commentators tend to assume that these stars represent the twelve apostles and that the woman clothed with the sun symbolizes the church. Daniel confirms and complements this idea when he says, "Those who are wise shall shine like the brightness of the firmament, and those who turn many to righteousness like the stars forever and ever" (Daniel 12:3). The prophet does not speak here of angels, and he doesn't speak here only of the apostles. All "who are wise" and "those who turn many to righteousness" shall shine "like the stars."

Thus, the Bible answers the question of who this host and the stars are. *They are God's angels and also His saints and faithful people.* In fact, the Bible refers to them as "fellow servants" to each other (Revelation 19:10), so it is not surprising that the same symbol represents both and that Satan is fighting against both of them.

How can the antichrist "cast down" and "trample" God's angels or His saints? Is the antichrist stronger than God? Did the antichrist manage to do what Satan himself failed to accomplish?

To answer these questions, we need to remember that the antichrist did the same thing to the sanctuary. The prophet Daniel uses the same Hebrew verb for "cast down" in relation to the sanctuary as he does for the casting down of the stars. How did the antichrist cast down the sanctuary? Remember that the main action of the antichrist in this passage is blasphemy—blasphemy not as a curse against God but as a counterfeit, as the appropriation of God's name or title, as identity theft of God's address, His temple in heaven. Satan is not strong enough to throw the temple of God to the ground, but by teaching people to believe that the church building is "the temple of God" and "heaven on earth," the antichrist, like Jeroboam, has established his own spiritual service and turned the hearts of the people from God's heavenly temple.

If we are not mistaken and have understood correctly the manner in which the antichrist "cast down" the sanctuary, then something similar should happen when he casts down "the host" and "the stars." Let's see if this is really so.

WHAT IS THE "ABOMINATION OF DESOLATION"?

We have already mentioned the words of John of Odzun and his document, "Laying the Foundation." He describes the manner of laying the foundation of a church building in the following words:

> And they take twelve stones, which are first washed with water, then with wine.
> These figure the twelve Apostles, whose feet the Lord washed in the Upper Room....
> Indeed these stones are placed in four corners of the church to indicate their directions toward the four corners of the world, and to be appropriate by [their] solidity to be the foundation for the Temple of God, for we are based on them, and they on Christ the Head.[3]

According to this document, there was a whole ceremony, or even a liturgy, of laying the foundation of a church building. Whenever construction of a temple began, there had to be twelve stones laid in its foundation, symbolizing the twelve apostles. Laying the foundation of a church is more like a worship service than construction, and its main preachers are stones. Surprisingly, this resonates with the words of Daniel that the sanctuary and the stars will be "cast down" to the ground and will be "trampled." While the sanctuary itself and the "stars" are beyond the power of the antichrist, and he cannot cast them down from heaven, still he "exalts" himself and begins to blaspheme by attributing heavenly names to the earthly objects and thus symbolically tramples them.

But sometimes a symbolic trampling does not seem to be sufficient enough. That is why the "sermon of stones" can speak to us more convincingly and eloquently at times. For example, St. Peter's Basilica in Rome, according to the claim of the Vatican, was literally built over the tomb of the apostle Peter. Unlike the stones of a church foundation, which no one can see, the burial place of Peter is arranged so that every visitor to this basilica pays attention to the fact that the apostle Peter was buried under the church building in Rome.

But what about the angels? They also are to be thrown down, are they not? Even if the Church ever decided to claim that some angel had been buried under some temple, it would be unlikely that anyone would believe it. Therefore, the Church reveres the angels, along with the saints, by constructing temples in their honor and worshiping them instead of God. Philip Schaff says, "To the saints, about the same period, were added angels as objects of worship. To angels there was ascribed in the church from the beginning a peculiar concern with the fortunes of the militant church, and a certain oversight of all lands and nations."[4] And the *Catholic Encyclopedia* adds: "In the fourth century we find Eusebius of Caesarea distinguishing accurately between the cult rendered to angels and the worship paid to God (Demonstratio evang., III, 3), and St. Ambrose recommended prayers to them. From the fifth century, churches were frequently dedicated to the angels."[5]

Not only did these innovations have nothing to do with the teaching of the Bible, they directly contradicted it. The apostle John, when he wanted to worship an angel, was told not to do it. "And I fell at his [the angel's] feet to worship him. But he said to me, 'See that you do not do that! I am your fellow servant, and of your brethren who have the testimony of Jesus. Worship God! For the testimony of Jesus is the spirit of prophecy' " (Revelation 19:10). Neither saints nor angels will receive worship because it belongs only to God.

So, how should we understand the prophecy that "the host" and "the stars" would be "cast down" and "trampled"? After studying the long and complex history of the development of Christian doctrine in the light of Daniel's prophecy, we come to the conclusion that the claim that the apostles or other saints are in the foundation of churches either symbolically or literally, along with the worship of saints or angels and the dedication of churches to them are only a means to an end and not the goal itself. *The victorious faith of saints and the ministry of the holy angels were needed only as a means of covering a godless agenda with their reputation and good name, that is, "to pump up" the pagan Roman basilica with a holiness that could be compared to, or even be declared superior to, the holiness of God's temple in the time of Solomon.*

A good example can be found in the advertising world. In order to increase the value of a product in the eyes of the consumer, the seller invites the "stars" of his time to endorse his product. In the light of their glory, a hitherto unknown product—maybe even a useless product—can become almost indispensable and highly desirable. This is the principle at work in what Daniel wrote when he said that the "little horn" would be able to employ "the host" and "the stars" in his service and "cast them down," making them a tool of his propaganda. It is his purpose to turn people away from the only true worship of God, to make them forget about the true temple in heaven, and to make people treat the church building as the temple of God. The antichrist has decided to join those whom the Bible calls "the stars" in order to keep warm in their glory. Thus, "the host" and "the stars" were cast down, and the truth was "trampled" (Daniel 8:10, 12).

The attack on the heavenly High Priest, His Ministry, and His Sanctuary (Actions no. 3, no. 4 and no. 5)

Daniel says, "He even exalted himself as high as the Prince of the host; and by him the daily sacrifices were taken away, and the place of His sanctuary was cast down" (Daniel 8:11). If we read this phrase once again with great attention, we'll recall that in the previous chapter we already began to explain its meaning.

When Daniel writes that the little horn "exalted himself as high as the Prince of the host," he is speaking about blasphemy. Note that in the parallel passage from the previous chapter (chapter 7) the prophet speaks repeatedly of the little horn speaking "pompous words" (verses 8, 11, 20, 25) and adds in the end that these words will be "against the Most High" (verse 25). In chapter 8, Daniel does not elaborate on this in detail, believing that his reader is able to understand that the phrase, "exalted himself as high as the Prince of the host" (verse 11) means the same as speaking "pompous words" against the Most High, that is—blasphemy.

Why would so many people be deceived in spite of the blasphemy of the antichrist? We repeat the answer again: Because blasphemy is not just cursing God but appropriating His names or titles. The antichrist may confess the sins of his Church, ask forgiveness of everyone, including the victims of the Inquisition or sexual minorities, wash the feet of prisoners or even kiss them. Looking at these great acts of humility, sacrifice, or charity, many are ready to exclaim, "Is not this an example of godliness?" But at the same time the antichrist has no intention of giving up his title of High Priest, which belongs only to Christ. If "Satan himself transforms himself into an angel of light" (2 Corinthians 11:14), then the antichrist can and will take the form of Christ. Moreover, the more the antichrist copies Christ, the stronger his deception is.

If we see blasphemy as being a form of identity theft, then the more information that is stolen and the more similarities are established, the stronger the credibility of the fraud is. Therefore, if the antichrist calls himself a high priest or a priest, the first and natural question that would be said to him would be, "Where is your temple?" In other words, "If you have no temple in which you serve, how can you be a priest?" That is why Daniel also wrote that "the place of His [God's] sanctuary was cast down" (verse 11). The antichrist definitely needs to call his church the temple of God. By doing so he not only gets the title of priest, but he also gets God's "address" or the temple.

However, this picture is not complete. There is something we have not yet mentioned. To seize the victim's name and address is undoubtedly a great success for the identity thief, but it is not enough to carry out a serious fraud. This is information that teenagers manipulate on social networks, but hardened criminals know that additional steps are needed for more serious crimes. For example, one needs to know the answer to certain questions to obtain the victim's password or social security number. With this information, the offender can contact the bank or other credit institution on the phone and convince the clerk that he is the one whom he pretends to be and can thus deprive his victim of all that he or she has.

The antichrist usurps the name and address of the heavenly High Priest. But what is the third thing, the password or social security number, that the antichrist finds so necessary? As always, the answer is in the Bible: "By him the daily sacrifices were taken away" (verse 11).* It is elementary, isn't it? If you're a priest and you have a temple, then where is the sacrifice? A temple is useless without sacrifices. Therefore, to carry out a complete identity theft, the antichrist needs a sacrifice. That's why the title, the temple, and the sacrifice are all parts of one whole—each one is an element of the bigger picture that complement the others.†

---

* The original text simply says "daily"; the word "sacrifice" is missing. Perhaps it also speaks about other daily duties of a priest and not only about offering sacrifices. In this book, we are not going to examine all of these functions but limit ourselves only to the sacrifice.

† See the previous chapter, specifically the subdivision "Architectural Theology."

Three Elements of One Picture, table 7

Three elements of the prophecy	Fulfillment	Theology	Illustration: "identity theft"
"Exalted himself as high as the Prince of the host" (verse 11).	High priest or priest	Theology of priesthood	Name and title
"The daily sacrifices were taken away" (verse 11).	Eucharist	Theology of liturgy	Social Security number
"The sanctuary ... trampled underfoot" (verse 13).	The church is God's temple on earth	Theology of temple/ architectural theology	Address

We learn from the pages of Scripture that sacrifices haven't always needed a temple, but a temple has always needed sacrifices. *This means that compared to attacking the sacrifice, the attack on the temple is a means rather than an end. The antichrist's purpose is an attack on the sacrifice of Christ; i.e., the gospel. This is at the heart of this prophecy.** Usurping Christ's title and His "address" is, of course, a serious crime, but it seems to be just a teenage prank compared to the attack on His atoning sacrifice. If the antichrist is able to make us believe his message about the sacrifice of our Savior, the gospel will lose its power. Christianity will not only have "a form of godliness" (2 Timothy 3:5) but will also be "denying its power" (verse 5). So Jesus and the prophet John say that before the end of the history of

---

* At times Christians do not like to study the Old Testament or its prophecies because they do not find the gospel in them. It's because they don't see the gospel in those verses, rather than because it is not there. In John 5:39, Jesus Himself warns us against such shortsightedness.

sin the gospel will be preached again (Matthew 24:14; Revelation 14:6). This is the everlasting gospel; it is pure and holy.

Christ is our only and true High Priest. "For such a High Priest was fitting for us, who is holy, harmless, undefiled, separate from sinners, and has become higher than the heavens" (Hebrews 7:26). We come to Him rather than to a man to confess our transgressions. When we behold His righteous and self-sacrificial life, our conscience is awakened, and we are repulsed by sin. It is Jesus who suffered and died for our sins, and it is Jesus only who can be a mediator between us and God. His sacrifice is enough to redeem us from the curse of sin. There is nothing we can add to the salvation that was granted to us and that we receive by faith. His righteousness becomes our righteousness. It is the gift of God, "not of works, lest anyone should boast" (Ephesians 2:9). After He offered Himself as a sacrifice, He entered into the heavenly sanctuary and became our High Priest. There He intercedes for us before His heavenly Father. The absence of an earthly priesthood cannot alienate us from the grace of God. We access grace by faith in Jesus Christ rather than through participation in the Eucharist.

But now another message is preached for a billion Catholics and several hundred million Orthodox Christians. It declares that the Eucharist is nothing less than the sacrifice of Christ Himself. In other words, whenever any Catholic or Orthodox priest performs the Eucharist, he is offering Jesus Christ's sacrifice, as if what He did on the cross was not enough. The catechism of the Catholic Church says,

> "The Eucharist is thus a sacrifice because it re-presents (makes present) the sacrifice of the cross. . . .
>
> The sacrifice of Christ and the sacrifice of the Eucharist are one single sacrifice: 'The victim is one and the same . . . only the manner of offering [bloody and unbloody] is different."[6]

Many Protestants were strongly against this understanding of the Eucharist as a sacrifice. They pointed out that Christ commanded us to perform this ritual only as a memorial, never as a sacrifice. To recognize the Eucharist as both a memorial and a sacrifice would mean that Jesus' sacrifice is not enough for salvation. They stressed that according to Scripture, the sacrifice had to be offered only once. They repeatedly quoted Hebrews: "[The High Priest, Jesus] does not need daily, as those high priests, to offer up sacrifices, first for His own sins and then for the people's, for this He did once for all when He offered up Himself" (Hebrews 7:27). To continue to offer Him as a sacrifice, even a bloodless one, would be to admit the imperfection of the Savior's sacrifice.

If we remember the lessons we have learned from chapter 3, we will be able to notice some parallels between Judaism and the Catholic (and Orthodox) doctrine. Here is a direct quote from Chapter 3:

> The Jews do not believe Jesus Christ to be the promised Messiah and do not embrace His death on the cross as a sacrifice for sin. So they don't see any reason for the temple service and sacrifices to end. In other words, those who wish to rebuild the temple and offer sacrifices there do so because they deny that Jesus is the Messiah. John warned us about this when he said that the antichrist (in the broad sense of the word) would deny that Jesus is the Messiah (1 John 2:22). Therefore, whenever we hear that the sacrifice of Jesus did not accomplish enough (and thus it is necessary to compensate this lack through other sacrifices), or that He did not do anything at all (since He was not the Messiah), we must recognize this as the handwriting of the antichrist. What an amazing thing to see Christians sponsoring and

inspiring the Jews to build the temple! The temple is useless without a sacrifice, and why does the God of the Bible need an earthly temple and its sacrifices if the Lamb of God has already been slain?*

However, neither the Papacy nor the Orthodox Church wants to agree with this and have continued to teach their parishioners that faith alone is not enough for attaining salvation (grace) and that we need the Eucharist and other sacraments of the Church as well. Therefore, to acquire grace every true Christian should confess his sins to a priest and receive communion from time to time in order to not reject Christ's sacrifice and fall away from grace. In this "different gospel" (Galatians 1:6), the sacraments, the Eucharist, and the priests are given the key role.

In his book, *101 Questions and Answers on the Eucharist,* a famous Catholic scientist and doctor of theology, Giles Dimock, explains in an accessible form the basics of the sacrament of the Eucharist.

> What is the priest's role in the Eucharist?
> ... It is clear that not just anyone could preside at the Eucharistic celebration, but only the apostles or one appointed by them. The one presiding represents Christ ...
> ... only a bishop or a priest can represent Christ, the Great High Priest.[7]

If we ask ourselves why this is so, we are told that we need to keep in mind that the Eucharist is a bloodless sacrifice, and the right to offer a sacrifice belongs only to the priest or his "representative."

---

* See conclusion to the third chapter of this book.

> Can we receive [grace] at a Protestant Eucharist?
>
> They [Protestants] do not see the Eucharist as we do, even though Lutherans may hold for "Real Presence" as opposed to the Zwinglianism of most Protestants. Still they do not see their ministers as priests and so lose the understanding of priesthood and sacrifice . . . thus intercommunion for us is an impossibility.[8]

Note how easily the terms are substituted. In the first quote cited above, there was a reference to the priests as "representatives." In the second quote, they are not "representatives" anymore, but real priests offering real sacrifices. Such a play on words is common in the theology of the Eucharist and the priesthood.

> Can Protestants receive Communion at Catholic Mass?
>
> . . . In effect if we allowed wide intercommunion we'd be saying that we are all one doctrinally, organically, and ecclesiastically, but that simply is not true . . . In general then, the Church does not allow Protestants to receive Catholic Communion.[9]

In other words, those who receive the Eucharist in the Catholic Church must also accept its doctrine about it.

> Why does the Church celebrate the Eucharist on Sunday?
>
> . . . The simple answer is because it is the day that the Lord rose from the dead."[10]

The logic of this reply probably was originally meant not to be clear to everyone. Jesus gathered his disciples in the upper room and performed communion on a Thursday. Why not follow His example? But if the sacrament is a commemoration of His death, then why not do it on Friday—on the day He died? Instead, Sunday is the main day for celebrating the Eucharist. In the future, when the fourth commandment of God's law will be fully rejected and people will be united in the observance of Sunday, rather than the seventh-day Sabbath (Saturday), the Eucharist will become the center of Sunday worship.

> How often may I receive Holy Communion?
> Curiously, as Mass was celebrated more frequently by monk priests, even daily in medieval times, fewer and fewer Christians went to Communion....
> ...Pope Pius X [A.D. 1903–1914] restored frequent or even daily Communion to all Catholics.[11]

So, the answer is clear. Every conscientious Catholic can receive the Eucharist daily. What a surprise that this coincides with Daniel's prophecy that the daily sacrifice, or even all daily service, will be taken from the Prince of the host. Instead of being taught to come to God, the people were taught to go to His "representative," gradually causing them to forget the true gospel. John Hooper, a Protestant pastor executed for his beliefs, could not remain silent watching what was happening and declared openly, "I believe and confess that the popish Mass is an invention of Antichrist, and a forsaking of the sacrifice of Jesus Christ . . . "[12]

The attack on the covenant (action no. 6)

Daniel writes about the antichrist's attack on the covenant:

> For ships from Cyprus shall come against him; therefore he shall be grieved, and return in rage against the holy covenant, and do damage.
>
> So he shall return and show regard for those who forsake the holy covenant. And forces shall be mustered by him, and they shall defile the sanctuary fortress; then they shall take away the daily sacrifices, and place there the abomination of desolation (Daniel 11:30, 31).

In this passage, the prophet is speaking of the king of the North, who at that time represented the Roman Empire. Unlike other prophecies, Daniel does not state here the exact number of days or years when these things will happen. This means that what is described in the prophecy is more a process than an event of one day or even a year. We need to pay attention to the whole epoch rather than a specific date. When did these things happen?

Rome exterminated the Vandals in Africa in A.D. 534–535, "but in the year 640 the Arabs built a fleet in Cyprus (Chittim) and captured Egypt."[13] As a result, "The Mediterranean Sea—the main economic backbone of the Roman Empire—was lost for many centuries."[14] Thus, we can conclude that the events described here probably occurred at this time (the fifth to the sixth centuries).

Amazingly, this period coincides with the time of the antichrist's coming to the arena, which we have discussed in chapters 1 and 2 of this book. According to this prophecy, at this time God's holy covenant would be abandoned or forgotten. How could this happen?

In order to understand how this prophecy was fulfilled, it is necessary to recall the words of Christ: "This cup is the new covenant in My blood. This do, as often as you drink it, in remembrance of Me" (1 Corinthians 11:25). This text, like the prophecy of Daniel, speaks about the covenant and about the necessity to remember it and not to abandon it. Is this coincidence accidental? If we remember that a sacrifice was offered when a covenant was made, it becomes clear that the prophet is speaking here of what we have mentioned above—the institution of the Eucharist as a sacrifice rather than as a commemoration. Jesus offered Himself as a sacrifice, and the rite of the communion was established in remembrance of this fact. Any attempt to give this ceremony a different meaning is an attack on the covenant, that is, on "the new covenant in My blood." This will become even more apparent when we examine the question of the "army" of the antichrist, or the apostates from the holy covenant.

The army of the antichrist (action no. 7)

Perhaps you have noticed that beginning in the previous chapter, we started to speak of temples and priests in the plural. It is natural to ask why. Does this mean that there are many antichrists and temples?

In fact, the answer is simple, and as always, it is in the Bible. Let's read the three following phrases of the prophecy:

1. "Because of transgression, an army was given over to the horn to oppose the daily sacrifices" (Daniel 8:12).
2. "So he shall return and show regard for those who forsake the holy covenant" (Daniel 11:30).
3. "And forces shall be mustered by him, and they shall defile the sanctuary fortress; then they shall take away the daily sacrifices" (verse 31).

Daniel speaks here of an "army,"* "those who forsake the holy covenant,"† and "forces."‡ Note that the antichrist will attack the sanctuary not by himself, but with an "army." The prophet uses

---

* Or "host," "troops."
† Or "apostates."
‡ Or "troops."

words that carry the idea of plurality rather than singularity. But let's take first things first. To understand what is going on, let's start with the fact that the "host" was delivered or "given over"* into the hands of the antichrist. It is appropriate to ask, "By whom was the host delivered into the hands of the antichrist?"

In the Old Testament, this expression, "delivered," often indicates that God has left (abandoned) a particular person or group of persons with the result that others will now have power over him or them. For example, the book of Judges says, "Again the children of Israel did evil in the sight of the Lord, and the Lord delivered them into the hand of the Philistines for forty years" (Judges 13:1). Note that the prophecy of Daniel 8:12 and Judges 13:1 are similar in that they both have three parallel concepts. First, the "children of Israel" in Judges can correspond to the "army" in Daniel. Second, both the "host" of Daniel and the children of Israel in the book of Judges were given over to the power of the enemy. And third, God "delivered" or gave over the "host" "because of transgression," and He "delivered" the "children of Israel" because they "did evil." In other words, in the light of such texts of Scripture as Judges 13:1, we can say that Daniel warns us here about great "wickedness" among the people of God, which will result in the delivery of His people into the hands of the antichrist.

The words of the prophet in Daniel 11:30 convince us that we are not mistaken in our conclusion.† "So he shall return and show regard for those who forsake the holy covenant." It is obvious that only those who once have been participants in the covenant can be

---

* Daniel 8:12 and Judges 13:1 use the same Hebrew word, נתן, [naw-*than*], which can be translated as "to give over" or "deliver."

† Some people try to interpret Daniel 11:30, 31 as events that took place before the life of Jesus Christ, but this is not correct. Besides the ships of "Chittim" there is other evidence. Daniel 11 describes the events chronologically, and the prophet tells us even in verse 22 that "both it [the overwhelming army] and a prince of the covenant will be destroyed." As this phrase can refer only to the crucifixion of Christ, the events of verses 30 and 31 must take place in New Testament times.

WHAT IS THE "ABOMINATION OF DESOLATION"?

apostates from it. A person cannot be divorced if he has never been married. God could do nothing but leave those who had left Him and hand them over.

At this point, it is appropriate to recall the question we asked at the end of the previous chapter, What kind apostasy is Paul speaking about in 2 Thessalonians 2:3? Now we can see more clearly that the prophecies of Paul and Daniel about the temple are closely related. Before the "man of sin" sits in the temple of God, there must be an apostasy, the nature of which is explained by Daniel.*

However, the situation of the people of God as described by Daniel is more serious than that in the book of Judges. The prophet reports that there will be three differences from the era of the judges of Israel:

1. The enemy will have an "army" or "forces."
2. "An army" will be delivered "to oppose" the sacrifice.
3. This "army" will defile the sanctuary.

Note that the "army" was delivered into the hands of the antichrist "to oppose the daily *sacrifices*." This indicates a close, or even inseparable, connection between the "army" and the priestly service. This phrase of Daniel gives us every reason to say that his reference is not only about Christians or, to be more precise, not only about *all* Christians, but also those who have something to do with the institution of the priesthood. Based on this, we come to the conclusion that this "army" is the institution of the priesthood, since according to the theology of the Eucharist, only the priests can offer this "sacrifice." One of the leading scholars in the field of Old Testament theology, Gerhard Hasel, confirms these conclusions: "This 'host' may be conceived to be either restrictively a 'clergy'

---

* That is, the host and its Prince, the sanctuary, and the sacrifice, would be trampled.

or non-restrictively a 'group of people' who are over or against the continual ministry of the 'Prince of the host' in the heavenly sanctuary."[15] Apparently, it is on them that God lays the primary responsibility for abandoning the holy covenant, because "for everyone to whom much is given, from him much will be required" (Luke 12:48).

Now it must be clear to us what it means when the prophecy says that God will lose His army. But from where will the antichrist get his army? Remember that the apostle Paul warned, "From among yourselves men will rise up, speaking perverse things, to draw away the disciples after themselves" (Acts 20:30). These are the same, mentioned by Daniel, as those "who forsake the holy covenant" (Daniel 11:30). They remained Christians but began to teach "perverse things." Already in the days of Paul, the "mystery of lawlessness [was] at work" (2 Thessalonians 2:7). He wrote to the Christians at Philippi, "For many walk, of whom I have told you often, and now tell you even weeping, that they are the enemies of the cross of Christ" (Philippians 3:18). It was painful for the apostle to watch as former servants of Christ became His enemies, often without realizing it.

This process of apostasy began in the time of Paul and continued for the next few centuries. The "host" gradually apostatized from the covenant and finally was given over to the power of delusions. But when they left the "army of God," they didn't just surrender but rather were employed in the service of the enemy. Jesus said, "He who is not with Me is against Me" (Matthew 12:30). *Thus, the army of God became the army of the antichrist, and those who were supposed to be His servants began to act as "the enemies of the cross of Christ."* It is not surprising that by the end of the sixth century the search for the antichrist reached a deadlock and soon stopped.

Now that we have seen who belongs to the army of the antichrist and where it comes from, we are ready to return to the question of why we are talking about temples and priests in the plural. For this purpose, let's read what this army will do: "And forces shall be mustered by him, and they shall defile the sanctuary fortress" (Daniel 11:31).

If the army spoken of here is the army of priests, then why is a whole army needed? After all, there is only one sanctuary. Let's find out.

First, we must remember that to defile the heavenly sanctuary the antichrist copies its service, that is, he copies both its priests and its high priest. In the biblical sanctuary, the priests offered a daily service, while the high priest performed the annual service. In the heavenly sanctuary, Christ does both. Therefore, Christ serves both as a priest and as High Priest. This means that it does not matter which of these titles a person appropriates; in both cases he is appropriating the title of Christ and becomes an antichrist.

Second, the antichrist replicates the story of Jeroboam and creates an extensive system of worship, with thousands of priests and temples, rather than Jeroboam's two centers of worship. The more the better. In each of these cases there must be three elements: the priest, the temple, and the sacrifice. At the head of this system there is, of course, the high priest in Rome—the pope. In this sense he is much more suited for the role of the chief antichrist because the more someone's title reflects the title of Christ, the higher the degree of blasphemy. He even has his throne in Rome where "Antipas . . . My faithful martyr, . . . was killed among you" (Revelation 2:13). *But the antichrist in Rome did not stop there; he cloned himself!* Why? The territory of the holy Roman Empire, and especially of the whole world, is much larger than the territory of the Northern Kingdom of Israel. If it was sufficient for Jeroboam to establish only two altars, the antichrist needs thousands of them because his territory is the entire world. So we can talk about the arch antichrist and antichrists. However, both an ordinary priest in a provincial temple and the high priest in the of St. Peter's Basilica in Rome are both a substitute for Christ, His ministry, and His heavenly temple. Both of them bear His title, both build a temple in the likeness of the heavenly temple, both set up a throne in it, and both offer a sacrifice.

Both the Catholic and the Orthodox Churches consider that most of the Old Testament laws were given only to the nation of Israel rather than to all mankind, and thus these laws have lost their relevance. However, it is surprising that they justify the legitimacy of the institution of priests on the basis of the laws of the Old Testament. But that's not the most interesting thing. The most interesting thing is that the Old Testament laws did not allow more than one temple. It would never have come to one's mind in the Old Testament to build twelve temples, one temple for each tribe, instead of the one and only temple in Jerusalem. Even when the tribes of Reuben, Gad, and half of the tribe of Manasseh decided to build an altar rather than a temple, the rest of the Israelites were ready to wipe them off the face of the earth for this crime. And they calmed down only when they heard that this altar was not intended as a place to offer sacrifices, but rather as a monument (Joshua 22:10–34). If Catholic and Orthodox Christians follow the temple traditions of the Old Testament, then why are there thousands and even tens of thousands of temples on the face of the earth today? Probably because this phenomenon has nothing to do with the true institution of the priesthood but fits perfectly with the logic of Jeroboam and the prophecy of Daniel.

Third, in Revelation the prophet John tells us that the antichrist and the false prophet will work counterfeit miracles (Revelation 16:13, 14). We can read in Matthew 24:24 of the same confederacy and of their "great signs" with the slight difference that in Matthew, Jesus uses the plural when referring to the individuals who are the actors in these prophetic scenes. In Revelation, John speaks of "the beast" and "the false prophet"; in Matthew, Jesus speaks of "false Christs" and "false prophets." Obviously, Jesus is not saying that in the end time there will be an increase in the number of people suffering from mental illness or delusions of grandeur in which they declare themselves to be the Messiah. Such people are easily diagnosed, and they could not mislead many. In addition, mentally ill persons are almost always isolated; they would not be able to work together effectively to deceive. Here, Christ is speaking not only of false Christs, but also of false prophets—all acting together. They have one message and one purpose. To prove their authenticity, both of them work wonders. If they contradicted each other, the deception would lose its power. They act as single front; they are part of one army, one system. These false Christs are the same "host," the same ones "who forsake the holy covenant" (Daniel 11:30), and the same "army" that Daniel was speaking about.

These words used by Daniel contain within them a plural connotation, and they give us three important lessons:

First, the antichrist has his "army"—false Christs. Each of these "warriors" is similar to the antichrist himself. Each copies the model of "priest-temple-sacrifice" and thus fulfills the prophecy. Nevertheless, the leading role belongs to the "high priest."

Second, it is wrong to talk about lay Catholic or Orthodox Christians as being the antichrist. They are victims of the deception rather than a part of it.

Third, from the point of view of this prophecy there is no fundamental difference between the Catholic and Orthodox priesthood. This is not surprising. By the middle of the eleventh century, when there was a split between the Catholic and Orthodox sections of Christianity, the theology of the priesthood, of the temple, and of the Eucharist took its basic shape. The split did not change the basic statements of these doctrines in both the Eastern and Western Church. In both, the "priest-temple-sacrifice" concepts went hand in hand. Sometimes it might appear that there is an insurmountable gap, or even hostility, between Catholicism and Orthodoxy, but this is only on the surface. The angel, who gave instruction to Daniel, drew his and our attention to the essence of things. From the point of view of Daniel's prophecy, the Orthodox priesthood in general, and the priests of the Orthodox Church in particular, are a part of the army of the antichrist. Like Catholics, the Orthodox are called priests, build temples, and offer sacrifices.

All the nations where Orthodoxy is the main religion would probably be interested to learn what place their Orthodox Church occupies in the light of the prophecies of Daniel. To face the truth, the Orthodox Church is just another form of the Catholic Church. From the perspective of the prophecy, there is no fundamental difference between them. The pope is the high priest on a global scale, and the Orthodox patriarchs are only younger and disobedient brothers, who are responsible for their sectors of the world, which are usually limited to one nation, language, or country. For example, The Declaration of Patriarch Cyril and Pope Francis confirms this, saying, "We are not competitors, but brothers." However, in this brotherhood the Orthodox Church has always had to take a back seat and be reduced to a secondary role.

The abomination of desolation (action no. 8)

To set up the abomination of desolation, the antichrist commits a series of actions rather than just a single one. The prophet Daniel reveals that the abomination of desolation is not a single, separate event, but only one link in a chain of interrelated events such as the attack on the heavenly host, the sanctuary, the sacrifice, the covenant, and so forth. Today, many of the attempts to explain the meaning of "the abomination of desolation" (Daniel 11:31) often completely omit these details of the prophecy and thus ignore the context. As a result, the abomination of desolation is not only made to stick out, but it is taken out of context and made an autonomous event. Its connection with the other parts of the prophecy is lost, which inevitably leads to misinterpretation.

If our conclusions are correct, then the abomination of desolation is to be set up somewhere in the Church's temple. But where?

WHAT IS THE "ABOMINATION OF DESOLATION"?

Let's read the prophecy again. "Then they shall take away the daily sacrifices, and place there the abomination of desolation" (Daniel 11:31).

Reading this prophecy again, we can see that whenever Daniel talks about the abomination of desolation, he always draws our attention to the "daily service," an integral part of which was the sacrifice. Such a close relationship between them causes us to take a closer look at the "sacrifice" offered by the Church in the liturgy and to study it in more detail.

Both in Catholicism and in Orthodoxy there are many rules prescribing the procedure of the Eucharist. However, we should consider one of them. Here's what the *Catholic Encyclopedia* says about this: "Mass may sometimes be celebrated outside a sacred place, but never without an altar, or at least an altar-stone."[16] In other words, the "sacrifice" of the Eucharist cannot be offered if there is no altar. The logic of such a rule is simple. *Just as there can be no priest without a sanctuary and just as there can be no sanctuary without sacrifices, so there can be no sacrifice without an altar or a place where it is offered.** Both a Catholic priest and a priest of the Orthodox Church need not only a temple and sacrifice but also an altar. Without an altar, it is impossible to conduct the Eucharist. To turn the hearts of the people from worshiping in Jerusalem, Jeroboam built two altars. To convince people to follow him, the antichrist is also in need of an altar.

However, the altar draws our attention not only because it is directly related to the daily sacrifice. The fact is that the expression, "the abomination of desolation" (Daniel 11:31), was closely associated with the defilement of the altar of the Jewish temple by the

---

* Both in the Catholic Church and in the Bible, an altar and a place where a sacrifice is offered are one and the same. In the Orthodox Church, a part of the temple corresponding to the Most Holy Place is called the altar, while the place to offer a sacrifice is called a table for the Eucharist.

Syrian king, Antiochus Epiphanes.* That is exactly what Christ's audience would have understood as the "abomination of desolation." They knew that "on the fifteenth day of the month Casleu, in the hundred and forty-fifth year, king Antiochus set up the abominable idol of desolation upon the altar of God" (1 Maccabees 1:57). The chronicle talking about this event was well known. King Antiochus, who had sacrificed a pig on the altar of the Jewish temple, defiled it by sacrificing an unclean animal in violation of a number of laws of the Torah.

Comparing one with the other, we come to the conclusion that in order to understand the "abomination of desolation," we need to pay attention to the altar—but to the altar in the Christian church rather than to the one in the Jewish temple. Why the altar in a Christian temple? Well, the prophecy of Daniel refers to "the time of the end" (Daniel 12:4, 9), and hence it was not talking about Antiochus Epiphanes, but rather about events which take place much later.

What is so special about the altars of Christian churches? The answer to this question we find again in the *Catholic Encyclopedia*: "This reverence for objects associated with a martyr gave rise to the custom of entombing such relics beneath the altars of newly erected churches, until it ultimately became the rule not to dedicate a church without them."[17]

What does this mean? It means that a Catholic or an Orthodox church cannot conduct the liturgy of the Eucharist if there are no relics. As the cloud of the glory of God sanctified and hallowed the Jewish temple with its presence, so relics "sanctify" a Christian temple with their presence. A temple cannot fully function without them; at best it can serve only as a chapel, that is, just a place for prayer. In Catholicism, relics are usually placed at the base of the

---

* Read why Antiochus is not the one who fulfills the prophecy: William H. Shea, *Selected Studies on Prophetic Interpretation*, Daniel and Revelation Committee Series, vol. 1, 25–55.

altar or inside it. In Orthodoxy, they are sewn into an antimins—a square wimple of silk or linen—and are put beside the altar on the so-called throne. To conduct the Eucharist, it is necessary to put gifts on the antimins. Either way, relics are reserved for a place of honor in the Christian temple—in the Holy of holies. But it would not be correct to place them on an equal footing with the other items of the temple. It is the relics that sanctify and hallow all that they come into contact, rather than vice versa.

What are relics? These are the remains of a human body of someone whom the Church honors, such as a saint or a martyr. It can be teeth, hair, nails, bones, or skulls. All that remains of a person after the process of decomposition can be used as a relic in order to "sanctify" the altar or the Eucharist.

The question arises, "If sacrificing a pig as an offering on the altar in the temple of God was called the 'abomination of desolation' because it defiled the whole temple, what does the Bible say about the presence of the remains of dead bodies in the temple of God?"

It is not difficult to answer this question since clear instructions have been given in this regard.

> The Lord said to Moses, "Speak to the priests, the sons of Aaron, and say to them: 'None shall defile himself for the dead among his people, except for his relatives who are nearest to him: his mother, his father, his son, his daughter, and his brother; also his virgin sister who is near to him, who has had no husband, for her he may defile himself. Otherwise he shall not defile himself, being a chief man among his people, to profane himself.
>
> 'They shall not make any bald place on their heads, nor shall they shave the edges of their beards nor make any cuttings in their flesh. They shall be holy to their God and not profane the name of their

God, for they offer the offerings of the Lord made by fire, and the bread of their God; therefore they shall be holy" (Leviticus 21:1–6).

It is clear from these words that in most cases a priest was not even allowed to touch a dead body. If he acted contrary to this rule, he became defiled and could not perform his ministry in the temple. Only if the deceased was his relative was he allowed to touch the dead body, but even then he had to go through a ritual of cleansing before he could return to his duties. The Lord warned, "Whoever touches the body of anyone who has died, and does not purify himself, defiles the tabernacle of the Lord" (Numbers 19:13). That means that to "defile the tabernacle of the Lord," it was enough for a priest just to touch a dead body before going out to serve in the temple.

If this was so, can we imagine what would happen if he brought that very dead body or some part of it into a holy place? Most likely the priest would be stoned, and the temple would cease its operation. What would happen if the remains of the dead were buried under the altar of the Jewish temple or if the temple itself was built on the site of a cemetery? I guess we would be unable to call this anything other than the "abomination of desolation"! However, all the things mentioned above take place in the Catholic or Orthodox temples for which it is claimed that everything that happens in them is a continuation of the service established by God in the sanctuary.

As we have already learned, one of the reasons why it is impossible to build the temple of the prophet Ezekiel is that a cemetery is located near the Eastern wall of old Jerusalem. The size of the temple is such that for its construction, the cemetery area would have to lie at its base. Anyone who is even slightly familiar with Judaism understands that no Jew would ever build the temple on the bones of the dead. However, Christians do the very opposite. The more relics—and the more well-known the deceased saint is to whom they belong—the holier the place is considered to be and the more it will gather pilgrims. St. Peter's Basilica became a special sacred place because of the apostle's tomb, where the pope performs the functions of a priest as the Bishop of Rome. Foreseeing such a perversion of the gospel and of the doctrine of the heavenly sanctuary, the priest, and His sacrifice, the angel was sent to tell Daniel about the "abomination of desolation," which would mark the arrival of the antichrist.

But that's not all. There is another interesting detail that cannot be ignored when we talk about the altar. The altar is famous not only for the fact that Jesus Christ is sacrificed there and relics are buried under it. According to the teachings of the Catholic Church, it is a throne upon which God Himself sits invisibly. Germanus wrote, "The Holy Table is the place of the Tomb where Christ was buried, and on it is set forth the true and heavenly bread, the mystic and unbloody sacrifice. . . . It is also the throne of God on which he seated."[18] In an effort to reproduce the Jewish temple where in the Holy of holies God sat between the cherubim, Christians began to teach that the altar is the throne upon which God himself sits invisibly. The Eastern Church was no different in this matter. Simeon of Thessalonica, an Orthodox Archbishop, taught,

> For this reason the Altar truly is the Table of Christ, the throne of glory, the dwelling of God, and the Tomb and monument of Christ and His resting-place. . . .
>
> The embroidered cloth . . . on the Altar is decorated because it signifies the glory of God, for the Altar is the throne of God.[19]

The modern Russian Orthodox Church is a little different from its predecessors because it is not the altar that the Russian Orthodox considers as the throne but rather the antimins* in which the relics are sewn up.

Why do we pay special attention to this fact? It is for the following reason. You will recall that we were searching for the throne of the antichrist in the previous chapter of this book, and we found that it is located right next to the altar and to the so-called throne of God. Most often both the throne of a priest and the altar are situated in the Most Holy Place. Consequently the question naturally arises, "How could it happen that God's throne is so close to the throne of the antichrist?"

Again the Bible gives us the answer. If we read the Bible, we understand that the throne of God is in heaven: "Thus says the Lord: 'Heaven is My throne, and earth is My footstool. Where is the house that you will build Me? And where is the place of My rest?'" (Isaiah 66:1). And Jesus says, "I also overcame and sat down with My Father on His throne" (Revelation 3:21). Apparently, the Bible teaches that the throne of God is in heaven rather than in a Christian temple. But if this is correct, then whose throne is the altar? Who can sit there invisible to our eyes?

To answer this question, let's recall a prophecy in Revelation chapter 2.

> And to the angel of the church in Pergamos write,
>
> "These things says He who has the sharp two-edged sword: 'I know your works, and where you dwell, where Satan's throne is. And you hold fast to My name, and did not deny My faith even in the days in which Antipas was My faithful martyr, who was killed among you, where Satan dwells" (Revelation 2:12, 13).

---

* Which means "instead of the throne."

WHAT IS THE "ABOMINATION OF DESOLATION"?

If we believe this prophecy, then it is possible to find the throne of Satan in Pergamos. The message to the church in Pergamos referred in particular to the contemporaries of John the Revelator and only then to future generations. In the previous chapter, we have discussed what it tells us. But what throne of Satan could the angel be speaking about to the inhabitants of ancient Pergamos?

The fact is that ancient Pergamos was known for its altar, gigantic in size and pretentious in architecture. This altar is one of the most significant monuments of the Hellenistic period that has been preserved to our day. If the angel referred to the Pergamos altar as the throne of Satan, then it becomes clear who is the "invisible" one present on the altar in a Christian temple. It becomes clear why millions will be deceived and worship both the dragon (Satan) and the beast (the antichrist). (See Revelation 13:3, 4.) As one orthodox theologian has said, "The world of Satan is the world inside out."[20] In the heavenly sanctuary, God sits on His throne and next to Him is His Son. Trying to imitate that, Satan has put his throne in the earthly temple, and next to him there is the throne of the antichrist. Finally, it becomes clear why God promises the last generation of Christians—those who do not worship the throne of the antichrist—a place on His throne (Revelation 3:21).

Another prophet who speaks about the throne of Satan is Isaiah.

> How you are fallen from heaven,
> O Lucifer, son of the morning!
> How you are cut down to the ground,
> You who weakened the nations!
> For you have said in your heart:
> "I will ascend into heaven,
> I will exalt my throne above the stars of God;
> I will also sit on the mount of the congregation
> On the farthest sides of the north;
> I will ascend above the heights of the clouds,
> I will be like the Most High" (Isaiah 14:12–14).

The "son of the morning" who wants to be like God is Satan. But note what he wanted to do. He says, "I will exalt my throne above the stars of God." His plan failed, and Satan was "cut down to the ground." However, he did not forget his intentions, and if their literal fulfillment is impossible, he uses symbols. Because he wants to take God's place, he imitates God in everything. Imitating God, he wants to set his throne in the likeness of God's throne; that's why he wants it also to be "above the stars of God." As we have already learned, the Bible calls those who are faithful to Him, both men and angels, stars. Satan cannot "sit" on the cherubim, and therefore he makes the relics his throne. In doing so, He continues the fight against God begun in heaven; He challenges God when trying to take His place and tricks people into worshiping himself. That is why in the Orthodox and Catholic Churches relics will always be associated with the throne of God. Thanks to the prophecies of Daniel and Isaiah this deception becomes obvious, and we have no doubt that it is nothing but "the abomination of desolation."

In conclusion, and in the interests of a complete, truthful account, it must be said that Protestants realized this error from the very beginning and, to put it mildly, did not feel a deep respect for the Church's theology of the Eucharist. For example, John Hooper, whom we have quoted earlier, wrote, "I believe and confess that the popish Mass is an invention of Antichrist, and a forsaking of the sacrifice of Jesus Christ, that is to say, of His death and passion; and that it is a stinking and infected sepulcher, which hideth and covereth the merit of the blood of Christ; and therefore ought the Mass to be abolished and the holy Supper of the Lord to be restored and set in his perfection again."[21]

The only thing Protestants were lacking was to see this in the light of biblical prophecy. But it was hidden from their eyes; otherwise it would inevitably have led them to an understanding of the time periods of prophecy, but they were hardly ready for that. According to the plan of God they were to "hold fast what you have"

(Revelation 3:11; cf. Philippians 3:16) without knowing the time and dates, because "the words are closed up and sealed till the time of the end" (Daniel 12:9).

The test of time or 1,335 days (action no. 9)

A wonderful feature of this prophecy is the clear time frame for its fulfillment. It is rare for a prophecy of the Bible to be characterized by such specifics, and therefore the question arises, "What is God's purpose when He states the exact time of the prophecy's fulfillment?" The answer would seem obvious: to warn us about the exact time of the beginning and end of its fulfillment. However, this is not really the correct answer.

Let's remember the lessons we have learned earlier in chapters 1 and 2. The prophecy of Daniel warned that the coming of the antichrist would be after the fall of the Roman Empire. It was a warning for those people who lived in the end of the fifth century and the beginning of the sixth. But for us it is a solemn reminder that the antichrist is already here. A warning is needed (and possible) only for those living during the time of the fulfillment of the prophecy. But if the prophecy has already been fulfilled, and the time God points to in the prophecy has come to an end, then the time factor becomes a reminder and a protection from error rather than a warning. Studying prophecy and paying attention to the time factor involved, we realize that we should not look for the antichrist among the famous politicians of the future or even of the present, because the antichrist's plane landed on planet Earth long ago, and he disappeared into the crowd almost unnoticed.

The same principle is found in the fulfillment of the prophecies about the Messiah. For all those living before or during His first coming, the prophetic periods and dates were a warning. But when the times predicted came to an end and the Messiah was crucified, their function changed, and they became the most powerful witness against false Messiahs and misconceptions.

The time factor is a kind of test of the validity of an interpretation of prophecy. God decides to tell us about time only in special cases when the power of deception and the price of delusion is great. To narrow down the "suspected" subjects of prophecy, to leave out all doubts and false interpretations, God appeals to an exact science—mathematics. God brings prophecy to another level, and the language of words is replaced by the language of numbers. It then becomes obvious if an interpretation is nothing more than far-fetched and speculative. This explains why most interpretations of the "abomination of desolation" prefer to remain silent about the 2,300 or 1,335 days mentioned in the prophecies.

Those who believe that the temple in Jerusalem must be rebuilt usually do not consider it necessary to explain Daniel 12. Moreover, they urge us not to believe anyone who tries to explain it because they say, it is a sealed prophecy (Daniel 12:9). However, they emphasize the word, *sealed,* and prefer not to discuss the words that follow—"till the time of the end."

In addition, if we continue to read, we see that Daniel says that "many shall run to and fro, and knowledge shall increase. . . . The wicked shall do wickedly; and none of the wicked shall understand, but the wise shall understand" (Daniel 12:4, 10). We can make only two possible conclusions out of this. Either we have not reached the specific time mentioned in the prophecy or we cannot be among the "wise" that "shall understand." But these commentators do not like either of these conclusions. The first contradicts their own words that we are the generation that is living in the time of the end and soon the temple will be rebuilt. But the second is even worse, because to acknowledge it would mean to admit their spiritual bankruptcy. So they try to avoid this question or remain silent.

The time factor puts in a difficult position even those who consider the "temple" in Paul's prophecy (2 Thessalonians 2:4) to be either the human body or the church as an assembly of believers. If the temple is the body, then the antichrist cannot literally sit in it. If it is the assembly of believers, then what is the abomination of desolation? But in both cases the proponents of these interpretations remain silent on the subject of the 1,335 days. The only way to explain how "the abomination of desolation" can be set up in the body or in the Church for 1,335 days is to completely disconnect Paul's prophecy from the book of Daniel, as if these individuals were talking about two different events. In this case, the antichrist just sits in the temple of God but does not set up the abomination of desolation. The prophecy of Paul becomes disconnected from all other prophecies about the temple.

This *disconnection* seems to satisfy those who interpret the temple as our bodies, but it does not entirely satisfy those who believe that the temple is the assembly of Christians. They note that both Paul's epistle and the prophecy of Daniel speak about the apostasy of the people of God. If there is still some connection between these prophecies, then they need to explain what the "abomination of desolation" is. Trying to find the answer, they assume that the apostasy and the "abomination of desolation" are things of the future, and their beginning will be the ratification of a Sunday law. Then after 1,335 days, the second coming of Christ will occur. However, we should give many of those holding this view credit for realizing that if this interpretation were true, it would be possible to calculate the day of the coming of Jesus Christ, which is contrary to His own words, that "of that day and hour no one knows, not even the angels of heaven, but My Father only" (Matthew 24:36). Thus, the question remains open.

To find the answer to the questions that arise and to reconcile all the contradictions, first and foremost we need to remember that Daniel 12—the "abomination of desolation" and the prophetic periods mentioned in it—are only the last part of the prophecies on this subject in Daniel's book. There are three of them:

1. Daniel 8:9–14 (2,300 days)
2. Daniel 11:30, 31
3. Daniel 12:9–13 (1,290 and 1,335 days)

We can understand what is said in Daniel 12 only when we study it in a close relationship with Daniel's entire book and look not only at the individual pieces, but at the whole picture. So let's turn to Daniel 8.

Chapter 8, like chapter 12, mentions the prophetic period, which is related to the sanctuary.

> "Then I heard a holy one speaking; and another holy one said to that certain one who was speaking, 'How long will the vision be, concerning the daily sacrifices and the transgression of desolation, the giving of both the sanctuary and the host to be trampled underfoot?'
> And he said to me, "For two thousand three hundred days; then the sanctuary shall be cleansed" (Daniel 8:13, 14).

Here the angel informs Daniel that the cleansing of the sanctuary will happen after 2,300 days or years. However, it is not mentioned here when the 2,300 years will begin.

In chapter 9, the angel is sent again to explain to Daniel that the beginning point of the 2,300 years is to be the decree to rebuild Jerusalem. "Know therefore and understand, that from the going forth of the command to restore and build Jerusalem until Messiah the Prince, there shall be seven weeks and sixty-two weeks; the street shall be built again, and the wall, even in troublesome times" (Daniel 9:25). Thus, the beginning of both periods—the 490 days and the 2,300 days—was to be 457 B.C. when the decree to rebuild

Jerusalem was issued.* The 490 days (years) had to do with the Messiah and "your people" (Daniel 12:1), that is, Daniel's people or the Jews. The second period (2,300 days/years) stretched much further and referred to "many days in the future" from Daniel's perspective (Daniel 8:26).

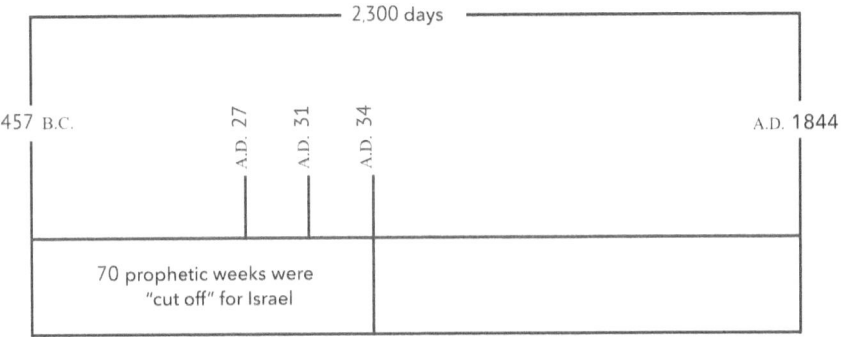

Due to the fact that both periods have the same starting point, we can definitely say when the 2,300 days ended. According to the prophecy, they ended in A.D. 1844. Until that time, the antichrist was supposed to do his work of defiling the sanctuary as described in Daniel 8:9–14.

So Daniel 8 tells us the ending date of the "abomination of desolation," but not its beginning, since the first part of the period referred to the Messiah and the Jews rather than to the sanctuary. We are given the beginning of the period related to the defilement of the sanctuary only in chapter 12, not in chapter 8. "And from the time that the daily sacrifice is taken away, and the abomination of desolation is set up, there shall be one thousand two hundred and ninety days. Blessed is he who waits, and comes to the one thousand three hundred and thirty-five days" (Daniel 12:11, 12). It is obvious that those waiting to the end of the 1,335 days are called

---

* For details see, *Symposium on Daniel*, vol. 2, 220-255.

blessed because they will reach the time when "the sanctuary shall be cleansed." This means that if the cleansing of the sanctuary was to happen in 1844, the setting up of the "abomination of desolation" was to occur 1,335 years earlier, that is, in A.D. 509.

What are these dates famous for? Do they have anything to do with the relics, the altar, the Eucharist, and the sanctuary? Let's read first what we know about some of the events of the year A.D. 509. "Images and relics of saints were, in after ages, laid on the altar, or communion table. In the Council of Paris, in the year 509,* it was decreed that no altars should be consecrated, except those which were made of stone only. After this, they were usually built as fixtures in the altar part of the church; and the relics of some favourite saint were deposited in some part of the erection."[22] Since that time, a mandatory part of the consecration of the altar has been placing relics in or under it. The Council of Paris, of course, was not an ecumenical council of the Church, but its decision was so much appreciated that soon after, in the year A.D. 517, it was supported by the Council of the Church in the synod of Epaon.[23]

We can't say that there were neither relics nor altars in the churches before A.D. 509. Both of them have a long history. For example, wooden tables and stone altars existed for a long time as parallels to each other. One church might use a table; another might build an altar. A similar situation existed with relics. Some churches placed them on the communion table and some in another place. However, the year 509 marked a turning point. The decision to build altars only of stone meant that it became seen not so much as a table, but only as an altar. It was decided that the altar should be consecrated with oil and that relics could not be placed anywhere else but in some part of an altar. Therefore, despite the fact that

---

* Some believe that such a decision was not made until A.D. 517. Yet even in A.D. 506, Synod in Agde instituted a canon about consecration of altars. Therefore, we consider it possible to assert that by A.D. 509, theological and liturgical roles of altars were formed anyway.

relics and altars existed before A.D. 509, the solution of that year "seems to be the first public act of this nature, that we have upon authentic record in ancient history."[24]

The prophecy says that "from the time that the daily sacrifice is taken away, and the abomination of desolation is set up, there shall be one thousand two hundred and ninety days" (Daniel 12:11). The angel does not explain this intermediate date, but it is most likely related to the completion of the period of persecution of three and a half years or 1,260 years (Daniel 12:7; 7:25; Revelation 11:2; 12:6; 13:5). In 1798, Pope Pius VI was taken prisoner, and in 1799 he died, finishing up a whole era of persecution of dissent (see Matthew 2:19, 20). Historians also consider 1799 to be the year of the completion of the French Revolution,* the events of which were described by John the Revelator in Revelation 11. These two dates are separated by exactly 1,290 years.

But the completion of the 1,335 prophetic days would be a much more important event. The angel said, "Blessed is he who waits, and comes to the one thousand three hundred and thirty-five days" (Daniel 12:12). Notice that the angel said that there would be those who would "wait" for the completion of the prophetic period. This means that there will be those who understand the prophetic times and seasons and understand them correctly. This is the only way they will be able to anticipate their fulfillment. Who are these people and what happened in 1844?

Turning to the history of the early- and mid-nineteenth century, we can find only one group of people who became known for its discoveries made on the basis of the study of the prophecies of Daniel. Among them was William Miller, who made the 2,300 days of Daniel 8:14 the subject of his special study. He came to

---

* Some believe that the prophecy about the 1,260 years could have been fulfilled between A.D. 539 and A.D. 1799.

the conclusion that this prophetic period would end in 1844 and continually preached about it beginning in 1831.

William Miller correctly identified the end of the prophetic period, but he was wrong about the event that would happen after 2,300 days. He believed the sanctuary to be our earth and consequently that the cleansing of the sanctuary meant the cleansing of the earth by fire at the coming of the Lord Jesus Christ. This error led him to begin preaching that the second coming of Christ would occur no later than 1844.

This message caused a great religious revival among Christians of different denominations. They confessed their sins and awaited the coming of their Savior. They rechecked the calculations of Miller and settled on October 22, 1844 as the date for Christ's return. Of course, it was their big mistake. But they were able to realize it the next day.

On October 23, Hiram Edson, with his friends and fellow believers, turned to the Scriptures again to understand the cause of their error. Based on the book of Hebrews, they came to understand clearly that Christ is our heavenly High Priest and that the sanctuary in Daniel 8:14 was not the earth but the sanctuary of heaven—the one not made with hands. They came to the conclusion that just as the cleansing of the earthly sanctuary involved a judgment, so the cleansing of the heavenly sanctuary meant the pre-verdict judgment in heaven in which Christ, our heavenly High Priest, was interceding for us before God. Since that time, the message of the heavenly sanctuary, the judgment, and the heavenly High Priest became the center of their preaching.

This message completely contradicted what was taught by the Catholic and Orthodox Churches. It was uncompromising and showed how earthly counterfeits had been substituted for the heavenly realities. In the light of the prophecies of Daniel, the earthly priests, led by their earthly high priest, their sacrifices, and temples, showed the essence of their true nature. They became not only useless, but dangerous, as they appeared as a part of the great deception of the antichrist.

Since the heavenly sanctuary was "cast down" with the lies of the antichrist, who "cast truth down to the ground . . . and prospered," so the cleansing of the heavenly sanctuary included not only the work of the heavenly judgment but also its justification on the earth.* The Hebrew word וְנִצְדַּק (*tsadak*) in Daniel 8:14, translated as "cleansed," in our opinion could and should be translated "will be justified," "declared righteous," or even "rehabilitated."† The translators found it difficult to translate this word literally because they didn't understand how the sanctuary could be justified. They knew that the sanctuary had to be cleansed from time to time (see Leviticus 16:29–34), but they had never heard that it should be justified.

Everything falls into place when we realize that Daniel describes that someone will pretend to be Christ and act on His behalf without His approval. That someone is the antichrist.‡ Just as a fraud who has claimed to be you, or hacked your account on a social network, ruins your reputation, so the antichrist shows God, His church, and the sacrifice of Jesus in a false light. And just as the victim of such a fraud needs to be justified, so does the sanctuary.

The message of the heavenly sanctuary and its High Priest, proclaimed in 1844, was the beginning of the justification of the truths that had been trampled for a long time. At the same time, along with the judgment in heaven, this message is to go around the entire earth to point out that the only true High Priest and His sacrifice is

---

* In other words, the heavenly sanctuary cannot be cleansed if it is not vindicated on earth. The cleansing of the heavenly sanctuary can be done only when people confess their sins before Jesus. It cannot happen as long as people are kept in delusion about the role of the true High Priest, His sacrifice, and His temple.

† For example, the same word occurs in the book of Exodus and is translated as "justify." "Keep yourself far from a false matter; do not kill the innocent and righteous. For I will not justify the wicked" (Exodus 23:7).

‡ The word literally means "instead of Christ."

our only hope for salvation. God, His sacrifice, and the temple will appear in their true light; they will be justified and glorified so that "whoever believes in Him should not perish but have everlasting life" (John 3:16).

Conclusion

In the book of Daniel, we find four passages that speak of the abomination of desolation:

1. Daniel 9:27 (Matthew 24:15; Mark 13:14; Luke 21:20)
2. Daniel 8:9–14 (2,300 days)
3. Daniel 11:30, 31
4. Daniel 12:9–13 (1,290 and 1,335 days)

If the first passage speaks of the destruction of Jerusalem in A.D. 70, the latter three extend far beyond the first century. Despite the fact that they are in different chapters, they are parts of the same prophecy and therefore need to be considered in relation to and seen as explanatory of each other. Paul's prophecy in 2 Thessalonians 2:4 is directly connected to these three passages; all attempts to understand it in isolation from the prophecies of Daniel are doomed to a limited or incorrect interpretation.

In the book of Daniel, we have a detailed description of how the "abomination of desolation" will be set up, and by studying history, we can see how the prophecy was fulfilled.

How Will the Antichrist Set Up the "Abomination of Desolation"?, table 8

Prophecy	Fulfillment
1. Will "cast down some of the host" (Daniel 8:10).	The Church began to teach that its temples, symbolically and literally, have famous apostles and saints as their foundation.
2. Will "cast down . . . some of the stars to the ground" (Daniel 8:10).	The Church began to dedicate its temples to the saints, angels, worship them, and assign them responsibility for different areas.
3. Will exalt "himself as high as the Prince of the host" (Daniel 8:11).	The Church began to teach that its head is the high priest.
4. "By him the daily sacrifices would be taken away" (Daniel 8:11).	The Church began to teach that the Eucharist is the sacrifice of Jesus Christ.
5. "The place of His sanctuary was cast down" (Daniel 8:11).	The Church began to teach that its buildings are the temple of God on earth.
6. The covenant with God will be forsaken (Daniel 11:30).	The Church lost the understanding of the significance of the communion service, which is "the new covenant in My blood" (Luke 22:20)
7. The antichrist will set the whole army against God (Daniel 8:12; 11:30, 31).	Through the apostasy, God's host, His ministers, were "put to the service" of the antichrist.

8. The abomination or transgression of desolation will be set up (Daniel 8:13; 11:31; 12:11).	The remains of dead bodies have become an integral part of a temple; they were put under the altar or the "Most Holy Place," to consecrate the Eucharist, the altar, and the temple.
9. After 2,300 days and 1,335 days the sanctuary will be cleansed (Daniel 8:14; 12:11, 12).	At the end of the 1,335 and 2,300 years in 1844, the message of the true High Priest and His intercession for us in the heavenly sanctuary began the beginning of its complete justification.

As we use table 8 as an answer to the question about the "abomination of desolation," it is extremely important for us to ask the reader to pay attention that in the Bible an act of idolatry is called an abomination (Deuteronomy 7:25; 27:15). It would not be fair to interpret the "abomination of desolation" only as point number 8 of the table. The conclusion that we should be coming to is that the "abomination of desolation" is a form of worship. It is a deviation and totality of all actions described above, where point number 8 is only a cherry on top. Although, the full picture can be seen in the Eucharist.

Sometimes the prophecies are unfairly underestimated. People prefer the Gospels, alleging that we need only them in order to know Jesus Christ. However, Jesus Himself said, "Search the Scriptures, for in them you think you have eternal life; and these are they which testify of Me" (John 5:39). This means that the Messiah and His sacrifice are always at the center of the narrative in all the books of both the Old and New Testaments. The book of Daniel is no exception. The High Priest and His sacrifice are at its center. But being a prophetic book, Daniel speaks about the antichrist, who takes the place of Christ and substitutes his own sacrifice and his gospel in the place of the sacrifice and gospel of Jesus Christ. Imitating God, the antichrist has established his own gospel with the Eucharist at its center. An angel was sent to Daniel to expose the essence of this substitution, because "It is indeed upon the Mass as on a rock that the whole papal system is built, with its monasteries, its bishoprics, its collegiate churches, its altars, its ministries, its doctrine, i.e., with all its guts. All this cannot fail to crumble once their sacrilegious and abominable Mass falls."[25] Uncovering this deception, Daniel proclaims the true and everlasting gospel uplifting the heavenly sanctuary, the sacrifice, and the High Priest before us.

At the end of his communication with Daniel the angel warned, "Many shall be purified, made white, and refined, but the wicked shall do wickedly; and none of the wicked shall understand, but the wise shall understand" (Daniel 12:10). This means that even when the seals preventing the understanding of this prophecy are broken, it still will not become clear to all. It is necessary to "be refined" to understand it. In order to cleanse us from the impurities of delusion, God sometimes needs to lead us through the fire so that we may be melted in trials. Often it is very difficult for a person to change his viewpoint, especially in matters of religion, so God has to melt us to separate truth from misconceptions and slag from precious metal. But "in this you greatly rejoice, though now for a little while, if need be, you have been grieved by various trials, that the genuineness of your faith, being much more precious than gold that perishes, though it is tested by fire, may be found to praise, honor, and glory at the revelation of Jesus Christ" (1Peter 1:6, 7).

Now as we finish this chapter and look back, we can say that Protestants were not wrong when they named the antichrist. Maybe they couldn't prove it as we can do today, but there were objective reasons for this. Their point of view finds more and more confirmation with every year and every century. However, the question arises, "If Protestants were right in the sixteenth century, then why are they uncertain about the identity of the antichrist today? The idea that the temple in Jerusalem should be rebuilt has a Protestant origin, doesn't it?"

In order to answer these questions, we need to examine the last prophecy cited as proof of the future reconstruction of the temple in Jerusalem. In chapter 3 "Will the Temple Be Rebuilt?" we have identified the four prophecies, which are usually referred to in order to prove that the temple will be rebuilt:

1. Daniel 9:27
2. Matthew 24:15
3. 2 Thessalonians 2:3, 4
4. Revelation 11:1

As we have already determined, the first three prophecies on this list do not have any relationship to the construction of a new temple in Jerusalem. But what does Revelation 11 speak about? We are going to seek answers to this question in the next chapter.

Notes

1. "Display of Flags in Catholic Churches," United States Conference of Catholic Bishops, accessed February 28, 2020, http://www.usccb.org/prayer-and-worship/sacred-art-and-music/architecture-and-environment/display-of-flags-in-catholic-churches.cfm.

2. "The Display of Flags in Roman Catholic Churches," Diocese of Richmond, Office of Worship, May 16, 2007, Studylib.net, https://studylib.net/doc/7265479/the-display-of-national-flags-in-roman-catholic-churches.

3. John of Odzun, "Laying the Foundation," quoted in John Wilkinson, *From Synagogue to Church the Traditional Design:Its Beginning, its Definition, its End* (New York: Routledge, 2002), 202.

4. Philip Schaff, *History of the Christian Church,* Nicene and Post-Nicene Christianity, vol. 3 (New York: Charles Scribner's Sons, 1891), 430.

5. *Catholic Encyclopedia*, s.v. "Early Christian Representations of Angels," accessed February 26, 2020, http://www.newadvent.org/cathen/01485a.htm.

6. "The Sacramental Sacrifice Thanksgiving, Memorial, Presence," *Catechism of the Catholic Church* , 2.2.1.3.5, accessed February 26, 2020, https://www.vatican.va/archive/ENG0015/__P41.HTM. This means that the One who offered Himself as a bloody sacrifice is offered again as a bloodless sacrifice in the Eucharist.

7. Giles Dimock, *101 Questions and Answers on the Eucharist* (New York: Paulist Press, 2006), 27.

8. Dimock, 79.

9. Dimock, 75, 76.

10. Dimock, 76.

11. Dimock, 69, 70.

12. John Hooper, *Later Writings of Bishop Hooper Together With His Letters and Other Pieces* (Cambridge: University Press, 1852), 32.

13. Rostislav Volkoslavsky, Secrets of Apocalypse (n.p.: Life Source, 2008), 136. Original quote and citation translated from Russian to English.

14. Volkoslavsky, 136.

15. Gerhard Hasel, "Establishing a Date for the Book of Daniel," *Symposium on Daniel,* Daniel and Revelation Committee Series, vol. 2, ed. Frank B. Holbrook, (Hagerstown, MD: Review and Herald', 1986), 417.

16. *Catholic Encyclopedia*, s.v. "Altar (In liturgy)," accessed February 26, 2020, http://www.newadvent.org/cathen/01346a.htm. In the Bible there are certain examples when a sacrifice was not offered in the temple but on an altar.

17. *Catholic Encyclopedia,* s.v. "History of the Christian Altar," accessed February 26, 2020, http://www.newadvent.org/cathen/01362a.htm.

18. Germanus, "Church Symbolism," quoted in Wilkinson, *From Synagogue to Church*, 199.

19. Simeon of Thessalonika, "The Eucharist," quoted in Wilkinson, *From Synagogue to Church*, 215.

20. "Interview with deacon Andrey Kuraev about Mikhail Bulgakov's novel, *Master and Margarita*," December 30, 2010, You Tube video, 29:16,

https://www.youtube.com/watch?v=gktuPnNqUa4&feature=youtu.be. Quote translated from Russian to English, video is in Russian.

21. J Hooper, *Later Writings*, 32.

22. "To the Editor of the Christian Instructor: On the Innovation Respecting the Communion Table," *The Edinburgh Christian Instructor*, vol. 23, July 1823, (Edinburgh: A. Balfour, 1823), 450.

23. Charles Joseph Hefele, *A History of the Councils of the Church, from the Original Documents,* vol. 4, trans. and ed. William Clark, (Edinburgh: T &T Clark, 1895), 112.

24. Joseph Bingham, *Origines Ecclesiasticæ: The Antiquities of the Christian Church,* vol. 1, (London: Henry G. Bohn, 1856), 302.

25. Jaroslav Pelikan, Helmut T. Lehmann, Hilton C. Oswald, eds., *Lectures on Psalms I,* Luther's Works (St. Louis, MO: Concordia Publishing House, 1966), 10:220.

Chapter 6

Who Is the False Prophet?

Besides purely theological questions, probably every Christian studying the book of Daniel comes to one very practical question: "Who are those whom God calls His people?" This question arises quite naturally. After all, if the Catholic priesthood with their temples and sacrifices is the "host" of the antichrist (and if the same phenomena in Orthodoxy are only a modification of the Catholic priesthood), then where can we find God's church, which has not been occupied by the antichrist? If it is neither Catholicism nor Orthodoxy, then what is it?

The only element in Christianity that has abandoned the priest-temple-sacrifice model is Protestantism. Protestants began to point to the similarities between the biblical antichrist and the papacy. Does this mean we should trust their message?

Perhaps so, but it is not that simple. The fact is that the Protestantism of the sixteenth century is not the same thing as modern Protestantism. Until the mid-nineteenth century, Protestants had no doubts about who the antichrist is; Protestants of our day do not have such confidence. Moreover, it has become popular to hold the opinion that the pope and the papacy cannot be the antichrist because of the belief that the coming of the antichrist is still in the future. Some Protestants also believe that the Jerusalem temple must be rebuilt and that the antichrist will sit in it. As far as this group is concerned, the papacy is above suspicion as being the antichrist because the popes haven't shown any interest in a rebuilt temple.

In this situation it turns out that, again, we can trust no one. Like Catholic and Orthodox believers, Protestants, too, became victims of misconceptions and have thus misled others. So again we ask the question, "Who are those whom God calls His people?"

The book of Revelation helps us understand this. Among the four most famous passages allegedly predicting the restoration of the temple in Jerusalem, there is one that we still have not explored. This prophecy is recorded in Revelation 11:1, 2. But to better understand what John says in this passage, we first need to read and understand two other passages that are directly connected to this prophecy. These are Revelation 16:13 and Revelation 10.

1. What do we know about the false prophet?

The first passage is Revelation 16:13. "And I saw three unclean spirits like frogs coming out of the mount of the dragon, out of the mouth of the beast, and out of the mouth of the false prophet" (Revelation 16:13). This text is already familiar to us. We have already dealt with it when we discussed the fact that in imitating Christ, the antichrist is a part of an ungodly trio. Just as Christ is in unity with the Father and the Holy Spirit, so the antichrist is inextricably linked with the dragon and the false prophet. Just as the Son has received power from the Father, so the antichrist received power from the dragon. Just as no one comes to the Father except through the Son, so the worship of the antichrist leads to the worship of the dragon. Just as the Holy Spirit is the source of the gift of prophecy, so the spirit of error is a source of false prophecy. And just as the Holy Spirit glorifies Christ, so the false prophet will glorify the antichrist.

Each member of this unholy trio performs its function. In Revelation 12, we read about the war in heaven in which the dragon opposed God but lost the battle and was cast out. The beast spoken of in Revelation 13 is the antichrist, who is fighting with the saints of the Most High who are the body of Christ. But whom does the false prophet fight? If the dragon fought with God in heaven and the antichrist fought with Christ on the earth, then whom does the false prophet oppose, and how does he go about it? It would seem the answer is obvious—he opposes the Holy Spirit. But who can resist the Holy Spirit? And how?

Running ahead ourselves, we can say that the false prophet confronts and fights with the true prophet of God. True prophecy is a gift of the Holy Spirit, "for prophecy never came by the will of man, but holy men of God spoke as they were moved by the Holy Spirit" (2 Peter 1:21). Therefore, to struggle against the gift of prophecy is to struggle against the Holy Spirit. And we need to understand that if a person does not have the gift of prophecy, that is, if he is not a prophet but he is preaching the true prophetic message, then the false prophet will oppose him as well, because his message will inevitably still expose the false prophet's deception. Thus, the false prophet leads the fight against true prophecy in all its forms—both the prophets and their message.

It looks like the Bible speaks very little of the false prophet. From Revelation 16:13, 14, we learn only that he will cooperate with the antichrist to work miracles. Many of those who today await the coming of the antichrist also know about the false prophet, but because of the almost complete lack of information about him in the Bible, it is even more difficult for them to identify him than it is to identify the antichrist.

However, we can and should understand who the false prophet is—not from any description of him in Scripture but from the description given of a true prophet. Why? Because imitation of the truth is a favorite method of Satan. Nobody is going to make a counterfeit $101 dollar bill. Why? Because neither the banks in America nor any other banks in the world would accept such a bill; the counterfeit would be worthless. A counterfeit is always linked to its original and must have a lot in common with it. Knowing what the true temple is and what kind of service goes in it, we were able to understand who the antichrist is. The antichrist and the false prophet are alike; as the saying goes, "They are indeed of the same breed." That is, they are driven by one spirit and their methods are the same. This means that the false prophet loves fakes. If we know who the true prophet is and what his message is, then we can identify the false prophet. *As the Antichrist will oppose the true ministry of the High Priest in the heavenly sanctuary by becoming its "reflection" on earth, so the message of the false prophet will resonate with the message of the true prophet and become its "echo," thus replacing the true prophecy with a false one.*

Today, many people know that the book of Revelation speaks of the false prophet, but not many of them know that it also speaks of the true gift of prophecy, which is to be manifested. Where can we read about the true prophet of God? What does John say about him? Whom does the false prophet copy and whom does he oppose?

2. What do we know about the true prophet?

Where in the book of Revelation do we find a prophecy of the true prophet of God? The answer is surprisingly simple: the true prophet of God in the book of Revelation is, of course, the prophet John himself. But as John died long ago, and we are interested in the prophet of God who will live in the end time, we need to find where John speaks of a prophet or a gift of prophecy in the end time. If we reread the book of Revelation, we will be able to find only one place with this rare phenomenon—John prophesies about himself, and even more surprisingly, this prophecy does not relate to the first century when he lived, but rather to the final events of human history. How can this be? Let's look at Revelation chapter 10. "I saw still another mighty angel coming down from heaven, clothed with a cloud. And a rainbow was on his head; his face was like the sun, and his feet like pillars of fire" (verse 1). This figure is described as an angel, but we have reason to think that it was Jesus Christ Himself. If we compare the description of Jesus in Revelation 1:12–16 and that of this "angel" in chapter 10, we'll find much in common. His face is compared to the sun (cf. Revelation 1:16; 10:1). His feet were "like fine brass, as if refined in a furnace" and "like pillars of fire" (Revelation 1:15; 10:1). His voice is as of "the Lion of the tribe of Judah" and "when a lion roars" (Revelation 5:5; 10:3). But what is He doing?

"He had a little book open in his hand. And he set his right foot on the sea and his left foot on the land" (verse 2).

Jesus appears to John holding an open book in His hand. Judging by many signs, we can guess that this book is the book of the prophet Daniel.[1] For example, we know that the only book of the Bible that was sealed, or closed to understanding, was the book of Daniel, so we immediately think of it when we see that the book is open. We can also note that after this vision—starting with the eleventh chapter and continuing until the end of the book—John refers to Daniel's prophecy of 1,260 days or 42 months. He also speaks about the persecution of the saints of the Most High, of the true and false worship, and of the temple of God. All these topics are found in the book of Daniel; the only difference is that Daniel sealed his book until the end time, but John saw the book open. The open book in Jesus' hand implies that the time has come for Daniel's book to be unsealed and that Jesus has appeared to explain what is written in it.

John continues:

> So I went to the angel and said to him, "Give me the little book."
>
> And he said to me, "Take and eat it; and it will make your stomach bitter, but it will be as sweet as honey in your mouth" (Revelation 10:9).

An invitation to eat the book is, of course, an invitation to read and understand it. And here the question arises, "What exactly was the prophet John supposed to understand after reading the book of Daniel? What was sealed and remained unclear?"

We can't say that no one could ever understand anything in the book of Daniel. For example, the content of the first six chapters either needs no explanation or explains itself. But when we come to the second part of the book, and especially to the prophetic periods, such as the 1,335 days and the 2,300 days, we can see that no one could understand them until the time of their fulfillment. These periods have a direct relation to the defilement and the cleansing of the sanctuary, and this means that Jesus invited John to understand those passages that we have studied in previous chapters of this book.

However, John died in the first century A.D.; he did not live until A.D.1844 when the 2,300 prophetic days were finished, and thus he was not able to understand this prophecy because it related "to many days in the future" (Daniel 8:26). Why, then, was he told in this vision to eat the book? The only explanation can be that in this vision, *John represented those who would live in this time, who would study and understand the sealed portion of the book of Daniel.* He was a symbol of those who would diligently study the prophecies and find the truth. Just as the prophet Elijah had been a symbol of the prophet John the Baptist, so John was to be a symbol of those who would prophesy in the last days. It had been predicted that Elijah was to come, but it was John the Baptist who came as the fulfillment of that prediction (Matthew 4:5; Matthew 11:13, 14). Likewise, it was not John himself who was to eat the open book, but rather those who would live in the time when the book would be unsealed. Like John, they will have a prophetic message, and so in a sense, they can also be called prophets. The same Spirit who gave the prophecies to Daniel and John will guide those who would be able to understand them. Neither Daniel nor John lived to see the day when the book of Daniel was unsealed, and that means that John's experience, in actuality, describes what would happen with those who would read and understand the prophecy.

John continues: "Then I took the little book out of the angel's hand and ate it, and it was as sweet as honey in my mouth. But when I had eaten it, my stomach became bitter" (Revelation 10:10).

The change of taste from sweet to bitter coincides miraculously with the experience of those who awaited the coming of Christ in 1844. After reading the prophecies of Daniel, they were happy to know that the sanctuary would be cleansed soon, and Jesus would return to earth as they believed. But that sweet anticipation gave way to bitter disappointment. The book of Daniel was sweet as honey in their mouths but became bitter in their bellies. However, they were not left without further guidance. Look at what the text says next: "And he said to me, 'You must prophesy again about many peoples, nations, tongues, and kings' " (Revelation 10:11).

After the book had been eaten, *after the sweet/bitter experience, they were told to "prophesy again."* These words, "prophesy again," are crucial for understanding the issue, which we have chosen as the title of this chapter. The reasons for that are the following:

First, as we can see, the false prophet came to oppose the true prophet. In order to find the true prophet, we have to find the place where it is written about him in the book of Revelation. And although chapter 11 also speaks of two prophets of God, we cannot discuss them because the time of their ministry was limited to the period of the 1,260 days and thus was finished before the end of the 2,300 or the 1,335 days. After this period, the only true prophet of whom John writes is himself. He is given the command to prophesy, which means he is called to the prophetic ministry and thus is the true prophet of God for whom we are looking. Having read and understood the book of Daniel, and having lived through the bittersweet experience, he was to "prophesy again."

Second, the word, "again," is very important. As far as we know, once being called, John never ceased his ministry of being a prophet. However, the word, "again," contains the idea of discontinuity, of stopping and starting once more. It is possible to explain this contradiction only if we understand that the events of Revelation 10 will happen *after* John's ministry and also after the ministry of the two prophets—that is after the 1,260 days. Their prophecies have ceased. In this case, the true prophet of God, who must "prophesy again," cannot be John; it must be those who will read the "open book." John was not supposed to rise from the grave to explain the book of Daniel; thus, he was only a symbol of those who would read and understand Daniel's prophecies. Just as the Old Testament foretold that the prophet Elijah would be sent again, yet it was John the Baptist who came to fulfill that prophecy. So Revelation says that John must "prophesy again," but it is not him who is to do this. In this regard, the angel told John in Revelation 19:10 that he would not be alone in his ministry. John wrote, "And I fell at his feet to worship him. But he said to me, 'See that you do not do that! I am your fellow servant, and of your brethren who have the testimony of Jesus. Worship God! For the testimony of Jesus is the spirit of prophecy.' " This means that John has "brethren," the prophets. These prophets, like John himself, will have the "testimony of Jesus," which "is the spirit of prophecy."

And third, the fact that John is told to "eat" the book tells us that the phrase, "prophesy again," does not necessarily mean that a true prophet must have visions; it is not visions that are important.* The important thing is that his prophetic message must be the message of the open book; i.e., of the book of Daniel. Prophetic times and seasons came to an end, the time has come, and Jesus sends His true prophets to explain what was sealed and incomprehensible.

---

* For example, we know nothing of John the Baptist having prophetic visions, but nevertheless Jesus called him the greatest among the prophets.

3. What will be the content of the message of the true prophet?

Only now are we ready to read the prophecy of Revelation 11:1, which some people claim to be the proof that there will be a new temple built in Jerusalem.* Why only now? Why could we not go directly to the text we are interested in? For the simple reason that John didn't divide his book into chapters. This was done by other people later on who sometimes failed to do so correctly, and this passage is a good example of such a failure. In fact, the first verse of chapter 11 is a continuation of the conversation between the angel and John recorded in chapter 10, and it can't be properly understood in isolation from that previous chapter. But if so, then think about what John is told to do immediately after the command to prophesy. "Then I was given a reed like a measuring rod. And the angel stood, saying, 'Rise and measure the temple of God, the altar, and those who worship there' " (Revelation 11:1).

Is it an accident that after reading the open book and being commanded to prophesy, the prophet is told to measure the temple? Of course not. This is not a new vision, but rather a continuation or explanation of the previous one. First, he should prophesy about "many peoples, nations, tongues, and kings," and that's what Daniel is speaking about in detail beginning with the seventh chapter of his book. Then John was told to measure the temple, and we read about the temple and its defilement in the eighth chapter of Daniel. In other words, we see how the angel explains to John the seventh and

---

* "While we recognize that many who take such position are devout Christians and earnest students of the Word, we feel that such interpretations make nonsense of Holy Scriptures. After the death of Christ, the New Testament ignores the Temple of Judaism, except to say that its rituals are now valueless, having met their fulfillment in Christ. See Heb. 9:8-14. To say that the Temple ritual and sacrifices will be inaugurated again with the blessing of God is to deny the once-for-all nature of the Cross of Christ to which the sacrifices pointed," Desmond Ford, *Crisis* (Newcastle, CA: Desmond Ford Publications, 1982), 486.

eighth chapters of the book of Daniel, the chapters that set the tone for all the subsequent chapters. This means that preaching on God's temple will be an integral part of his prophetic ministry.

We have already said that a true prophet of God is to explain the prophecies of Daniel, especially those that are difficult to understand. But continuing his command to John, the angel explains what should be the basis of his message and urges him to pay special attention to the temple. This emphasis is understandable, as it is the prophecies about the 1,335 and the 2,300 days that remained closed to understanding and that spoke about the defilement and the cleansing of the sanctuary. Now it was time to understand and explain them.* In addition, the bitterness of disappointment had to be corrected, and the angel came to help. John was commanded to measure the temple, because it is "measuring," or the study of the sanctuary, that helped Bible students following 1844 to understand that the sanctuary should be understood as the heavenly temple, rather than as symbolizing our earth.

Another object that was supposed to be "measured" was the altar (Revelation 11:1). Sometimes interpreters find it difficult to determine which altar was meant. The fact is that the temple had two of them—the altar of burnt offering and the altar of incense. The first one was in the outer court, and the second one was before the veil separating the Holy Place from the Most Holy Place. It would seem that Revelation 11:1 is speaking of the altar of incense, since John was specifically told not to measure the outer court, the place where the altar of burnt offering was situated (verse 2). But in John's day, Herod's temple had an outer court for the Gentiles where there was no altar of burnt offerings and where sacrifices were not offered. Based on this, some believe that the altar John was told to measure is the altar of burnt offering.

---

* The measuring of the temple in Ezekiel 40:2–43:12 was made to study its size and to rebuild it afterwards. In this case, the command to measure the temple means to explore and restore the truth about the heavenly sanctuary.

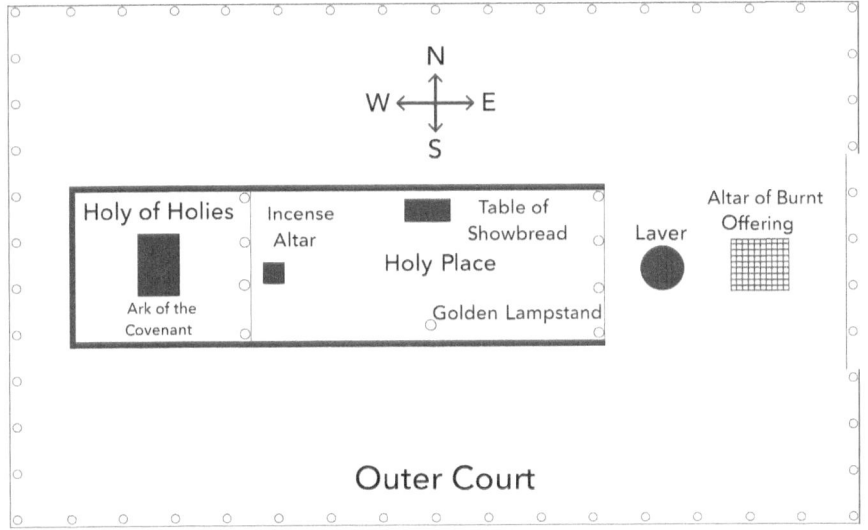

Moses placed the altar of burnt offering in the outer court.

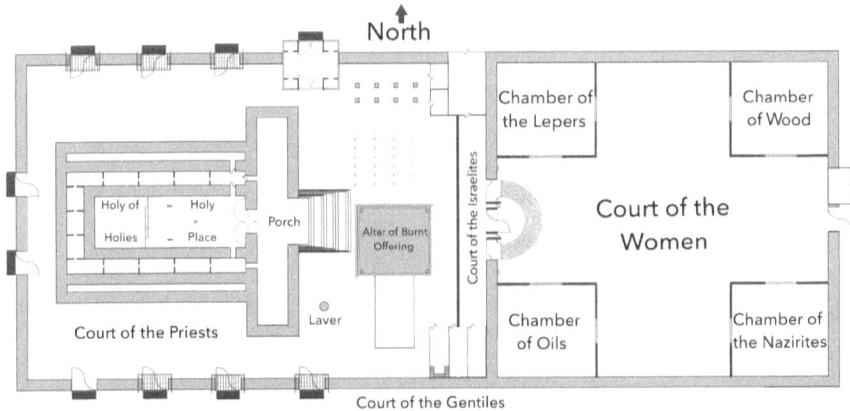

Herod's temple had an outer court for the Gentiles where there was no altar of burnt offerings.

We'll be able to understand correctly what is said here only if we understand who the "Gentiles" are and what the "outer court" is. The text of Daniel 9:24 helps us with this: "Seventy weeks are determined for your people." The seventy weeks mentioned here are 490 years that are to extend from the decree to rebuild Jerusalem to the time of Christ. It is said about them that they "are determined for your people" (Daniel 9:24). The literal translation is "cut" or "cut off" for your people. There is no doubt that the "people" refers to the Jews and that the 490 days (years) are the years of testing that ended with the people crucifying their Messiah. But here the question arises, "If the first 490 years were determined, or cut off, for the Jews, whom did the remaining years belong to and how many years were there?"

The first part of the question is easier to answer than the second part. If the first 490 years were given to the Jews, then the rest of the time belongs to the Gentiles. Jesus Himself said that some amount of time was determined for the Gentiles: "And Jerusalem will be trampled by Gentiles until the times of the Gentiles are fulfilled" (Luke 21:24). This means that both the Jews and the Gentiles were given some "time." What time?

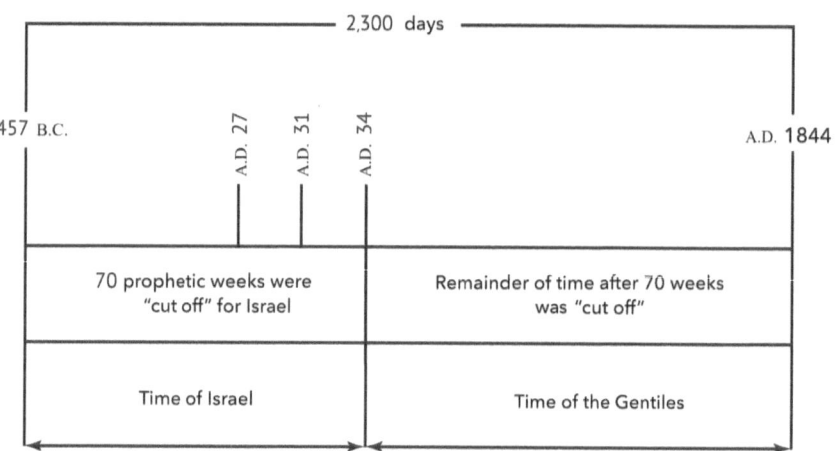

We already know that both the 490 and the 2,300 prophetic days begin from the time of the decree to rebuild Jerusalem. This means that the first 490 years were cut off from the 2,300 years and given to the Jews, while the rest were given to the Gentiles. The times of the Jews ended in the year A.D. 34, and the times of the Gentiles is the period from A.D. 34 to A.D. 1844. Out of these 1,810 years, 1,260 years would be the era of persecution, and 1,335 years would be the years of the defilement of the sanctuary.

Therefore, when the angel says that the outer court will be given to the Gentiles (Revelation 11:2), *he refers to the second part of the 2,300 days and to the "times of the Gentiles" rather than to nationality*. He points to specific places in the book of Daniel, which is now open and which he has come to explain. He refers to Daniel 8:13, 14.

The proof of this is the second part of his phrase—"They will tread the holy city underfoot for forty-two months" (Revelation 11:2). It resonates like an echo of the words of Daniel's prophecy: "Then I heard a holy one speaking; and another holy one said to that certain one who was speaking, 'How long will the vision be, concerning the daily sacrifices and the transgression of desolation, the giving of both the sanctuary and the host to be trampled underfoot?' " (Daniel 8:13).

Although both Jerusalem and the outer court will be *trodden down*, it is unlikely that we can say *Jerusalem* and *sanctuary* are interchangeable words in this prophecy. Jerusalem is a city, but the outer court is an area of the sanctuary. The Gentiles could be in Jerusalem, but only Jews could go into the sanctuary. However, both were given to be *trodden under foot*. But while Jerusalem was to be *trampled* for 42 months, the sanctuary would be *trampled* until the end of the 1,335 or the 2,300 days. Only with the help of Daniel 8 is it possible to understand what outer court the angel was talking about and how it would be *trampled*, since only Daniel speaks about the *trampling* of the sanctuary.

ANTICHRIST AND HIS TEMPLE

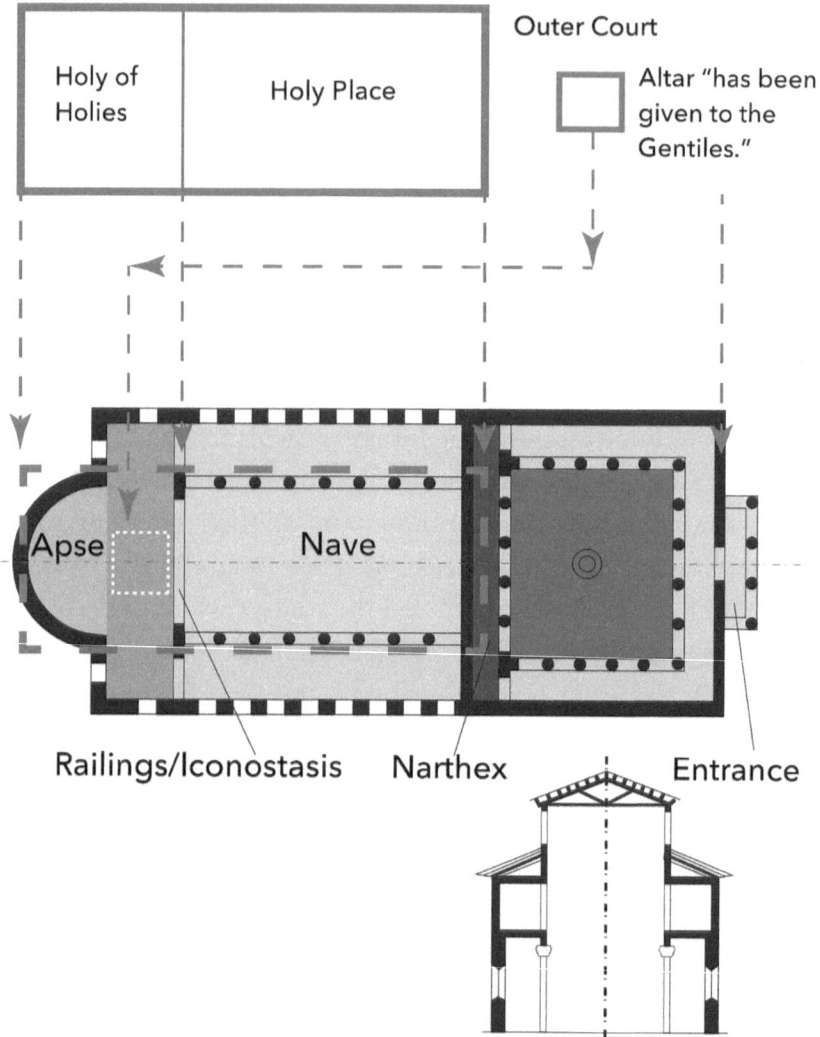

Railings/Iconostasis   Narthex   Entrance

In previous chapters, we have examined in detail how the sanctuary was trampled and have seen that the sacrifice was taken away and trampled, but the sacrifice has always been connected only with the altar of burnt offering. This means that when the angel told John to measure the altar, he was speaking of the altar of incense, because the altar of burnt offering, which was located in the outer court, did not need to be measured. Also it was given up to be trodden by the Gentiles who did not act any better than did the Jews and in the Gentile's time crucified the Savior, too, by offering Him as the "bloodless sacrifice" of the Eucharist. By this it was proven that "both Jews and Greeks . . . are all under sin" (Romans 3:9), and that "all have sinned and fall short of the glory of God" (Romans 3:23). Salvation is only by faith for everyone "since there is one God who will justify the circumcised by faith and the uncircumcised through faith" (Romans 3:30). Is this not the true and everlasting gospel?

This message was especially appropriate in the mid-nineteenth century when "reformers began to raise questions on the nature of the Eucharist and the participation of the assembly."[2] In the churches of different denominations, attention was suddenly drawn to the altars in the church. In 1839, a book was published in London with the title, *The Great Apostasy; or, the Church of Rome Proved to Be Not the Church of Christ, but the Greatest Enemy to Christ, to His Doctrine, and to His Religion, That God Ever Permitted to Arise in the World.*[3] One subsection of this book was titled, "The Mass Altars of the Apostate Church of Rome." A few years later in 1846, in another part of the world, a book was printed in America called, *Reasons for Refusing to Consecrate a Church Having an Altar Instead of a Communion Table, or the Doctrine of Scripture, and of the Protestant Episcopal Church, as to a Sacrifice in the Lord's Supper, and a Priesthood in the Christian Ministry.* In it the author complains that "within some five or six years"[4] he has observed the ministers of the Episcopal Church in Europe and America beginning to apostatize from the truth, actively setting up altars, instead of tables, for communion. He tries to remind his brothers in the faith that "it has always indeed been decidedly the usage of our Church to have a literal table as distinguished from an altar-form structure."[5] He indicates that

> in the Lord's Supper, 'you need no other sacrifice or oblation, (than that of Christ on the Cross:) 'no

sacrificing Priest, no mass, no means established by man's invention.' But the revolutionary effort, which is best known as the Tractarian,* directly contradicts this language of our Church, teaching that we do need another oblation and sacrifice; that the sacrifice of Christ on the cross cannot avail us, unless it be applied by what is called the "unbloody" sacrifice of his body and upon the altar of the Eucharist; that we must have a mediation of a 'sacrificing priest' at that altar, or we cannot partake in the mediation of our Great High Priest before the mercy-seat in the sanctuary in the heavens; and consequently, that the Lord's Supper is not a mere 'memory' of a sacrifice, but is a real propitiatory sacrifice for sin. This is Popery in the essence.[6]

The author delves into history and finds that the year 509 was the year when the wooden tables were replaced by stone altars, and since then the theology of the Eucharist as the sacrifice quickly began to supplant the truth.[7]

It is hard to imagine what could have happened if the authors of these books and their churches had seen everything in the light of the prophecies of Daniel and John and if they had listened to the words of the angel to measure and to understand what the temple was. If only they could have seen that the "outer court" and the altar were given to the trampling of the Gentiles. Perhaps they could have also seen that the angel had commanded to measure the altar of incense and the worshipers in the temple. It would not be difficult for them to understand that the measurement of a human being had

---

* A movement of 1833–1841 led to the "Branch Theory," according to which Anglicanism was considered to be one of the branches of the Roman Catholic Church. As its views were publicized in a series of tracts (*Tracts for the Times*), the movement was known as the Tractarian Movement.

always pointed to the judgment and that the altar of incense pointed to the intercessory prayers of Jesus brought to His heavenly Father at this judgment. If only they could have understood what dates the prophecy about the cleansing of the sanctuary and the beginning of the judgment had pointed to, it could have been the beginning of a great religious awakening. For this reason, the angel sent John to "prophesy again." Those who studied the prophecies of Daniel had a special message, which the world needed so much, and they were called by God to proclaim it.

4. What will be the message of the false prophet?

If we do not take Revelation 11:1–13 out of its context, we can understand that the whole passage is an explanation of the command to "prophesy again."* This means that the preaching of the prophet of God is inseparably linked with the "open book" and with all that it says about the temple of God. However, there are other chapters of the book of Daniel that will become a part of this proclamation. In Revelation 11:2–13, we see the angel paying special attention to the events of the three and a half years or the 1,260 days. And although this period speaks of the time of persecution of God's people, it is also a part of the 1,335 or the 2,300 days and connected one way or another with the sanctuary, and therefore it is also to become a part of the preaching of the true prophet.

Now that we know exactly what the prophet of God will do, it is not difficult for us to determine who the false prophet is, and it will be impossible to argue with this conclusion since the false prophet is one who tells false prophecies. *He will also preach about the temple, the antichrist sitting in it, the abomination of desolation, and the three and a half years of persecution, but it will be a message*

---

* Revelation 10:11 also resonates with Revelation 14:6 where, too, a message is to be preached to "every nation, tribe, tongue, and people."

full of errors. And who does this today if not those who say that the temple will be rebuilt?

Today, many of the Protestant churches confidently preach that the construction of the temple in Jerusalem is about to begin. It is not Catholics or the Orthodox who do this; both of them have nothing to do with this business. It is the Protestants, those who once preached that the papacy is the antichrist. Today they are not sure of this anymore and are waiting for the coming of the antichrist in the future. This "man of sin," as they think, will sit in the temple of God in Jerusalem and will persecute the Jews for three and a half literal years. And of course, he is to defile the temple and set up the abomination of desolation in it. As proof, they quote Daniel 9:27; Matthew 24:15; 2 Thessalonians 2:3, 4; and Revelation 11:1. We have studied all these texts and have been able to make sure that none of them say that the temple must be rebuilt.

These Protestants have their eyes on every newscast in order to know what's happening in Jerusalem or who among the politicians will be the one who will stop the war in the Middle East. Unfortunately, this approach often resonates in people's hearts because it is easier to follow the news than it is to explore history and Scripture. By expecting the reconstruction of the temple in the future, they have successfully traded one message for another; that is, they are doing what the false prophet is supposed to do. But as they utter the prophecies, they are speaking contrary to the Scriptures and are doomed to fail. They themselves do not notice how clearly they prove that they bear the title given to them in the prophecy of John.

5. There is nothing new under the sun

In the beginning, the Protestant churches had proper and noble intentions. Their sincere desire was to help the Church get rid of error and return to the pure and everlasting gospel. Being deeply religious and committed to the body of Christ, they firmly believed that once ignorance was defeated, the Church would be able to improve and carry out all necessary reforms. All their efforts were focused on a reformation inside the Church to which they already belonged rather than on creating a new church. However, they were wrong. It turned out that education was not enough. The problem was much deeper and lay not only in the neglect of the Scriptures but also in an unwillingness to follow it. The system rejected the light, declared these Protestants to be heretics, and anathematized them. In response, the Protestants could do nothing but continue to develop independently. It is hardly fair to accuse them of divisiveness, since they did not reject the Church, but the Church rejected them.

Some also blamed Protestantism for allowing interest on loans and private appropriations that led to a global economic crisis.[8] Although that may seem credible from the point of view of history and economic science, the picture changes when we look at it through the prism of the prophetic Word. Describing the events of the Reformation, Daniel said, "But many shall join with them by intrigue" (Daniel 11:34). When we read these words, it becomes clear to us what actually happened. Like the Egyptians who joined Israel when they came out of Egypt (and who probably had never been happy with Pharaoh), so the moneylenders pursued their own goals when they joined the Reformation movement. The only thing that usurers and reformers (moneylenders and Protestants) had in common is that the Church prohibited the views and practices of both groups. But if it was a disagreement on the matters of theology and faith for Protestants, then for moneylenders it was the Church's ban on interest loan. By themselves, they failed to be an independent and strong movement, but they were able to join the Reformation movement, and so they joined "with them by intrigue." Unfortunately, these moneylenders were able to exert a strong influence on the camp of the Protestants for several centuries, with the result that those living in the most developed countries of the world are tempted more than others to serve both God and mammon at the same time. However, with the help of the prophetic Word, we understand that "many . . . join with them by intrigue." Their influence discredited the whole movement, and the risk is that many will toss the baby out with the bath water. To prevent this, Daniel was given a message that helps to weed out the tares from the wheat. He explains to us that *we should not be reading the Bible from the point of view of economic science but that we need to study economics through the prism of the Bible.*

For Protestantism, as for Catholicism or Orthodoxy, the main claims of the Bible lie not in the sphere of economic crimes or any other crimes. Such things incur condemnation even from those who have never been acquainted with the Scriptures. The main problem in biblical matters has always been confusion in matters of faith.

Protestants were to do a huge work revising traditions and testing their conformity to the Scriptures. This was nothing new; in all times God has sent His messengers to draw a clear line between error and truth, between tradition and Scripture (see Matthew 15:3, 9). During the Reformation, many people had access to the Scriptures in their own language for the first time in many centuries. Now they had to restore the lost gospel doctrine bit by bit. Step by step, they moved forward, making new discoveries. "The path of the just is like the shining sun, that shines ever brighter unto the perfect day" (Proverbs 4:18). God led them in this way until in the nineteenth century, they finally reached the time when God opened the book of the prophet Daniel before them, and here came the moment of truth. It was a time of serious trials for the whole Protestant movement.

Those who understood correctly who the antichrist is were now ready to understand the prophecy of the sanctuary as no one had ever understood it before. Without much difficulty, they determined when the 2,300 prophetic days should end, but they made a mistake in the matter of defining the sanctuary. Just like Jesus' disciples, who recognized the Messiah but were mistaken concerning the purpose of His coming, these Bible students correctly understood one thing but misunderstood the other. Like the disciples who after the crucifixion continued to search the Scriptures to find reasons for their mistake and disappointment, so these continued to explore the prophecy after 1844.

However, instead of reviewing every detail of the prophecy and determining exactly where they made a mistake, the majority were quick to call the entire logic of the argument one big mistake. As a result, not only did they question the year 1844 as the ending date of the 2,300 days and the relevance of the sanctuary in heaven, but they also questioned the identity of the antichrist. The historical-grammatical method of interpreting Scripture was rejected, and there appeared new approaches to interpretation that suggested looking for the antichrist in the future. Wheat was not sifted from the chaff, and the baby was tossed out with the bath water.

Since then, discussion of the antichrist has ceased to be straightforward. Protestants began to look for new ways of explaining the prophecies, which were intended to exclude the papacy from the "circle of suspects." Therefore, in the early twentieth century, a Protestant pastor, Arthur Pink, discontinued believing that the pope is the antichrist. Today, for many Protestants, the pope is neither the antichrist nor any other prophetic character. Slowly but surely, Protestants are renouncing their theological heritage, which makes them ready to "extend a hand of fellowship to the papacy."

Solomon shared with us his wisdom and warned, "That which has been is what will be, that which is done is what will be done, and there is nothing new under the sun" (Ecclesiastes 1:9). There will not be anything new in the history of the false prophet, as he will repeat the antichrist's history of "success." The apple never falls far from the tree. As the apostasy from "the Holy Covenant" (Daniel 11:30) made servants of God into hosts of the antichrist, so rejecting the truth about the heavenly sanctuary will make Protestants into false prophets. They are two peas in a pod. Their union will have a huge, enticing force. Various differences may still hinder the unity of the antichrist and the false prophet today, but they will be forgotten in the face of the global turmoil predicted in the Bible. "For false christs and false prophets will rise and show great signs and wonders to deceive, if possible, even the elect" (Matthew 24:24).

> How the Roman Church can clear herself from the charge of idolatry we cannot see. . . .
>
> And this is the religion which Protestants are beginning to look upon with so much favor, and which will eventually be united with Protestantism. This union will not, however, be effected by a change in Catholicism; for Rome never changes. She claims infallibility. It is Protestantism that will change. The adoption of liberal ideas on its part, will bring it where it can clasp the hand of Catholicism.[9]

6. Who are "the rest of her offspring"?

Concluding our study, we must again turn to the question, "Whom does God call His people?" This is not an idle question because according to our findings, there is no one whom we can trust in matters of faith. Prejudices and misconceptions have been so firmly established in Christianity that sometimes it is almost impossible to distinguish them from the truth.

However, God has not left us in the dark about the coming of antichrists and false prophets. He has also pointed out where we can find His people. In Revelation 18, John hears a voice commanding, "Come out of her, my people, lest you share in her sins, and lest you receive of her plagues" (Revelation 18:4). The Babylon that God's people must leave is the apostate Church (Revelation 17:1-5); therefore, strange as it is, God says that His people are still there!

God's people are in the Catholic Church and in the Orthodox Church and in the Protestant churches. God calls them to come out, but if they reject light, they will turn into Babylon. "Among the Catholics there are many who are most conscientious Christians, and who walk in all the light that shines upon them, and God will work in their behalf."[10] The same can be said about sincere Orthodox and Protestant believers. They live and act according to the light that shines on them. Whenever they learn new truths, they gladly accept them and follow their Savior. So as soon as they clearly see the deception of the antichrist and the false prophet, they will be called out of Babylon. It won't be easy, but they will obey God's command and do it.

Jesus said, "And other sheep I have which are not of this fold; them also I must bring, and they will hear My voice; and there will be one flock and one shepherd" (John 10:16). Here Jesus promises to gather His children from different places. Wherever they are, they will hear and know His voice. He will gather them into one place, and "there will be one flock and one shepherd." This flock will be the remnant of God's people with whom Satan will struggle. "And the dragon was enraged with the woman, and he went to make war with the rest of her offspring, who keep the commandments of God and have the testimony of Jesus Christ" (Revelation 12:17). "The rest of her offspring" are God's people. *They keep the commandments of God and have the testimony of Jesus Christ, which is the spirit of prophecy* (Revelation 19:10). In order not to "share in her sins, and ... receive of her plagues" (Revelation 18:4), we need to continually study the Scriptures. Our only hope is the everlasting gospel, pure and true. This is not *a part* of the Bible—that part which we like more than others. It is *all* of the Scriptures. It is God's two witnesses—the Old and New Testaments. Only in them can we trust.

Notes

1. *Symposium on Revelation,* book 1, Daniel and Revelation Committee Series, vol. 6, ed. Frank B. Holbrook, (Hagerstown, MD: Review and Herald', 1986), 298–301.

2. Richard Vosko, *God's House Is Our House* (Collegeville, MN: Liturgical Press, 2006), 61.

3. *The Great Apostasy; or, the Church of Rome Proved to Be Not the Church of Christ, but the Greatest Enemy to Christ, to His Doctrine, and to His Religion, That God Ever Permitted to Arise in the World* (London: Hamilton, Adams, and Co., Paternoster-Row, 1839).

4. Charles Pettit M'Ilvaine, *Reasons for Refusing to Consecrate a Church Having an Altar Instead of a Communion Table, or the Doctrine of Scripture, and of the Protestant Episcopal Church, as to a Sacrifice in the Lord's Supper, and a Priesthood in the Christian Ministry* (New York: Stanford and Swords, 1846), 6.

5. M'Ilvaine, 7.

6. *Reasons for Refusing to Consecrate a Church Having an Altar Instead of a Communion Table,* 11, 12.

7. *Reasons for Refusing to Consecrate a Church Having an Altar Instead of a Communion Table,* 15, 16.

8. Valentin Katasonov, *Interest: Loan, Justifiable, Reckless: "The Money Civilization" and the Present-Day Crisis,* (Denver: Outskirts Press, 2015), 60.

9. Ellen G. White, "Visit to the Vaudois Valleys," *Advent Review and Sabbath Herald,* June 1, 1886.

10. Ellen G. White, *Testimonies for the Church* (Nampa, ID: Pacific Press', 2002), 9:243.

Epilogue

While our quest for answers to the questions asked in this book has forced us to consult a variety of scriptures, our focus has always been on the book of Daniel. Its mysterious language and the importance and scale of the events it describes have fascinated its readers for a long time. From the earliest days of its existence the church has tried to "decode" the prophecies of Daniel and, in general, proposed an accurate interpretation, yet according to the words of the angel who communicated the message to the prophet, the last generation on earth will understand this book better than their predecessors. To the prophet, the angel's words must have sounded like the angel was pronouncing a sentence upon him: "Go your way, Daniel, for the words are closed up and sealed till the time of the end" (Daniel 12:9). This means that the key to the "code" of the prophet's book has always been in the hands of God rather than in the hands of men. He is the God "who reveals secrets" (Daniel 2:28), and only He can reveal "what will be in the latter days" (verse 28). By studying the prophecies of Daniel and how they have found their fulfillment in history, we once again see that "God is not a man, that He should lie, nor a son of man, that He should repent. Has He said, and will He not do? Or has He spoken, and will He not make it good?" (Numbers 23:19).

However, we can see that even though the prophecy was "sealed," God has not left previous generations completely in the dark. Almost always there were those who could not accept the teachings of the antichrist, not based on Daniel's prophecies but rather based on intuition and did not worship him. Perhaps they could not explain their beliefs using the prophecies of Daniel, but they had enough other reasons to doubt that the teachings spread by the Church came from divine inspiration. Some, reading the Pentateuch, noticed that the Church had dared to change the Ten Commandments. Others, reading Paul's writings, understood that we are saved only by faith in Christ, who has been sacrificed once and for all (Hebrews 7:27; 10:10, 14, 18). A third group, studying the regulations of the Church councils, drew attention to their internal contradictions. And a fourth group just could not agree with the paganism that had been brought into the Church. Whatever their reasons, all of these opposed the authority of the antichrist and his teaching. If we look at Paul's words about the Gentiles, "who do not have the law, [but] by nature do the things in the law" (Romans 2:14), it can be said that these people who did not understand the prophet Daniel intuitively rejected the doctrine of the antichrist.

It can seem difficult to understand what Daniel wrote, but that is only at first glance. In fact, there is no need to become a theologian to do so. Jesus once said, "If anyone wills to do His will, he shall know concerning the doctrine, whether it is from God or whether I speak on My own authority" (John 7:17). In other words, the most necessary qualification for anyone who wants to understand the Word of God is not the power of his intellect or the quality of his education, but rather his desire to do the will of God. Such people can claim the promise that God Himself will be their teacher: "The entrance of Your words gives light; It gives understanding to the simple" (Psalm 119:130). It may be that they cannot always argue convincingly the grounds of their faith, but they will be keenly attuned to all sorts of hypocrisy, formalism, and the substitution of a lie for the truth. As in the past there were those who were unwilling to worship the antichrist, so today there are those who will read and understand the book of Daniel.

In the course of our research, it became obvious to us that all of Christianity—Catholicism, Orthodoxy, and Protestantism—have been influenced by the antichrist and his teachings in varying degrees. What should the believer do? Wherever we go there will be priests, sacrifices, altars, and temples, and at best we will be told that the temple is going to be rebuilt in Jerusalem and that the antichrist will come soon. But what is even worse, we will be told that sinners cannot be reconciled to God. For repentance and faith, the antichrist has substituted religious formalism and salvation by works. What is the solution?

First, we need to make sure that the Bible is the main rule of our faith. Religious truth is not determined by tradition, by the majority opinion, nor the authority of the clergy, by the expert opinion of a narrow circle of persons, nor even by a miracle or a sign from heaven, but by the pure, plain Word of God. Too often and too easily we are ready to turn away from the Scriptures and, instead, trust someone who is supposed to be "trustworthy." The so-called faith of the fathers often takes us hostage, and unfortunately, we often don't even notice how loyalty to tradition supersedes loyalty to the gospel. Affiliation with and love for one's people become a higher priority and stronger than love for God. That is why Jesus said, "He who loves father or mother more than Me is not worthy of Me. And he who loves son or daughter more than Me is not worthy of Me" (Matthew 10:37).

A powerful tool in the antichrist's armory against the Bible has always been majority opinion. Nonsense said once will not be noticed by anyone. But if it is repeated by thousands of people, it will be listened to. A million repetitions may turn into a request for a new political power structure, but a billion repetitions are destined to become a sacred world religion where no one will dare say that "the emperor has no clothes." In such circumstances, we need to remember the words of Christ:

> "Enter by the narrow gate; for wide is the gate and broad is the way that leads to destruction, and there are many who go in by it.
> Because narrow is the gate and difficult is the way which leads to life, and there are few who find it" (Matthew 7:13, 14).

However, if other means of seduction are not effective and do not achieve the desired result of no one daring to resist the "sacred" tradition, Satan sets in motion healings, communications with the dead, and other miracles. The mind that is not grounded in the Scripture is simply not able to resist these deceptions and becomes an easy prey, unable to provide any resistance, and becomes a part of the army of the antichrist. Jesus warned that these false signs would have tremendous power because they would be performed by professed Christians in the name of Christianity. "Many will say to Me in that day, 'Lord, Lord, have we not prophesied in Your name, cast out demons in Your name, and done many wonders in Your name?' " However, His answer tells us that they have nothing to do with the truth. "And then I will declare to them, 'I never knew you; depart from Me, you who practice lawlessness!' " (Matthew 7:22, 23).

The prophet Isaiah invites us to compare every opinion, teaching, or doctrine—especially miracles—to the teachings of the Scripture. "And when they say to you, 'Seek those who are mediums and wizards, who whisper and mutter,' should not a people seek their God? Should they seek the dead on behalf of the living? To the law and to the testimony! If they do not speak according to this word, it is because there is no light in them" (Isaiah 8:19, 20).

This work cannot be delegated to someone else; it is our personal responsibility before God.

In the course of our reflections on the main theme of this book, *we have touched on many auxiliary issues that could not be fully discussed* but that will certainly attract the attention of the inquisitive reader. *Maybe this will encourage him or her to find effective ways to answer questions about these issues.* If the reader now has a desire to take up the Word of God and study it with prayer, the author will consider that he achieved his goal.

Second, we need to have a living, personal communion with our heavenly High Priest, Jesus Christ. Scripture says that the law is "our tutor to bring us to Christ" (Galatians 3:24). This means that we will understand that we need a Savior only when we look at ourselves in the light of His holy law. We will also begin to understand that "all have sinned and fall short of the glory of God" (Romans 3:23), and therefore no earthly priest can ever be a mediator between us and God. Christ's sacrifice on the cross was enough to pay for all our sins, and we can't add anything to it to improve it. As we look at Jesus as our High Priest, we start to remember His words that the time is near when all earthly temples and their sacrifices will be useless because "the hour is coming when you will neither on this mountain, nor in Jerusalem, worship the Father. . . . But the hour is coming, and now is, when the true worshipers will worship the Father in spirit and truth; for the Father is seeking such to worship Him" (John 4:21–23). In light of the book of Daniel, we start to understand that to claim to forgive sins in God's name is blasphemy and that confession to a priest does not bring those participating in it closer to God, but only alienates them from Him.

Seeing Jesus as our High Priest helps us understand the truth about righteousness by faith as nothing else can. By faith we enter into the heavenly sanctuary "where the forerunner has entered for us, even Jesus, having become High Priest forever" (Hebrews 6:20). There we can see His holy and unchangeable law according to which God judges. We understand that we can't cover our sin by any goodness of our own and that our only hope is in God's forgivingness. We see that Jesus paid our debt, and therefore we turn to God asking Him to forgive us for the sake of the blood shed by Jesus Christ.

When we approach God in this way, with repentance, it is not some charlatan or intermediary who give us assurance that our sins are covered; it is God Himself. The gift of the Holy Spirit, a new life, and a desire to help others receive this forgiveness become the proof of our sincere repentance and forgiveness. We understand that no priest can declare us forgiven or grant us forgiveness. A human being is not God and cannot see the heart. Even we, who believe we are forgiven, may be prone to wishful thinking, not any different from the Jews to whom John the Baptist said, "Do not think to say to yourselves, 'We have Abraham as our father' " (Matthew 3:9). Our new life in the Holy Spirit becomes the undeniable evidence of our sincere repentance and forgiveness, but no matter how righteously we live after our conversion, we can't earn salvation and avoid judgment. Jesus is our Advocate in this judgment; as the One who, though without sin, took our punishment on Himself. He has the right to forgive our sins and cover us with the garments of His righteousness.

When the judgment is over, Jesus will come again to render to every man according to his works. Just as the high priest came out of the sanctuary to announce the end of the judgment on the Day of Atonement, so Jesus will come out of the heavenly sanctuary to return to the earth and save His people.

Today, the true meaning of repentance and forgiveness has been distorted; the ministry of our heavenly High Priest has gone by the wayside and is forgotten. According to the prophecy of Daniel, at the end-time impostors will be exposed, the heavenly sanctuary will be justified, its High Priest and sacrifice will be exalted, and God's people will be saved. But for this to happen we will need to play our role.

Third, we need to tell the world about God's love and salvation; we need to win the information war waged by the antichrist against Christ and His sacrifice. Jesus predicted this proclamation when He said, "And this gospel of the kingdom will be preached in all the world as a witness to all the nations, and then the end will come" (Matthew 24:14). This gospel is of universal scale; it does not belong to any single nation, and therefore every nation, tribe, tongue, and people will have to hear it.

The natural human reaction is to worry about one's friends and blood relatives more than others. It is unnatural not to love one's parents, who nurtured and raised us, whatever they may have been. Likewise, it is unnatural not to love one's country, one's culture, and one's people. There is an incredible power in such love, a power that has made many people praise it in poetry and songs. This inspiration arises spontaneously, and suddenly we realize that homeland, family, and tradition are more than just words.

In the moments when we feel such inspiration and feel something holy, we may be tempted to assume that the source of this bliss is not God but rather the traditions of the fathers. At times like this, it is easy to be deceived. The Creator gets replaced by His creation. Our bloodline, family, tradition, and religion can become our god. As a result, belief in one's own exceptionality is growing. Such faith and love for tradition is idolized and has become a kind of religion, creating an insurmountable barrier between nations and peoples.

There is nothing new in this. The preaching of the gospel has always faced many racial, cultural, social, and other obstacles. Selfishness, racism masquerading as patriotism, snobbery, and other "isms" have always blinded us and hindered obedience to the gospel. Overcoming these things is like being melted in a crucible. Just as metal is melted and cleansed and reformed, so must we be transformed. We must be cleansed from false ideas that are so attached to us that they seem to be the very foundation of our existence. This process has always been extremely painful, and for some it is totally impossible. It is possible to absorb with our mother's milk a religion infected by the antichrist, and recognizing this possibility is one of the strongest tests that can come to us who live in the end of time. To undergo such a transformation is like being born again. That's why the angel warned, "Many shall be purified, made white, and refined, but the wicked shall do wickedly; and none of the wicked shall understand, but the wise shall understand" (Daniel 12:10).

Children of God can be found among all tribes and peoples, and each one needs to hear the gospel. It is shortsighted and selfish to think that God prefers one nation over another. The angel did not say that the Slavs will understand, and Americans will remain in the dark, or that Catholics or Protestants will gain the needed knowledge while the Orthodox will not be awarded this privilege. The angel who appeared to Daniel was not a racist and did not divide people based on their DNA or place of residence. Unfortunately, it is sometimes difficult for humans to understand and accept the idea that "God shows no partiality. But in every nation whoever fears Him and works righteousness is accepted by Him" (Acts 10:34, 35). On this same principle, the angel divided all people into only two categories—the wise and the foolish, the righteous and the wicked (Daniel 12:9, 10). What matters is not a skin color or national origin but a desire to do the will of God.

God's grace and the gospel have touched the hearts of people in all nations and in all times; each one of them has dearly loved and prayed for all God's people. Whether they understand it or not, when a person today prays for his family, he is motivated by the Holy Spirit who inspired Moses to pray, "Forgive their [Israel's] sin—but if not, I pray, blot me out of Your book which You have written" (Exodus 32:32). The same Spirit motivated the apostle Paul, who was willing to lose the kingdom of heaven himself in order for his brethren, the Jews, to be saved. "I could wish that I myself were accursed from Christ for my brethren, my countrymen according to the flesh, who are Israelites" (Romans 9:3, 4). Even though Paul suffered much from his people, he continued to love them and followed the example of Christ by blessing those who persecuted him.

Paul wouldn't be Paul, and he would never have become the apostle to the Gentiles if he had decided to "privatize" God. He knew that God did not prefer one nation over another. In this, Paul differs greatly from some today who are not above declaring themselves to be God's favorites based on their ethnic or cultural origin.

A love for one's parents and homeland does not mean that we believe they are infallible. Paul loved the Jews, but he also knew that they were guilty of crucifying Christ. His love for his people was blind until he began to see the light in every sense of the word. Then he saw that if his people did not repent for not recognizing and accepting Christ as the Son of God, they would be lost. They had replaced the living God with "the faith of their fathers." He understood that those things of which the Jews were so proud and that he had loved so much—the traditions and ceremonies of their fathers, a culture and history extending back for more than a thousand years, even their religion itself—that those things overshadowed Christ and His gospel. For him, this became the "antichrist"* he had once loved and worshiped.

So what should the believer do if he or she wants to serve God? Is there any way out? Probably the answer is found in the example of the apostle Paul. He wanted to help his brothers understand their fatal mistake, and he told them about his experience of enlightenment. Therefore, if our reader is a Catholic and loves his people, then as no one else does, he has everything that is needed to tell other Catholics about what he has learned from the book of Daniel. He can now show others how to receive true forgiveness of their sins; he can protect them from participating in the liturgy of the

---

* Instead of Christ.

antichrist and from the influence of his false doctrines. Orthodox or Protestant believers who communicate with their brothers or sisters in faith can do the same for them.

The ideal, but probably impossible, scenario would be for the Church to reform. God calls Christians to turn to the Bible and to admit their mistakes. Those who realize what is wrong can help others realize their mistakes like no one else. If we follow this advice, we may soon find that among the ministers of the Church there are those who have tried to change it but failed. The system has always resisted reform. History and prophecy convince us that the antichrist might change forms, but he never changes his nature. So when the system refuses to be reformed, Christians have no choice but to organize themselves and to worship God in the way that their conscience prompts. When all pleas to repentance are rejected by the system of the antichrist, God will call His people to come out of it (Revelation 18:4).

Fourth, we need to understand that we have entered the final phase of the history of sin and that we need to be prepared for the fact that its time will soon expire. Daniel was told, "The words are closed up and sealed till the time of the end" (Daniel 12:9). Thus, if the mysteries of his prophecies have become understandable, this means that this "time of the end" has come. What's going to happen? The angel answered: "Many shall be purified, made white, and refined, but the wicked shall do wickedly" (Daniel 12:10). If you read these words carefully, you can see that the author of the book of Revelation, the apostle John, used a similar expression to describe the events of the last days before the Second Coming: "He who is unjust, let him be unjust still; he who is filthy, let him be filthy still; he who is righteous, let him be righteous still; he who is holy, let him be holy still" (Revelation 22:11). Here Daniel and John speak about the same thing. In Daniel, the book is sealed, but it is unsealed in John's Revelation. But in both cases the opening of the book results in a division of people into those who become hardened and those who accept. In other words, people will choose their own fate. Therefore, the words of the Lord follow immediately: "And behold, I am coming quickly, and My reward is with Me, to give to everyone according to his work" (Revelation 22:12).

We have no reason to doubt the truth of the prophetic Word. As surely and inevitably as the prophecies have been fulfilled in the past, so they will be fulfilled in the future. Their fulfillment does not depend on whether we believe in them or not. It does not depend on whether we want, or don't want, them to be fulfilled. The fulfillment of God's Word depends on God Himself. Whenever we study history together with the Bible, we see it again and again. We need to study history in order not to lose historical memory. But along with history, we need to examine God's Word because, when we study them together, they reveal to us the plans and character of our Creator. The Scripture says,

> Remember the former things of old,
> For I am God, and there is no other;
> I am God, and there is none like Me,
> Declaring the end from the beginning,
> And from ancient times things that are not yet done,
> Saying, "My counsel shall stand,
> And I will do all My pleasure" (Isaiah 46:9, 10).

God has done everything to warn us about the deception of the antichrist and the danger of future events. Therefore, only when we heed God's warnings will we be ready for them.

www.ingramcontent.com/pod-product-compliance
Lightning Source LLC
Chambersburg PA
CBHW030000110526
44587CB00011BA/814